LUISA DE CARVAJAL Y MENDOZA

# INTERACTIONS
in the Early Modern Age

*Series Editor*
**David Whitford**

*Advisory Board*
**Surekha Davies**
**Kathryn A. Edwards**
**Tryntje Hellferich**
**Nicholas R. Jones**
**Nicholas Terpstra**
**Merry Wiesner-Hanks**

New religious expressions, technological advances, emerging cross-continental empires, environmental and social upheavals, and interactions among previously unconnected peoples and states both demanded and created a new worldview, promoting change among some and retrenchment among others. Books in this series explore these changes, and their reception, from multiple perspectives. Topics covered include women and gender, race and ethnicity, religious expression and dissent, popular culture, technology, economics, politics and power, and war and military practice.

A previous version of this series was published as Early Modern Studies by Truman State University Press through 2018 and by The Pennsylvania State University Press through 2020.

# LUISA DE CARVAJAL Y MENDOZA

The Politics of an Anglo-Spanish Life

Freddy Cristóbal Domínguez

The Pennsylvania State University Press
*University Park, Pennsylvania*

Library of Congress Cataloging-in-Publication Data

Names: Domínguez, Freddy Cristóbal, 1982– author
Title: Luisa de Carvajal y Mendoza : the politics of an Anglo-Spanish life / Freddy Cristóbal Domínguez.
Other titles: Interactions in the early modern age
Description: University Park, Pennsylvania : The Pennsylvania State University Press, [2025] | Series: Interactions in the early modern age | Includes bibliographical references and index.
Summary: "Examines how piety and politics interact in early modern Europe. It explores the political interventions of the Spanish noblewoman, Luisa de Carvajal y Mendoza, a woman known for her holiness and for her missionary efforts in Protestant England in the seventeenth century"—Provided by publisher.
Identifiers: LCCN 2025039209 | ISBN 9780271100371 hardback | ISBN 9780271100388 paperback
Subjects: LCSH: Carvajal y Mendoza, Luisa de, 1566–1614 | Carvajal y Mendoza, Luisa de, 1566–1614 —Political activity | Catholic women—Spain—Biography | Catholic women—England—Biography | Catholics—Spain—Biography | Catholics—England—Biography | LCGFT: Biographies
Classification: LCC BX4705.C334 D55 2025
LC record available at https://lccn.loc.gov/2025039209

Copyright © 2025 Freddy Cristóbal Domínguez
All rights reserved
Printed in the United States of America
Published by The Pennsylvania State University Press,
University Park, PA 16802–1003

The Pennsylvania State University Press is a member of the Association of University Presses.

It is the policy of The Pennsylvania State University Press to use acid-free paper. Publications on uncoated stock satisfy the minimum requirements of American National Standard for Information Sciences—Permanence of Paper for Printed Library Material, ANSI Z39.48–1992.

For Mary

# CONTENTS

Acknowledgments / viii

**Introduction** / 1
1 Lessons of Her Youth / 14
2 Pious Publicity in Spain / 37
3 On the Verge of England / 56
4 An English Life / 87
5 Carvajal's Spanish Diplomacy / 110

**Conclusion** / 132

Notes / 139
Bibliography / 155
Index / 163

## ACKNOWLEDGMENTS

Although it would be years before I picked up the project, this book first reared its head in 2016 after Hillary Clinton's loss to Donald Trump. In the aftermath of all that, I thought it would be interesting and worthwhile to consider gender and politics historically. Wouldn't it be interesting to study a woman navigating her world with something like Clinton's grit and determination?

I wrote most of this book groggily over a period of dark early mornings. To survive, I had to chug coffee and find inspiration. I thought about and often thumbed through the works of my heroes: Carlo Ginzburg, Roger Chartier, Anthony Grafton, Michael Questier, and Peter Lake. One day I picked up an extraordinary book on things completely unrelated to this project by my colleague Trish Starks—*Smoking Under the Tsars*—and was blown away. To read their work feels unabashedly decadent. There is pleasure to be had.

No book has been as important for the completion this monograph as Mary Beth Long's *Marian Maternity in Late-Medieval England*. It has little to do with my research, but its most dazzling qualities inspired me to write again.

Putting this book together has been solitary work, but I am grateful for the few who provided much. I am especially indebted to three people plus two anonymous readers who read the whole thing: Michael Questier, Anne J. Cruz, and Mary Beth Long.

I'm grateful for the kind support provided by the Huntington Library, the American Philosophical Society, and the Pandemic Research Recovery Grant at the University of Arkansas.

I'm indebted to the Department of History here at the University of Arkansas, including its extraordinary staff: Brenda Foster, Melinda Adams, and Stephanie Caley.

Advising graduate students is the most rewarding part of my teaching portfolio. Seeing the hard work my students put into their research and the level of wonder they bring to it is refreshing and inspiring. Special thanks to Nathan Harkey, Cole Younger, and Earth Anderson, who have been working with me throughout the writing of this book and who are always forgiving of my eccentricities.

My parents, Lourdes and Freddy, have been integral to finishing this book. Their kindness is true and the love they show their grandchildren inspires me to be a better parent. Their help in schooling our preschooler provided peace of mind and time to read.

My children provide perspective. Rose's senior year in college is just around the corner; Vivian's freshman year is there too. Santi has started kindergarten and Laura is on her way to middle school. I think about the fragilities and possibilities of their young lives and writing seems like nothing much at all. I cannot count the ways I love you.

Finally, Mary Beth (again). She had to endure the highs and lows of this book, my yammering when I thought it was going well and my tantrums when I thought it wasn't. In both cases, her support was always loving and strong. As I finish this book, it's inevitable that I think of you who brings joy to every beginning, middle, and end.

# Introduction

Hilary Mantel, author of *Wolf Hall*, wrote an exquisite essay on monarchical bodies, past and present.[1] Although not specifically about the female body—old, sick, fat Henry VIII gets his—some of its most revealing parts deal with the specifics of femininity and its discourses. The women she deals with are, in the end, defined by others—sometimes cannibalized by them. She herself recalls encountering Elizabeth II only to regret it: "I passed my eyes over her as a cannibal views his dinner." Royal women are things to be ogled, and their prominence waxes and wanes depending on how they carry their bodies. Mantel laments how once Kate Middleton, now Princess of Wales, became a royal, she morphed into a cipher. She recalls noticing Middleton turn into "a jointed doll on which rags are hung." In the early days of her journey to monarchical eminence, people only cared about what she wore; then, later, she became nothing more than an expectant mother. Mantel predicted Middleton would emerge from the mess of childbirth to become a radiant figure, even if that radiance could only be a reflection of her motherhood or her potential for conception. Mantel assumed that the public would make it so "that this young woman's life until now was nothing, her only point and purpose being to give birth." Although some misinterpreted Mantel's analysis as criticism of the princess, in fact it was a critique of social inflictions upon a living, breathing body, transformed by gawkers who only cared about the carapace, the shell.

This is not a new story. Middleton's deceased mother-in-law, Lady Diana, was a victim of similar abuse, or sociocultural use, with tragic consequences: "Something in her personality, her receptivity, her passivity, fitted her to be the carrier of myth." Mantel reaches further back to early modernity for other prominent examples. In eighteenth-century France, there was the extremely image-conscious Marie Antoinette, with all her wigs and frocks, a woman configured as "all body and no soul: no soul, no sense, no sensitivity," who became emblematic of everything wrong with the kingdom, a woman "who focused the rays of misogyny." There was also Anne Boleyn, Henry VIII's wife, who despite being a power player was ultimately valued "for her body parts, not her intellect or soul."

Despite her elegant analysis, Mantel's understanding of the monarchical body, especially the female body, hearkens back to narratives of feminine disempowerment that remain prominent in the public sphere. Female royals become prey to misogyny, prisoners of superficiality, and it is not clear that they can escape the institutional and mediatic strictures imposed on them. Mantel's is a story of victimhood, of what society does to these overtaxed bodies: "We don't cut off heads of royal ladies these days, but we do sacrifice them, and we did memorably drive one to destruction a scant generation ago." There is a miserable truth to all this, but there are also complexities that require attention.

In her lectures on women and power, classicist Mary Beard reminds us that the silence imposed on women in the patriarchal West has deep roots in Greek and Roman times. She suggests that the ancients were alive to the problem of female silence in the manly terrain of power and reflected on it time and again. For example, Ovid told the story of Philomela, who was brutalized and raped by Tereus, king of Thrace. To hide the horrible act, Tereus cuts out her tongue, but she lives to tell her story through the feminine communicative art of weaving. Her rapist cannot keep her silent, despite his most gruesome efforts. Centuries later, when Shakespeare drew from Ovid's story for *Titus Andronicus*, he ensured that the assaulted woman of his play, Lavinia, would be more fully and spectacularly mutilated: her hands would be cut off along with her wagging tongue. And yet she "spoke," nudging open a printed copy of Ovid's *Metamorphoses* and wielding a stick to write the names of her assailants on the ground. In these meaningful gestures, strange but nevertheless bookish and writerly, we bear witness to how pre- and early modern women could become expert actors and communicators even against severe cultural, institutional, and physical limitations rooted in testicular hegemony.[2]

If women like Lavinia could speak, even in their silence, to what extent could they participate in that most masculine activity, early modern politics? To be sure, as with men, the answer depends on many factors, including time and place, race and class. Still, it is plain to see that women were often politically engaged. There is now a substantial body of literature concerning the power of queens and regents who navigated their gender roles, most prominently Elizabeth I of England, but we can add to these a host of others in early modern Europe and elsewhere, such as Njinga of Angola.[3] Indeed, Allyson Poska has underlined how studies of women monarchs serve as prime evidence for what she rightly conceptualizes as normative female agentic roles.[4] And yet scholarship on the most exalted classes is still a work in progress. Studies of great figures such as Catherine de Medici and Mary Tudor are still ripe for further specialized treatment, and some powerful figures are just being rediscovered. For example, Silvia Mitchell's recent monograph on Mariana of Austria pushes against old narratives marginalizing her, even during her decade as regent to the future King Charles II in seventeenth-century Spain.[5]

Of course, the stories of early modern women and politics must include nonroyals. This was not always the case, but scholarship in the past three decades (at least) has delved deeply into how elites lacking monarchical blood still wielded formal and informal power. Research has shown the ways in which women established important kinship networks that served the needs of the family—how, in certain circumstances, they served as heads of households, and how, by means of patronage, they held vital roles within the concentric circles of courtly power.[6] Still in its early stages, scholarship has begun to describe how learned and noble women contributed to modes of political thought.[7] As exemplified in Poska's pathbreaking work, some scholarship has turned away from elite women altogether by showing how women of humbler classes could be key players within frameworks of power as well.[8]

This book focuses specifically on a category of early modern women who can be described as "holy." The precise meaning of the term can be contested. Although it resonates with sanctity, I use it here to refer to individuals who aspire to and are recognized for possessing spiritual gifts—by divine will and/or forms of self-sacrifice—above and beyond most others and whose identity is firmly marked by such spiritual acuity.

As relatively recent scholarship has pointed out, embedding holy women—especially in Anglo-American contexts—into political narratives has been fitful. F. Thomas Luongo's *The Saintly Politics of Catherine of Siena*, for example, is a punchy piece of revisionist history showing how one of the most famous medieval saints emerged from and participated in local and international politics.[9] He claims to go against centuries of tradition that have obscured her role in earthly matters and thus simplified her public life and her status in it. Luongo argues that such a blind spot results from modern scholarship that has accepted premodern categories of femininity such as the holy woman, a discursive type that hinges on sharp distinctions between the spiritual and the secular. Unsurprisingly, though we historians claim to create distance from our historical subjects, we tend to swallow their stories whole. Thus, to follow the Catherine of Siena example, the political side of her life is still being explored in dribs and drabs. Unn Falkeid's intellectual history of late medieval papal politics, *The Avignon Papacy Contested*, is still redressing the fact that Catherine and contemporaries such as Birgitta of Sweden have been "essentially wiped out of the historical-political scenery."[10] This claim might be a little overblown, given the work of scholars like Renate Blumenfeld-Kosinski, but the general sentiment is not misplaced.[11]

Especially in regard to pious women, there is a lingering sense that studying politics is a matter of secularization. When Luongo describes Catherine of Siena's political work, he emphatically underscores how she became immersed in the power dynamics of her family and their worldly interests, which were also embedded within broader ecclesiastical struggles. But, surprisingly, matters of piety and devotion and religious practices sometimes seem exiguous. On the other hand, in studies of "secular" women, their religious commitments can be taken as epiphenomenal. Mihoko Suzuki's excellent book *Antigone's Example* seeks to reinscribe women within the realm of the political by showing them doing political work at revolutionary moments. Even though she acknowledges and deeply understands ecclesiastical and spiritual matters, Suzuki seems to undermine confessional allegiances and motivations. As she explains it, the women in her book and their writings constitute a "political critique of a largely secular nature, though the authors' religious affiliations ... certainly marked their political critique."[12] Such a tendency has something to do with a sense that modernization is distinct from the religious and spiritual.[13]

Whatever its forms and limitations, the inclusion of women in "politics"—and, by extension, the inclusion of "holy women" in that realm—has required a more malleable notion of political action.[14] For our purposes, politics can be thought of as participation in public affairs and, separately or entwined, how the individual (subject or citizen) ensures that participation. Such a broad definition embraces scholarly movements away from an exclusive focus on the history of kings and queens and institutions such as parliament, where women were excluded. Such a shift occurred with the retooling and reemergence of cultural history and an emphasis on "political culture" that refocused scholarship on symbolic/performative acts and beliefs/perceptions as opposed to history "as it really was." As a result, historians have reconceptualized loci of political "work" and have cast an eye toward activities outside of official seats of governance, toward other places and spaces real and imagined. For example, political history as practiced today cannot afford to neglect the world of polemic, articulated in town squares by citizens and street prophets or set aflutter in bustling, intangible spheres created by ephemeral printed material. Historians now hold as a near truism that there is a whole world of political actors and influencers in and out of, independent and in concert with, centers of governance during a period in which the notion of "government" itself was amorphous. The range of participants in political debates and policymaking helps prove the emergent consensus that the early modern period saw the rise of a "public sphere" with both a knowledge and an understanding of the workings of "state," which the state itself could not ignore.[15]

No book has married a deep understanding of public spheres and the activities of holy women more than Peter Lake and Michael Questier's *The Trials of Margaret Clitherow*. Clitherow was a secular woman of relatively common stock in late sixteenth-century York who got into trouble for her aggressive Catholicism and her protection of priests during a time of acute religious turmoil. Ultimately crushed to death by the authorities, she went on to become an exemplar of saintly piety for some contemporaries and, in retrospect, for confessionally motivated historians centuries later. Lake and Questier have shown that her story is a prime example of how the behaviors, performances, and utterances of saintly women could be, and were, at the center of a range of political conflicts, both between Catholics and the state and among Catholics themselves. The current volume could not have been conceptualized without *The Trials of Margaret Clitherow*, in part because, as Lake and Questier suggest, the woman we will soon meet can be seen as an aristocratic version of Clitherow, with the benefits of diplomatic immunity.[16]

ENTER LUISA

Luisa de Carvajal y Mendoza was a Spanish noblewoman who decided to shun (in theory) the trappings of wealth and power to lead a life of spiritual nourishment and worldly abnegation. In Spain, as soon as she could escape the strictures of her station, Carvajal lived a humble life in the company of her onetime servants. More astoundingly, she went on to establish a similar form of lay communal living in England, where she died as a missionary to English heretics and a sustainer of English Catholicism at the start of the seventeenth century. Although her kinship ties allowed access to men and women with extraordinary political power, she emphatically tried to leave that world behind, or at least to participate in it from what she construed as the margins. Carvajal, as we will see, was part of an ample public sphere, an expansive formal/informal realm of politicking.

Before the twentieth century, Carvajal's life was treated hagiographically. Michael Walpole, her confessor, wrote what is likely the first spiritual biography of Carvajal shortly after her death.[17] It seems to have circulated among a relatively restricted circle of readers, including perhaps some nobles, the monarchy, and English Catholic exiles in Spain. Walpole meant to underline Carvajal's many virtues: her forbearance, her drive to serve God, the trials and tribulations she experienced, her successes in converting English heretics, and her suffering amid English Protestant abuse. Perhaps Walpole had an eye on Carvajal's potential beatification, but the narrative and its framing seem more focused on providing readers (English seminarians, for example) with a positive exemplar.

Two decades after Carvajal's death, Luis Muñoz, a prolific hagiographer, published the first printed book based on Walpole and a range of other sources with the explicit aim of supporting her canonization proceedings. Aside from underlining Carvajal's virtues—her singular drive to overcome hardship in the name of Christ and the salvation of souls—Muñoz also added a forceful apology for her efforts against possible criticisms of her overabundant zeal, insisting that her actions were done in compliance with, and with the permission of, her superiors. She was cast in the mold of biblical and ancient women who lived lives of abnegation and (public) sacrifice against oppressors, ultimately achieving martyrdom. Carvajal was not killed by heretical hands, but her final illness *was* exacerbated by imprisonment. Muñoz emphasizes that she too was a martyr, and at her death she became a relic and a saint by popular acclamation.[18] His book reveals "the ardent faith of a woman who with a delicate body and delicate limbs seized virtue's rigors [lo arduo de la virtud], showing through her manly efforts that in the soul and spirit there is no difference between man and woman."[19] The lessons of her life well lived should thus be embraced unreservedly among all good Catholics, regardless of gender.

Carvajal's next biography emerged from a swell of nineteenth-century English Catholic activity. In 1873, Lady Georgiana Fullerton compiled a book about Carvajal based on Muñoz's. It came out during a push for canonizing early modern English martyrs and it seems to have functioned as a pitch for Carvajal's pertinence to that exalted group. Fullerton introduced Carvajal to English audiences among whom she had become "all but unknown," even though she had once "spent nine years in the exercise of every spiritual and temporal work of mercy toward her persecuted brethren in the faith."[20] Fullerton hoped that her book would speak to broad issues of piety and reform. In a telling aside, she wonders what would become of a person of conviction such as Carvajal in nineteenth-century England. She would not be jailed but would have been considered a nuisance by all. In a jab at what she considered enfeebled (nineteenth-century) Catholicism, Fullerton wonders "whether Catholics in our days do not carry too far a system of absolute silence on religious subjects." Maybe, she wonders, ceding to Protestants and "free-thinking friends and relatives" precludes hashing out serious differences and ultimately, she implies, misses the opportunity to convert others.[21] Carvajal, as a missionary, is diametrically opposed to any armchair Catholic. Fullerton's biography intended to relay the ways in which Carvajal's interior spirituality played out publicly in service to the church and the fortification of the English Catholic faith.

The first full treatment of Carvajal's life employing modern historical techniques and deep archival research came in the 1960s. After editing Carvajal's correspondence, her life writings, and her poetry, the Jesuit Camilo Abad wrote a full biography stuffed with details about her activities and her whereabouts from birth to death. He makes a special effort to reconstruct some social and political contexts that informed Carvajal's life, especially after her arrival in England. For all that, however, Abad's book is concerned with portraying her as a spiritual figure to inspire, among others, the many "young Spanish women, that generously leave their homeland today, their family and friends, to teach the Gospel of Jesus Christ in pagan regions whether civilized or savage."[22] Within this context, Carvajal's life is meant, once again, to edify by showing off a special spiritual grit that underlay her missionary zeal.

For centuries, then, whenever Carvajal's life story was told, it was under the veil of holiness. The marks of sanctity and its proof overwhelmed any other concerns.

While it is safe to say that scholarship on Carvajal since Abad has not been written in hagiographical modes, the biographical literature has tended to amend and reconfigure, not wholly overturn, precedent narratives. María Nieves Pinillos Iglesias wrote a useful, fact-rich biography of Carvajal that follows closely and accepts at face value the narrative Carvajal and her confessors produced in the seventeenth century. Although there is no explicit confessional pulse to the book, it is a survey of the ways in which Carvajal practiced her faith and accomplished her spiritual journey. Occasionally, Pinillos intently occludes any narratives that might, in theory, contravene this holy path. When the specter of politics manifests itself, she insists that Carvajal's intentions were purer than that. For example, when she discusses Carvajal's concerns about a simmering alliance between Holland and England and her efforts to thwart such a rapprochement, Pinillos seems to undermine Carvajal's political initiative, telling us that she was only involved in these affairs because of "the religious consequence."[23] By doing this, the author implies some discomfort with—though not rejection of—the intermingling of politics and religion, something that is embedded in much of the literature on Carvajal.

Margaret A. Rees, in *The Writings of Doña Luisa de Carvajal*, emphasizes spiritual qualities independent of other fields of action. Her work is divided into three sections, one recounting (in a sense ventriloquizing) Carvajal's biography, another delving into an analysis of her poetry, and the last providing a series of documents, mostly writings by Carvajal herself. The justifications for her project are enlightening. Rees argues that there is something inherently dramatic about Carvajal's story in England during a period of religious repression. Fundamentally, though, what is most interesting about Carvajal's life (and output) is its representative quality "as an expression of mysticism in action, or at least ecstatic devoutness."[24] Following in this vein, Rees's treatment of Carvajal's poetry—punctilious in its description of rhetorical forms—focuses on how it reflects the interior movements of her soul, lonely meditation, and a particular brand of Ignatian spirituality. The story of Carvajal's life in England is a hodgepodge of episodes and descriptions of events and circumstances that all amount to an account of her holy toil. Rees speaks of Carvajal in heroic tones—she is likened to conquistadors—but "in her case motives were certainly untainted by anything other than religious concerns."[25]

In *The She-Apostle*, Glyn Redworth deviates from previous approaches. More than any other book on Carvajal, his work places her activities in a range of political, cultural, and religious situations, thus teasing out a fuller story about her as a historical figure. Unlike past biographers, Redworth shows a sensitivity to gender and the limits imposed on women. In the book's introduction, he says that Carvajal's story "raises uncomfortable questions about how far she was in charge of her own destiny." He concludes that "for all her aristocratic feistiness—and an apparent powerlessness to take no for an answer—her desire to risk death . . . was undoubtedly influenced by men of the cloth."[26] While Redworth recognizes that Carvajal "was a political animal to her fingertips," at several points it seems that all the politics happens around her, that she had uninteresting political opinions, and that the men in her life were the real doers.[27] Indeed, Redworth sometimes talks about Carvajal's own obtrusive political interventions in passing or talks about those occasions as missteps, ultimately the result of unintended consequences.[28] Moreover, although politics and political intrigue abound, these details sometimes seem external to the story of Carvajal's piety.

There is no doubt that Redworth's book is crucial and that it is based on impeccable knowledge of the available sources. He provides plausible interpretations of those sources, and his understanding of English and Spanish contexts is unsurpassed. However, I suspect the book steers close to the well-established narratological impulses of previous works to ensure (much-welcome) accessibility for broad audiences. As a result, analysis and nuance are occasionally hidden beneath the surface of storytelling. Readers would do well to grapple with Redworth's editorial notes to his translation of Carvajal's letters for a richer narrative of her politics.[29]

On the monographic level, very few books have covered as much interpretive ground as Michaela Bill-Mrziglod has in her published dissertation. *Luisa de Carvajal y Mendoza und ihre "Gesellschaft Mariens"* is a relatively neglected work that has some claim to cutting-edge status owing to its theological and ecclesiological bent. These themes are embedded within a varied—sometimes chaotic—series of discussions engaging with a broad range of scholarly interventions. Amid all this, she helpfully gestures at the breadth of Carvajal's political engagements and is among the very few scholars who have explicitly considered her activities as part of a broader Catholic political culture. Her discussion on this point is not exhaustive, but she underlines how Carvajal's occupations speak to confessionalization or how states solidify sovereignty by delineating religious in- and out-groups. Just as this framing helps us understand Carvajal's political ambitions, Bill-Mrziglod shows that there is also a story to be told about religious politics itself. Her assessment reflects a tendency to separate the political (mainly in its geopolitical form) from the religious (mainly in the form of complex proselytization), even if the book rightly hesitates at those very distinctions.[30]

To my mind, the most stimulating work on Carvajal has been through a feminist lens. Elizabeth Rhodes was the first scholar to fully consider her in tandem with issues of female subjectivity. She argues that her spiritual stance and her embrace of Counter-Reformation ideals were sources of authority and agency.[31] While Rhodes states unequivocally that Carvajal was a political actor, she implies that Carvajal could be an *unwilling* one, and she is generally not interested in the kind of "public" political engagement that this book discusses.[32]

For all the secular-religious entanglements that Rhodes recognizes, she nevertheless accentuates two separate spheres in Carvajal's life: one secular, one religious. In her curt critique of Redworth's biography, she asks, "What does one make of a fanatically Catholic noblewoman who gave her inheritance away and begged with the poor but fretted about having her own mattress in London, whose writings and actions manifest arrogance even as she claimed humility and who, according to all evidence, was full of life, but who also took a vow of martyrdom before leaving for England?" Rhodes here suggests that Carvajal lived in a bifurcated world between the flesh and the soul, a model that I don't think fully works.[33] While tensions between body and spirit existed—Carvajal would have recognized them—the reconciliation of both has proven more difficult for modern scholars than for Carvajal's contemporaries.

Anne J. Cruz is the foremost feminist voice in Carvajal scholarship. Her most important contribution thus far has been an edition of Carvajal's writings, which, among other things, has an introduction that is the most succinct, evenhanded, and even-tempered biography of the noblewoman.[34] The close attention paid to Carvajal's story within her cultural landscape and to the literary qualities of her writings is a core virtue in Cruz's work. As we might expect, some of Carvajal's political interventions, or attempted interventions, appear, but they tend to be marginal to the exposition of spiritual travails and the ways in which she navigated her gendered role (admittedly a kind of political act in itself). Cruz's treatment of the latter theme leaps off the page in several important articles emphasizing the multivocality of Carvajal's poetry and its rhetorical creativity as well as the ways in which Carvajal assumed a "transgendered" voice.[35] Elsewhere, Cruz has commented on how Carvajal worked and flourished as a woman within the boundaries established by male superiors, especially Jesuits.³⁶ In an essay she wrote for Helen Nader's groundbreaking edited volume about power and gender among women who belonged to the powerful Mendoza family, Cruz describes how Carvajal's writings tried to subvert masculine expectations, how they reveal women's desire "for the subjectivity so often denied them and for which they must constantly negotiate with the dominant hierarchies on their numerous sites of crossing."³⁷ Tellingly, while Nader's book highlights how several women played a dominant role in raw politics, Cruz focuses instead on matters of self-fulfillment and self-actualization as opposed to fully fledged public engagement.

Although all the preceding work informs the current volume, it draws more direct inspiration from several articles that take politics as their organizing principle. Miguel Iglesias has written an essay with what is likely still the most cogent description of Carvajal's "religio-patriotic" activities in Jacobean England.³⁸ His understanding of her political involvement highlights her epistolary exchanges with Spanish elites written largely in a diplomatic mode. Elena Levy-Navarro has described the kinds of rhetorical tools Carvajal used to gain a political voice within Spain's royal court by examining a batch of Carvajal's letters to the courtier Rodrigo Calderón.³⁹ While these articles generally stay in the realm of "high politics," other additions to the Carvajal canon insist on a more capacious understanding of politics and political tools. María Pando-Canteli has shown the ways in which Carvajal used the martyrological—indeed, the very flesh of martyrs—within a repertoire of activities aiming to convince people to support the English Catholic cause. Nieves Romero-Díaz has written a very important article on how Carvajal intruded into various public spaces to make her voice heard.⁴⁰ Much of the focus on Carvajal's politics has dealt with her time in England, but only recently have students of English history taken Carvajal seriously as a political figure during that crucial period of her life. I have done my part as a quasi-English historian in a very tentative article on Carvajal's life writings, but, aside from Redworth's, by far the most important work on the subject belongs to Kathryn Marshalek, who subtly treats Carvajal's public interventions in the streets of London and its prisons within very precise and archivally grounded contexts.⁴¹

I suspect that by the time this monograph appears in print, even more scholarship along these lines will have emerged. That said, there are three reasons why this book deserves its paper and ink. Understandably, scholarship on Carvajal's politics has tended to focus on her time in England, but because of this the Spanish side of the story is somewhat neglected.

While, as in my first book, I try to keep Anglo-Spanish issues central, this book offers something different in its emphasis on Spanish elements of the story.[42] This monograph also grapples with the problem of holiness and politics as a guiding narratological and analytical feature, something that current scholarship on Carvajal does not explore in any consistent or ample way. Perhaps most importantly, these previous two contributions are valuable within the parameters of a "life" that is woven with "political" threads. Here I want to explore how Carvajal put herself in, and was absorbed into, a realm of contestation over power by means of polemic, often about "matters of state." I do this with full knowledge that such matters were also construed as religious and were sometimes—though some scholarship has missed this—imbued with spiritual and devotional traits. In other words, here I describe how and why Carvajal became a voice in various interlaced politico-religious skirmishes and how she became a political actor within various "public spheres" as she tried to lobby for specific actions of remarkable importance among superpowers on the European scene. Moreover, I show how she encouraged certain behaviors that would be of real-world consequence in the realms of both the spirit and the flesh.

This is not a totalizing biography. The pages that follow do not attempt a full narrative of Carvajal's life and times, nor do they aspire to completion in any form, as most large-scale works on her have. This book provides shards of a life. My interest in individuals is idiosyncratic and linked to a set of restricted themes and my own concerns, together with a sense that a particular life reveals larger historical dynamics. In this, I draw inspiration from the work of scholars like Natalie Zemon Davis, who, as a teller of lives, has been drawn to those that allow for partial and incomplete explorations. While she respects her subjects, she also uses them. As Davis has put it, her interest "is always triggered by some prior question that I think I can fathom better through their lives."[43] Such partial—I use the word advisedly—biographies are inevitable and necessary. Real lives are always incomplete to those who write about them. So, we must be creative; an addition here, an omission there, lets us tell the story that we want to tell. These stories are rarely, if ever, innocent of the author's concerns and preferences, although ideally, peculiar interests are constrained by the historical record and an elusive quest for "truth." It's wise to acknowledge, as Bob Dylan—the subject of my previous book—has one of his musical characters say: "You can't open up your minds, boys / to every conceivable point of view." Perhaps it would even be wise to follow the advice from his later, amended version of the phrase: *"Don't* open up your mind, boys / to every conceivable point of view." Indeed, while there are myriad ways of studying and writing about Carvajal's life, from my point of view, politics, expansively defined, is crucial. The implicit mantra of this book is: no politics, no Luisa.

But even within the realm of politics, this book is not written with the intention of providing a painstaking description of all her machinations. I have tried to give the reader a sense of the *kinds* of activities she took part in to better understand her mode of political involvement.

In many ways, Carvajal's life fits a specific "type" that we can find replicated many times over in medieval and early modern Europe and beyond. Here we have the well-worn story of a noblewoman who leaves her nobility behind in search of a special communion with God. Although underemphasized in the literature, she also conforms to conventions concerning political involvement and even activism by lay (and pointedly non-ecstatic) women of a distinct spiritual acuity.[44] Indeed, given the realities of the time, there was no way a woman with her interests and social possibilities could escape what we can now call politics. Women of Carvajal's caste were expected to play a public role and, in so doing, to carry out, and exemplify, forms of public engagement legitimated by salubrious religiopolitical ends.

Despite the extent to which Golden Age Spain witnessed the popularity of intense and even extravagant female piety, not everyone followed that path, and thus there is an inherent exceptionality in Carvajal's story.[45] She is also "strange" because the form her active life took was unprecedented and not repeated in the early modern period. Although plenty of women aspired to martyrdom in pagan—often Muslim—lands, no other Spanish woman went to missionize in England amid its confessional strife.

Carvajal's story, or the story I've chosen to tell, is useful in that it works on two registers fundamental to the microhistorical project at hand. This case study stakes its validity on the idea that eccentricity is capacious enough to contain the coordinates of the normative. Further, Carvajal was a "political creature" who existed on the margins and in the center of her society *at the same time*. By considering aspects of her life, we witness her extraordinary political interventions while acknowledging that these were carried out using available and familiar political tools. Because of this, her presence in public spheres reveals the very nature of those spheres in early modern Europe.

Ultimately, this project is simple. I want to talk about a woman who took what her culture offered and ran.

CHAPTER 1

# Lessons of Her Youth

Luisa de Carvajal y Mendoza was born in the small *extremeño* town of Jaraicejo. The region had suffered a stretch of frigid weather that kept the family stuck at home, but as soon as it thawed, they trudged to the parish church. Baby Luisa was dunked into its baptismal font to everyone's joy and relief. Carvajal could not have had any memory of this, but she fixated on one troubling detail: the ritual was performed two weeks after her birth. Much later in life she lamented the gap—"fourteen wretched unbaptized days"—presumably because of the dangers posed to her mortal soul and the horror of ever having lived outside of the church.[1] The temporal space between sin and possible salvation, though not uncommon at the time, foreshadowed ambivalences that she claimed marked her early childhood home.

Her parents, María de Mendoza y Chacón and Francisco de Carvajal, had impressive pedigrees, belonging to the cream of Spain's landed nobility. Of the two, however, Carvajal's mother guaranteed more prestige, because there were few Spanish clans greater than the Mendoza.[2] Familial status mattered to Carvajal, but María was, above all, her mother, a luminous presence in life and memory. Carvajal recalled her spiritual devotions and revered her grace and faith. Her father was more worldly, and her treatment of him is curt. He was learned, with a noble bearing, but despite having been given gifts by God, "he did not apply them with the same devotion or virtue" as her mother. Her early childhood unfurled, or so she implied, amid the light of her mother and the pale gray of her father.[3]

The contrast she understood between mother and father resulted from what she knew about them and Carvajal's desire to evoke a past with which she wanted to live.[4] She wanted her experiences to conform to patterns and archetypes of saints' lives, in which maternal piety often augured that of daughters. How much could Luisa truly remember about her parents? They both died of typhus in 1572. She was only six.

Although an orphan from childhood, Carvajal would always reap the benefits of her bloodline. Her identity, as perceived by others, was defined by her nobility. Indeed, all formal discussions of her by biographers have begun with descriptions, often detailed descriptions, of her lineage. In more recent times, talk of her familial past has been flattened to evoke mere context, but the further back we go into the early modern period, that past proved her inherent worth. Ancestry dictated Carvajal's place in the social hierarchy and even proved her purity of blood, given the antiquity of her family and its roots in strongly Christian (importantly, non-Muslim) territories.

Coming from a wealthy and storied clan ensured ready-made kinship and social networks and alliances that would provide moral, political, and financial support throughout Carvajal's life. For this reason, when orphaned, she did not flail and descend into obscurity. She was resettled with wealthy, well-connected, and powerful family members who could help govern and educate her in a way befitting her class and station.

This chapter considers Carvajal's education—taken broadly—to understand her political ideals and assumptions about public engagement.

PLAYTIME

Contemporaries believed that an education started at the breast, where milk produced both nourishment and behavioral dispositions, but more formal and structured learning began—or should have begun, according to contemporary theorists—around the fragile age when Carvajal lost her parents. To hear Carvajal tell it, even before her formal studies had begun, her mother had already helped establish a sturdy foundation by providing an education in devotion and moral rectitude. What Carvajal ultimately missed from her mother's future education would be regained in a theater of grandeur. She was whisked away to live with her aunt, María Chacón, at the Descalzas Reales, an institution established by Juana of Austria (Philip II's sister)—the only female Jesuit—that housed and would house some of the most powerful women in Habsburg Spain within its conventual and adjacent palatial walls. This new setting started an educational experience that would have provided an entrée into a world of courtliness in which piety and power, faith and politics, intertwined. There, fervent prayer and pressing matters of state coexisted and even coalesced.

During four rambunctious years, Carvajal lived and played at the Descalzas with Philip II's children, her contemporaries Isabel Clara Eugenia, Catalina Micaela, and the one-year-old Infante, Fernando. She moved in an atmosphere of royalty with her exalted little companions, especially during playtime. She remembered that the cloisters were accessible from the Infantas' room and that they would raucously romp about, an experience that would have taught Carvajal the porosity between sacred and secular spaces. When they weren't running around, they spent much of their days playing dolls and dress-up, recreations that were thought to have great pedagogical importance and during which children would be socialized, where they could—at least within a royal context—pretend and prepare to be kings and queens.[5] Carvajal felt herself part of the royal troupe, as her little superiors did not show any "of the hierarchy and authority which their upbringing conferred on them."[6] Given this proximity, it is hard to imagine that Carvajal would have been excluded from other aspects of regal learning, a "curriculum" that was profoundly influenced by the unique exigencies of grooming future monarchs.[7]

Carvajal was very young when she joined her regal playmates and was introduced to the rudiments of the Infantas' educational program. It was a program that was, at the time of Carvajal's arrival, becoming more focused on the essentials of reading and writing as standardized by a recently appointed official tutor, Juan de Zúñiga. Beyond this, to what extent might Carvajal—still a child, after all—have followed along as Isabel and Catalina were introduced to a world of books that included worldly Cicero as much as holy Luis de Granada? To what extent would she have been exposed to the workaday aspects of "political practice" undertaken by Isabel, a little girl who from very early on wanted to emulate her father's penchant for writing and who from the age of six or seven was already helping her father in the workings of state? (The king would write missives, the queen would sand his letters, and Philip's daughters would deliver papers to the appropriate secretary.)[8] Ultimately, more important than any one lesson learned, or any specific academic track, was the assumption (or presumption) of rulership that little Luisa would have developed—or perhaps an inchoate understanding that upper-crust women had a place in politico-religious spheres. Admittedly, this might be stretching things. We can only know for sure that Carvajal's earliest formational phase insinuated feelings about power; a realm of possibilities opened up to an impressionable and no doubt very special child. It would only be in her next and crucial phase of maturation and growth that Carvajal's "political" education began.

## WOMAN OF THE HOUSE

After what seem to have been elysian years in Madrid, Carvajal's life took a more austere, perhaps darker turn. She left consecrated and regal walls for the estates of her maternal uncle, Francisco Hurtado de Mendoza, count of the Monteagudo and marquis of Almazán. Initially, she remained under the strict care of Isabel de Ayllón, her parents' servant and direct custodian since their death. Later, her uncle's wife, Ana María de Cárdenas, took over her tutelage. As Carvajal tells it, the marquise was a key figure in propelling her to adulthood. Conforming to the requisites of good motherhood, she would have provided a measure of exemplarity that Carvajal might replicate.

There were troubles.

Cárdenas did not like her niece. On more than one occasion, Carvajal says that her aunt spoke highly of her in public but didn't show such regard at home. We can almost hear a sigh when she recalled how "*they said* that the marquise cared for me" (my emphasis). The impersonal feel of her remembrance suggests that she never believed her aunt really did. Carvajal clearly considered her aunt's kind words mere performances meant to keep tensions between them hidden from view. In the end, she could only go by what she experienced: when her aunt wasn't ignoring her, she was scolding her—sometimes viciously.[9]

Why?

Most certainly, their personalities clashed. Neither Carvajal nor her aunt was a wallflower. Carvajal strained to remain respectful, but in her autobiographical writings she could be brutally honest (or prone to exaggeration?). Her aunt was sweet with those she liked, but to those who did not interest her, "she caused no little suffering." According to Carvajal, she had a "harsh personality" and exhibited imperiousness and jealousy. She would not truck what she perceived as challenges to her authority from faithful servants—or even from her own husband. There is another side to this story as well. Carvajal openly admits (or at least claims) that even as a five-year-old, she was a priggish brat who would tut-tut her mother's peccadilloes. This holier-than-thou posture likely made her insufferable. Without a doubt, Carvajal's aunt did not like, or approve of, her niece's asceticism as it developed. She considered it a mark not of sanctity but of excess.[10]

Carvajal and the marquise simply saw things from different points of view. For example, Carvajal remembers how she struggled to avoid indulgences at the dinner table: she would be moderate in what she ate and would sometimes have to hide food in her napkin to do so. Her unwillingness to eat a whole meal might have been a mark of modesty—that is how Carvajal told it—but the marquise would have read it as an attention-grabbing ploy that betrayed an infelicitous rejection of courtly customs and mores. To her, Carvajal wallowed in histrionics; to Carvajal, the marquise seemed to favor earthly comestible comforts, if not for herself, then at least for her children.[11]

Carvajal's aunt fits the spiritual roadblock trope of so many *vitae*, but if we accept that the relationship between aunt and niece was, indeed, toxic, they nevertheless adhered to social expectations of public cordiality and familial decorum. When they lived together, Carvajal answered to her aunt because, as she explained, within the household hierarchy women submitted to the matriarch. Especially in the two years that Carvajal spent under her aunt's wing in Almazán, while the marquis was away in Madrid, the marquise controlled her education. Under her care, Carvajal says she "learned how to write well and read any kind of handwriting, and to do arithmetic." Carvajal also remembers that the marquise wanted her to learn Latin—to continue studies begun at the Descalzas?—though it seems that she did not make too much progress.[12] These, of course, were skills related to public as well as private spheres, where readerly abilities (deciphering diverse hands, for example) and advanced numeracy would help in an array of intellectual and administrative pursuits. These activities were no less typical for a woman of Carvajal's stature than handicrafts, which were also key to her formation.

Notably, Carvajal would have been schooled in the public arts of "devotional practices." This would not have been something learned from any manual but through observation of her aunt, who was, again, despite everything, Luisa's primary (living) exemplar of feminine nobility. Indeed, although there was no hiding her aunt's "dry and harsh" personality, such unpleasantness was softened by admirable Christian virtue. The marquise was "a devoutly Christian woman full of Christian piety." As such, she never stopped performing devotions of all kinds, and she participated in any and all religious rituals, including masses, processions, and sermons. She also followed a rigorous regime of prayer and was avid in her acts of charity. (There were a lot of hospital visits.) Her public demonstrations of faith were so extensive that Carvajal even admits that she and her cousins "would tire of going to Church with her so often."[13]

There is another side to this apparent praise. Carvajal implies that her aunt was ultimately more about exterior show than internal growth. It is striking that her memories of spiritual nourishment are linked primarily to the aforementioned Ayllón, whom Carvajal saw as a taskmaster, and her uncle.[14] Be that as it may, we can assume that Carvajal would have assimilated the marquise's performativity, the external shows of piety, even if they alone would have been insufficient.

The marquise's serial churchgoing did not impede her terrestrial duties. Carvajal described how her aunt "spent time writing and taking care of business." When away, the marquis left his wife wholly in charge of the household. This was a heavy load, considering their substantial estate and the array of duties involved in its maintenance: she had to oversee vassals, take care of finances, and deal with any problems faced by the marquis's subjects. This involved, for example, caring for the poor and seeing that their necessities were met. Carvajal tells of how, during droughts, the marquise would ensure that they would have cheap bread.[15]

Her charitable work required establishing connections with a range of secular officials and ecclesiastical authorities. Wherever she lived, the marquise—employing a key tool of feminine nobility, the letter—"would write to all those concerned, magistrates, councilmen, merchants, patrons of hospitals and brotherhoods, bishops, and other ecclesiastical dignitaries."[16] As her husband's assistant, as a woman in charge of the home, the marquise must have made important social ties that would create a dynamic of mutual benefit between local institutions and the family. In observing her aunt's networking skills, Carvajal would have learned the extent to which pious, charitable ends required establishing and deepening worldly connections. Godly aims were thus not incompatible with a range of secular considerations essential for the flourishing of her uncle's estates.

This kind of embeddedness within a complex and mixed social environment would have extended beyond the home and the marquise's immediate surroundings. Although she does not mention this explicitly, Carvajal would have been told about her guardians' past deeds and would have known that her aunt had been fully integrated in the marquis's foreign political entanglements.[17] For example, during his storied time as Philip II's representative at the court of Rudolf II in Vienna, his wife worked hard to gather intelligence, pass on her husband's messages, and facilitate all sorts of political intrigue in her role as lady-in-waiting to the empress, herself an incredibly important power broker.[18]

In all this, the marquise was not unique. There is now a vast literature on the formal and informal roles women played in the maintenance of their husbands' estates—indeed, they were reared for such a role.[19] Wives of powerful men were expected to establish important alliances with women and men of their same status. They could become benefactors on a large scale to religious institutions, and they sustained individuals as well. Women often pulled strings for men seeking higher offices and other rewards.[20]

Noblewomen were involved in subtler forms of politics as well. Prescriptive literature of the time—books on ideal families, manuals for being a good wife—dwells on the importance of "home economics," but it also emphasizes how, in an ideal situation, women could and should be sources of spiritual uplift. The highly regarded scholar Juan Luis Vives—not a feminist of any sort—says of the good wife that she should exhort her husband "to innocence, piety, and mindfulness of divine goodness and power." Citing St. Paul, Vives asserts that "an unfaithful husband is sanctified by a faithful woman" (1 Cor. 7:14). This sanctification does not impinge on the salvation of the husband alone, though this is what mattered most. It is also the font of all his worldly success. By following God's will, "great resources and immense wealth are obtained." Vives recalls scripture to the effect that "there is no one who neglects anything in this world for his [God's] sake that will not receive much more, both in the next world and in this one as well" (Luke 18:29–30).[21]

Vives is not alone in emphasizing the high-stakes advisory role of women in marriage; it is a commonplace.[22] For example, decades after Vives wrote, Luis de León, an Augustinian friar, admits that if anyone can reform a straying husband, it is his wife.[23] Moreover, the notion that good advice for an errant husband would serve him well in matters not only spiritual but also material pervaded and could be as relevant to a merchant's ledger as it was to a monarch's *potestas*. Juan de la Cerda, a Franciscan friar, puts an explicitly political spin on this truism when he provides several examples of women who had turned rulers' wrath into pity, or, put another way, women who had steered their husbands from tyranny to good governance.[24]

In Carvajal's home, this dynamic must have been visible and legible. Although the marquis was master of his family and a pious exemplar above most others, his wife played an important role in his spiritual life as well.

Indeed, people said that the marquise tempered him at home, saving her husband from overzealous abnegation. This is surely something Carvajal would not have admired, but it nevertheless speaks to the fact that the good wife had a teacherly and uplifting role to play. She too could affect the spiritual affairs of men.[25]

It was once easy to relegate the maintenance of the home and spousal counsel to a sphere of domesticity apart from politics proper, the latter being the domain of men. But making gendered distinctions between public and private spheres, especially during the early modern period, does not make much sense. Such a separation did not exist in any simple way during Carvajal's lifetime, when forms of domesticity were integral to the functioning of governance, where the royal court was a space of intimacy and publicity, and where guardians of morality (confessors, for example) played an important role in the maintenance of the state.

In sum, Carvajal's aunt seems to have fit a model of noble behavior that conformed to essential cultural desires, even if her niece considered her profoundly imperfect. Carvajal would have watched her aunt and thus learned from her that women could be players in the game of international diplomacy, that they could function as heads of households, that they were expected to perform acts of public piety, that acts of piety could require a great deal of networking, and that they were expected to be agents of purification. As we will see in later chapters, Carvajal behaved as her aunt did with remarkable assurance.

### AN ARCHETYPE

The kind of near perfection Carvajal admired would have existed mostly in books. Without a doubt, the lives of saints were crucial to Carvajal's spiritual development, but while we know that she hung on every word of every saint's story, she does not elaborate on how these narratives informed her decisions. Nevertheless, commentators and biographers, by comparing her to female saints and martyrs of long ago, probably reflected Carvajal's own instincts and self-perception. Like those women, she too relished contradicting societal norms in defense of the true faith.[26]

More contemporary stories mattered as well. For our purposes, in the context of noble exemplarity, it's worth thinking about at least one woman she would have encountered (textually) before she left her uncle's home: Catherine of Aragon. There is no doubt that Carvajal would have read Pedro de Ribadeneyra's tremendously popular *Historia ecclesiastica del scisma de Inglaterra* (The ecclesiastical history of the English schism), first published in 1588, when Carvajal was twenty-two. Strikingly, Ribadeneyra described the book as "a mirror of princesses," because three women stand out as the most important defenders of Catholicism against Protestant attacks: Catherine of Aragon, Henry VIII's wife; Mary Tudor, queen of England; and Mary Stuart, onetime queen of Scotland. Among these three, Ribadeneyra emphasizes Catherine, largely because (for a Spanish audience) she manifested the ideals of her "nation."[27]

Unsurprisingly, Catherine is described as the good wife. Ribadeneyra insists that though she had all the necessary attributes, she refused to enter a convent or do anything to "prejudice her marriage." Taking on the role generally attributed to the exalted spouse mentioned above, Catherine was the responsible advisor, warning her husband until the very end "to care for his soul."[28] Within the context of Henry VIII's reign, conforming to Catherine's "wise" counsel would have meant the salvation of an individual king as well as the salvation of the kingdom over which he reigned.

The gesture at spousal acuity was a way to further emphasize her prodigious piety. The queen's life was marked by self-abnegation, which included fasting and painful prayer; it seemed meaningful to Ribadeneyra that she placed her knees directly on the ground while she spoke to God. She was also said to have worn a tertiary habit. No wonder Henry VIII got bored of her: "although the queen was not more than five years older than the king, in her life and customs she seemed a thousand years older." Her constancy was repaid by tears, because "our Lord wanted the sweet odor of her great virtues to spread throughout the world and so he allowed these virtues to melt in the fires of turbulence that she experienced."[29]

Such ethereal virtue was combined with worldly abilities. In her quest to save king and kingdom, Catherine needed to be proactive, using the terrestrial (political) tools at her disposal to achieve her dual ends. Catherine's sanctity was defined—as it was for ancient female martyrs, for example—by resistance. Hers was also informed by political prudence. Once Catherine saw the writing on the wall, understanding that Henry VIII would divorce her and turn his back on the church, she immediately tried to lean into her family networks by means of fiery correspondence with, above all, her nephew Charles V, to whom she explained the workings of the royal court and the schemes of Henry's evil counselors. She emphasized that she was the linchpin for maintaining what was left of virtue at the king's court. If she were gone, Catherine argued, her supporters would vanish, too, leaving the court a darker, more sinful place. Aside from writing to

Charles, Ribadeneyra reminds us, Catherine also quickly contacted the pope, predictably inserting herself into the complicated world of international diplomacy. While Rome tried to figure out a way to deal with the divorce issue in England, Catherine, having heard murmurs about papal plans, insisted that to allow the king to adjudicate the matter would be "making the king judge in his own case." She persisted in her uphill battle. Ribadeneyra tells us that papal ambassadors tried to shuffle her off to a convent or into some other kind of seclusion. She berated them and reminded them that they were "wanting to treat things that have already been decided, not only among counselors of two most prudent kings, but also in the Roman consistory . . . and accepted by acclamation of the world."[30]

Catherine, as Ribadeneyra describes it, reconciled such intransigence with supportive kindness. This was best exemplified by her relationship with her Franciscan confessor, John Forest, on his march toward incineration. To an extent, Ribadeneyra's rendering shows how the roles of confessor and penitent were reversed: while, through an exchange of letters, Forest encouraged the queen, she wanted to fortify him in return, insisting that he suffer tribulations "with happiness" knowing, she said, "that you will receive your eternal reward."[31] Forest responded that although he was aware of the ways of the world, she had awoken and reinforced his will to reject it. Catherine had not only assumed a confessorial persona—common in narratives of holy women—but by extension had confirmed her role as a publicly engaged woman standing up to the state by supporting an individual martyr seeking to reject it. In other words, she was taking part in, and encouraging, a battle against state authority (Henry VIII) by cultivating a priestly resistance fighter whose death would be solidifying to coreligionists, who would then resist the king as well.

Catherine also actively promoted a form of public piety in her daughter, Mary I. In a letter reprinted by Ribadeneyra, Catherine advised her in the ways of political dexterity, proper obedience, and survival. She instructed Mary to respond to the king and his ministers "with very few words" and to render obedience in those things not against God or her conscience. While Catherine exhorted her toward deepened piety and a pristine spirit, she pointedly told Mary *not* to take a habit. Her life, Catherine insisted, was to be a public one, one that promoted virtue by showing it in high relief against her father's sin.[32]

For readers like Carvajal, Catherine could epitomize the potential of a noblewoman at her most devout and God-serving. Her story, as presented by Ribadeneyra, offers a set of aspirational possibilities that were both active and extra-claustral. They formed the mental and behavioral tool kit that Carvajal drew from to provide guidance and justification for her own life, both in its self-sacrificing devotion and in its forward engagement in realms of action (politico-religious, intellectual, and the like) that might be thought of as masculine but were open to certain women of stature, authority, and spiritual strength. As we will see in more detail below, Carvajal's life followed some of the contours of Catherine's: she would go on to influence the behaviors and dispositions of the elite by means of thoughtfully cultivated networks and alliances with those who had politico-religious power in Spain and elsewhere. She would seek to live by the rules of rigorous devotion and thus become an advisor and nurturer of priests and statesmen. She would endeavor to become a purifying element of society. This, in turn, required some toil in matters very much of this world and with people whose power and purview were largely terrestrial.

POLITICAL LESSONS FOR THE WOULD-BE WIFE

Because Carvajal's uncle assumed she would live her life "in the world," he expected her to take part in the dynastic machinations by which the rich and powerful established kinship networks, financial ties, and political alliances. Simply put, the marquis assumed that his niece would find a match worthy of the Mendozas. In autobiographical writings, she recalls having had several suitors and that her uncle presented her to at least one. By the time he did, she had already decided against marriage in favor of a life of devotion to Christ. In retrospect, Carvajal was amazed that her uncle "with his great understanding and spirit, did not see the doctrine of perfection and mortification that he taught me could not be followed or bear fruit [in matrimony] ... that this [marriage] would be to ask pears of elm trees."[33] Too modest and obedient to reject her uncle's desires outright, she demurred, dissimulated, and smiled. He got the point but didn't like it.

Why would the marquis try to take Luisa off her religious course? In part it was simply a matter of insisting that a young woman do what was expected of her. It was also a matter of divergent understandings of (earthly) marriage. While Carvajal saw it as an impediment to her spiritual fulfilment, the marquis believed that marriage was not antithetical to exalted piety. He himself was proof of that. The marquis maintained a rich spiritual life and retained spiritual sensitivity even with both feet firmly planted on the ground. Carvajal remembered her uncle insisting that marriage could—as discussed above—even promote piety. Men needed good women to serve as models: the "state [marriage] was in need of persons who could give a great example of sanctity."[34] Carvajal agreed that this was often the case and that some women's piety was best exercised in their activities as wives. But such was not her calling.

The marriage issue ended up being a sticking point between uncle and niece, but there is no doubt that he was the single most influential person in her life. From her early teenage years he loved Carvajal dearly, as much as he did his own daughters. In fact, he developed a very special relationship with her based on what he saw as their shared Christian devotion. Keeping with contemporary expectations, the marquis took his role as spiritual guide to his entire family seriously. After dinner, he would take Carvajal and her cousins to a sitting room, where he would read from "sacred scriptures or church Doctors," sometimes for hours at a time.[35] Although her cousins would escape after a while, Carvajal stayed for the rest of her uncle's bloviations. Even when he was not around, she could gain access to the windows of his mind through his vast library, to the point that, as Anne Cruz has put it, she was reading over her uncle's shoulder.[36] Carvajal tells us that she habitually carried a spiritual treatise "as a perpetual companion" and insists that she preferred "mystical and substantial" books most, consulting them time after time.[37]

Because, as mentioned above, the role of the good wife colored the marquis's vision of Carvajal's future, his educational program would have included worldly topics. He surely expected Luisa to be equipped to be a diplomatic power player and mistress of her household, just as his own wife was. There were plenty of opportunities for quasi-formal and informal lessons on such topics, because Carvajal seems to have been around her uncle even while he tended to secular affairs. As Carvajal's confessor told it, the marquis would write at his desk, either by himself or with his scriveners and secretaries, while Carvajal sat on the ground doing her prodigious spiritual reading. Strikingly, when important visitors came, the marquis would usher her into a nearby oratory or behind a curtain, separated but not removed from his affairs.[38] There is no way that Carvajal would have closed her ears off to conversations within earshot. Indeed, by her own account, she had been an avid listener since childhood. From the time of her stay at the Descalzas, she "listened with extraordinary attention to people of some importance who spoke . . . about whatever grave thing, or ingenious matter, for a long time, without tiring."[39] Thus, aside from his devotional exemplarity, Carvajal's uncle epitomized a kind of political engagement very much intertwined with matters of salvation.

When Carvajal thought back to him, she emphasized the marquis's political prowess. He was "a man of great presence and intelligence, the most important and experienced of all the king's ministers and from what we know of the saintly King David, his image in many ways." By offering a Davidic comparison, Carvajal goes so far as to suggest that her uncle was a piously monarchical figure. She claims that one could see it in his regal eyes. She mentions with pride his religious zeal and the ways in which he defended the church, especially during his stint as ambassador to the empire. He was "a relentless exterminator of public and scandalous sins and devoted himself . . . to reconciling enmities and disbanding factions and dissensions."[40] Aside from his personal piety and theological learning, Carvajal admired how the marquis blended effective governance and true faith, how his service was oriented toward the public good, and how that public good was linked to the defense of the church and the diminishment of sin. As another David, the marquis was wise and temperate but also fierce; David was triumphant in battle against the sinful and was remembered for his ardent and successful fighting against the Philistines.[41]

Such parallels seem hyperbolic, but Carvajal's assessment conforms to the pious image that survived the marquis in circles beyond his home. For example, Ribadeneyra recalls the marquis with affection and admiration in his biography of Diego Laynez, onetime Jesuit General. Ribadeneyra remembers the marquis's close friendship with Laynez (whose parents were his vassals) and his unwavering devotion to the Society of Jesus. His sentiments were chiseled into the sumptuous tomb he had built in Almazán to commemorate the dead Jesuit. The marquis felt compelled to patronize the ostentatious monument owing to the honor he felt knowing that "such a distinguished man came from Almazán who with his sanctity and admirable doctrine not only represented his religion, but also served and defended the Holy Catholic Church in so many ways." To ensure proper homage to Laynez's memory, the marquis convoked the whole town to take part in acts of public commemoration, a spectacle of such solemnity that those present might have thought "father master Laynez was [the marquis's] lord."[42] Aside from a sense that the marquis was a supporter of good priests, this latter claim of inversion (momentary and imaginary, to be sure) between a secular lord and a religious figure was probably the highest compliment someone like Ribadeneyra could pay. The marquis, the old Jesuit suggested, displayed the superiority of the ecclesiastical and spiritual to that of the mundane and secular, a cornerstone assumption among those who embraced a vision of politics in which matters of faith ultimately trumped things of this world.

Carvajal's uncle was undoubtedly a man of faith and a man of business. In the years Carvajal was under his watch he formed part of the Councils of State and War, was named viceroy in Navarre, and would finish his career as president of the Council of Orders in Madrid. He was well-versed in the subtleties of negotiation and the rules of dissimulation, and he had a abiding interest in power. And yet there is no doubt that he was concerned about ecclesiastical matters and salvation, which he tended to with special urgency as the king's representative at local church councils and, above all, during his time as Philip's ambassador to the empire. Judging from Carvajal's remembrances—borrowed memories of her uncle's time in and around Vienna—his ambassadorial experience helped solidify his position as the monarchy's pious and effective servant.

To be an ambassador during the second half of the sixteenth century was to be sent into the wildfires of political and religious unrest.[43] The marquis knew his job was delicate, and he wrote trembling reports about how northern Europe—England, Denmark, and Sweden in particular—appeared to be ever more in the grasp of Calvinism. A good deal of his job centered on trying to avoid the same fate for the rest of Europe. At the very least, he wanted to maintain the piecemeal peace established by Philip II's father, Charles V, that allowed different confessions in different imperial territories. But more than such an expedient minimum, he wanted to convince good Catholic rulers to pivot toward decidedly Catholic interests, which in turn would help quell the spread of heresy in France and ultimately ensure that no aid be given by German princes to Netherlandish subjects who rebelled against Philip II's authority. Still, he was no fool. He understood that the emperor was in a bind, given the challenges posed by Protestant rulers within the patchwork empire. Despite his hatred for heretics, the marquis knew that rash action against them might mean the end of Catholic and Habsburg imperial rule, and so he did not advocate thoughtless zeal. In parts of the empire where "matters of religion cannot be ameliorated," he worked so that "they not get worse nor that we see any positive edicts against them [Catholics] in favor of heretics."[44]

Notwithstanding political nuances, the marquis was also frustrated by what he clearly saw as the emperor's failures to fully support the Catholic cause. He looked on desolately as imperial authorities kowtowed to Protestant pressures, so much so that Catholic concerns were neglected.

He witnessed how rulers spoke confidently about their own faith and their allegiance to Philip II while doing little to defend Catholics and promote the church. The times were such that authorities talked out of both sides of their mouths, promising anything on paper while rarely following through. Protestants did everything "under the pretext of religion," while the emperor chose dissimulation and seemed to countenance forms of toleration that the marquis thought to be the worst option possible.[45] The marquis thus had to push against a form of what he identified as "reasons of state" that seemed to minimize religion.[46] He was a voice of constant pressure on behalf of Philip II for continued loyalty toward Rome, for the protection of priests, and for the fight against Protestantism to the extent reasonably possible given the circumstances.

Even if he had to settle for a dubious status quo, as his (and his wife's) duties receded into memory and family lore, unpleasant diplomatic compromises would have faded. Admirers would hearken back to his time on the front lines against Protestantism, and they would vaunt his role as a hardliner. His efforts at the imperial court thus could be painted as an effort to promote a form of political engagement that, while savvy and rational, did its best to uphold the tenets of true faith.

Despite or perhaps because of the spiritual seriousness with which he tended to his affairs, the marquis struggled to attain a balance between his political and religious concerns. Unsurprisingly, he sought advice from priests to ensure that the secular did not overwhelm the spiritual. In fact, he sought the counsel of one of the most famous and respected spiritual guides of the sixteenth century, Juan de Ávila. Ávila's letter to the marquis on ideals of governance became one of his most important statements on the relationship between secular rulers and the church.[47] In it he suggested that the two realms, church and state, were distinct but fundamentally intertwined. The good governor is one deeply rooted in his faith, with an abiding respect for God's laws. Religion should always supersede concerns about "health, honor, and even his life when he might have to offer it all up to the good execution of his office."[48] The governor's actions should not be guided by self-interest but by the common good, because his office was executed not for lucre or power but out of charity. The good governor is necessarily a protector of the church and the ensurer of his subjects' virtue. As such, he should follow Christ's example: he should teach subjects how to be good, obedient, and faithful. Ávila's vision of the good ruler is one who eschews delight in savage punishments because the links between him and those he governs are those of love, and such bonds require the sustenance of his subjects' souls. Although Ávila does not question the need for secular governors to distribute justice, his understanding of successful governance hinges on the intentions and the moral underpinnings of the ruler's every action: punishments based on sinful motives like vengeance would be ineffective. The ruler should avoid "human prudence" (humana prudencia) and instead govern with godly prudence, the only kind that can lead to the positive "government of souls." To achieve this, the good governor must seek advice from the church when making decisions. This involved obtaining the proper guidance of confessors and, more broadly, securing the aid of ecclesiastical governors, mainly bishops. Ávila is careful to note that their advice was valuable not because of their political acumen but because they possessed a greater "celestial light that lives in them resulting from the contemplation in God."[49] It's crucial to Ávila's conceptualization of the well-run republic that an understanding of good governance depends on a spiritual disposition allowing for a lucid assessment of earthly politics through the lens of godliness.

The marquis was personally edified by Ávila's words, and he may have imparted that wisdom to Carvajal. But even without his direct intervention, her environment was saturated with—admittedly not unique—ideas and images that underscored the entwinement of church and state, of Christian ethics and secular rule. From testamentary records, we know that the marquis's possessions reflected a man who was, as Fernando Bouza has put it, both "learned and devout."[50] Carvajal would have been intimately familiar with the marquis's substantial art collection, including devotional images and reliquaries alongside what must have been a remarkable series of portraits of modern statesmen and historical emperors. In Almazán, she would have seen biblical images that brought both worlds together: lush tapestries depicting Moses, secular ruler par excellence; David and Goliath; the evil Old Testament king of Syria; and a painting of Judith cutting off Holofernes's head that the marquis kept in a chapel.[51] Most importantly, as mentioned above, Carvajal had access to her uncle's library, which included, apart from devotional and theological texts, a vast range of books on historical and, broadly speaking, "political" matters. She would have had access, for example, to a collection of Ávila's letters printed in 1578 that included the one originally written to the marquis.

We cannot trace with much precision the extent to which Carvajal read this or that book on "politics," but the marquis's library can at least allow us to suggest something about the general political orientation that would have been textually available to her. If we look at the prescriptive contemporary literature on political ideals and good rulership that he owned at the time of his death (in 1591), we see a definite interest in works advocating for the moral imperatives of the secular ruler as defender of the faith and the good servant of the church, works written by clerics who emphasize the close connection, as José María Iñurritegui Rodríguez has described it, between God's grace and the well-being of the republic.[52]

Here, one author will suffice. After returning from the empire, the marquis went back to Madrid between 1576 and 1578. There, among other things, he was involved in discussions about the looming conflict in Portugal about Philip II's claims to that crown (which the king would take by conquest in 1580). Interestingly, the marquis's library held two volumes by the famed Portuguese bishop of Silves, Jerónimo Osório. These were on Portuguese affairs, including a history of the reign of Manuel I and an advice manual on princely learning written to the young King Sebastian, both in their 1578 editions.[53] Osório today is a largely neglected figure, but in the sixteenth century, his voice had international resonances, in part because he wrote a book offering counsel to Elizabeth I of England. In it, he hurled one of the earliest full-fledged rebukes of Niccolò Machiavelli, whose books were said to have spawned "Machiavellian" political behaviors that critics believed nurtured man's basic instincts for power and glory while maliciously separating politics from Christian aspirations and the aims of salvation.[54] For all we know, the marquis may have read or at one point owned this book, too, but the books we know he possessed stay close to a traditional script that enmeshed piety with political success while promoting Christian ethics as the path toward good governance. Importantly, the Osório books we know he had emphasize and glorify traditional virtues of prudence, justice, and liberality as well as the king's duty to the public good, which is inevitably bound up with caring for the soul of the kingdom. They insist on both the necessity of true piety for good governance and, in line with Ávila and many others, the feebleness of "human prudence" without divine counsel.[55]

## THINKING POLITICALLY

Carvajal did not leave behind a formal political treatise, but we can glimpse how she perceived the political world in a somewhat unexpected place—among her musings about family life.

The idea that the household was a microcosm of the state was prevalent in early modern Europe (and well before and after). Not only did civilizations emerge from family units over the course of history but, for many, the well-run household mirrored the well-run state, and vice versa. Thus it should not be surprising—although it has gone mostly unnoticed thus far—that Carvajal's autobiographical writings contain the most vivid snapshot of how she conceptualized the relationship between church and state through the lens of her familial experiences.

When Carvajal discusses being caught between her uncle's encouragement of greater self-mortification and her aunt's displeasure about her asceticism, she comments on much more than domestic squabbles. How was a young woman to cope with contrary guidance from her two guardians, her two masters? It is worth quoting her reminiscence in full:

> I was especially pleased under his [the marquis's] rule, and did nothing without his permission, not even leave the house with my aunt or my married cousins, or go to the orchard, which was far from everyone, or wear special clothes or head cover for feast days. Since it was usually up to my aunt to give permission, my uncle preferred that I ask him first, for if he said no (as he often did) it would not be appropriate for her to grant it and I fail to follow her wish, as it would have upset her terribly. As I said, as regards earthly guidance, I was subject to her rule because I was a woman; yet the marquis was my spiritual advisor, whose advice also touched on things of a temporal nature. Therefore, it took no little care and skill to balance the two when she was at home, for she often stayed away a long time in other lands. My guidance, in those cases, involved my following the marquis's orders first, as he was head of household, and his authority more spiritual and of greater benefit to my soul, for it was permanent and enduring. For those things that I could not ask him without being noticed, I would remain quiet and let myself be blamed for what seemed my fault in not following their wishes, and even then, they at times guessed my reasons. In what I could freely choose without my uncle expressly wishing to grant permission, I obeyed the marquise, happy that I could please her in something. Whenever I was at liberty or in small things that she had ordered me to do, in both their presence, I always followed her orders rather than his, and my uncle was made to appreciate the discretion and tact this entailed.[56]

Although Carvajal's thinking exposes gendered norms and distributions of power, this passage is also fundamentally about the relationship between spiritual and secular spheres. Indeed, the disparity between her uncle's authority and her aunt's is not defined by gender (although this could have been assumed) but by the foundations of their power. As described here, the marquise was invested with temporal power, while the marquis oversaw the spirit. While Carvajal admits that there is a distinction between secular and religious authority, clearly one surmounts the other—or perhaps better put, one is implied in the other, given that the realm of the spirit ultimately governs the realm of the flesh.

This ambiguity between exclusive and overlapping jurisdictions at the heart of so much political theorizing at this time—the division and co-involvement of state and ecclesiastical power—might be reconciled on paper by thinkers of various stripes, but things became messy in the real world. Carvajal seems very aware of this as she describes the ways that politico-religious leaders and their subjects needed to perform a nimble dance. Clearly, her uncle trumped everything and her devotion to him was absolute, but the effectuation of this total submission required some sensitivity so that her aunt's (the state's) power might be placated. Success from this standpoint required her to circumvent her aunt's direct authority but also, on more than one occasion, to perform obedience in those things pertaining to her aunt's purview. In other words, Carvajal describes submission to earthly law, devoid of (direct) spiritual intervention, when doable. This was not simply or primarily a function of the proper distribution of power but also a game of dissimulation, a pragmatic, licit, and prudent way of keeping both regimes of power happy and satisfied and assuring some semblance of household comity.

That said, Carvajal upheld providential ideals consonant with what writers like Ávila maintained. As this story unfolds, we will see time and again that certain virtuous assumptions informed and even defined the course of action Carvajal took. For now, it's worth asserting that the politico-religious languages and ideologies briefly described above entered her frame of mind and mode of thought. Her correspondence is littered with references to "reasons of state" and distinctions between concerns that were "of an earthly nature" and those "of heaven."[57] In many letters she also wields the language of "prudence" in specialized ways, emphasizing (especially as it pertained to her own experiences) that there was a clear divide between its human and its godly form. In general, Carvajal held fast to the notion that "Our Lord often settles matters in such a way that their outcome defies the expectations of human prudence."[58] For her, then, human prudence alone was fundamentally defective without spiritual buttressing. In other words, decision-making based on earthly concerns alone often resulted in unhappy outcomes. But Carvajal was no amateur. Like her uncle, she could think through the earthly political logics she often found distasteful, especially when trying to decipher the thoughts of Protestant enemies (who were, she believed, invariably moved by secular objectives).[59] However, thinking in a distinctly secular mode does not necessarily mean succumbing to it. She just knew the enemy.

It makes sense to consider her public or semipublic comments on politics and political considerations to be polemical. Contemporaries often tried to (and did) delineate realms of secular and spiritual activity, lines that divided church and state, but Carvajal was brought up to believe that there could be no ecclesiastical and spiritual reforms without a supportive, godly state. Furthermore, she and like-minded contemporaries believed that the state was not viable without the help, guidance, and sometimes dominance of the church. Contemporary challenges to these assumptions were deemed not only deeply troubling but scarily dangerous. As a result, any public discussions dealing with complex politico-religious dynamics necessary for safeguarding the republic should not be taken as regurgitated pieties but as real interventions within a political discourse. While the promotion of spiritual objectives in the realm of politics was serious, the fact that things we take as assumptions needed articulation and rearticulation proves that thinkers, writers, and doers like Carvajal intended to go against the grain of perceived reality and, increasingly, against what was seen as the secularizing trends of political praxis.

Although Carvajal was not a political thinker by trade, she was nevertheless politically thoughtful.[60] This thoughtfulness was the product of the schooling discussed above. It would be simplistic and even demeaning to suggest that in her conception of religiopolitical values she learned everything from her uncle. Still, it is important to underscore that her worldview was a result of her upbringing, which helps us make sense of the methodical political actor and observer she would become.

## POLITICS IN THE FLESH

I don't want to suggest—indeed, it would go against the spirit of this book—that the marquis's "political" lessons existed separately from the spiritual guidance he offered. To the contrary, his understanding of the social order was predicated on the assumption that a greater communion with God was fundamental for everyone, from the monarch down. The fulfillment of the individual or the state required severe action. The concrete effects of necessary devotion should be printed on the skin. This is certainly how Carvajal came to see it; a witness could say without hesitation that "one could talk forever [seria nunca acabar de contar] about the inventions and means that she found to torture herself for God's love."[61]

Carvajal's life story, as she constructed it and as it was constructed by contemporaries, hinged on the idea that her spiritual aptitude was evident from an early age, but she would reach a higher plane of spiritual enlightenment later in her youth. When Carvajal was in her early teens, the marquis decided he could push her more than the other women in his household. He procured the assistance of an unnamed woman who was directly in charge of her penitential activities. Carvajal was commanded to disrobe to the waist, though out of modesty she covered her breasts "with a cloth that I held under my skin." Then her uncle's maidservant would use whips made of guitar strings to flagellate her "as long as she wished with such well-aimed blows" that Carvajal "could barely stand them." To hide her pain, she would clasp her hands together tightly.[62]

In keeping with the logic of penance as an act subsequent to an interior movement of the soul, Carvajal insisted that before the torments began, she would offer God the sacrifice she was about to endure. If she had not made the offer "from the bottom of her heart," she did not think she "could ever have had the strength to withstand such violence."[63] Such divinely inspired fortitude left lasting marks, sufferings beyond the moment of her imposed torments. The bodily damage was so severe that sometimes her clothes would stick to her bloody body. One time her uncle had asked her to fetch him a little desk, and when she did so, her wounds tore apart, gushing blood and pus.[64]

Scholars have made much of the marquis's violent impositions. Anne Cruz sees them as legible within the realm of contemporary (Spanish) Catholic culture.[65] Others see something more dubious and perverse going on. Indeed, scholars have labeled Carvajal's severe penitential sufferings as a form of sexual abuse and, although they have no solid evidence, some have even conjectured that the marquis secretly leered at his suffering niece.[66] While Carvajal's actions do need to be seen as part of a penitential culture, it is also true that Carvajal herself was aware that she was subjected to particularly nasty punishments. She admitted (along with others, including her confessor) to the *extraordinary* nature of her uncle's program.[67]

Although her uncle may have taken the notion of bodily penance to its limits, Carvajal consciously decided to embrace those behaviors, sometimes beyond her uncle's will. For example, it was said that once, when they were living in Madrid, she went to him for spiritual advice. It was six in the morning, and he asked her to meet him at the oratory, where he would talk to her. But other duties got in the way. He hurried off to court, where he had council work to do, and did not get home until around five o'clock. Carvajal stayed enclosed in the oratory. The marquise was distressed that her niece had been locked up, groaning that her husband was going to "kill her before her time," judging that he was being cruel. She did not know that Carvajal had the key and could have left at any time. She had not budged for fear of disobeying the marquis. When her uncle got home, he was confused. It was not so much that she was locked away—he had done that before—but he was presumably amazed because he had not intended for this visit to the oratory to be a penitential act or one of such rigor. When he asked her why she had confined herself, she did not respond much, enjoying the fact of her humility.[68]

If Carvajal wanted to escape the material world, she nevertheless amassed a collection of penitential objects. According to Isabel de la Cruz, she had two crucifixes with nails on them, an array of studded chains, and whips. She used an iron gag (*mordaza*) with tightening screws as well as little ropes with which she would tie her wrists together or that she tied around her neck.[69]

Carvajal believed that through severe penitential practices, she had achieved spiritual enlightenment and came to understand the lengths to which Christians had to punish themselves for their inherent sin. Her suffering was imitative and humble in her desire to experience Christ's pain, efforts "that both enriched me and increased my disillusion of the world."[70] So Carvajal's self-harm was thus a process of self-recognition and a path to an assessment of society at large, allowing her to comprehend how the kingdom of man was plagued by the attendant dangers of sin and how forms of purification were essential not only for the individual but for all people (and polities). Such insight fundamentally informed how she "read" the world around her and how she would maneuver through the cesspools in which she trod for the rest of her life. The microcosmic experience of devotion, and devotional suffering, had macrocosmic consequences in generating a way to imagine a communal experience or sets of experiences that were required for the godly state.

CONCLUSION

Luisa de Carvajal did not spend restless nights thinking about how she would one day be a participant in European diplomacy or how she would someday be written about as a "political" actor. Nevertheless, this chapter has shown how her upbringing created infrastructures of thought and action that would stay with her for the rest of her life. Put simply, Carvajal was brought up to be a noblewoman, and as such she depended on both the pointed lessons offered by her stand-in parents and the more implicit ones that were the result of everyday life and observation. She assimilated a sense of feminine authority in worldly and spiritual matters, she developed a strong sense of private and public performances of piety, she came to believe in the entwinement of worldly and spiritual things, and she acquired an advanced sense that correction and purification would be the only viable path for the maintenance and salvation of the individual and of Christendom at large.

CHAPTER 2

# Pious Publicity in Spain

Carvajal's uncle, in sharp contrast to her tight-lipped aunt, bragged about his niece loudly and promiscuously. Her patient bodily sufferings, her devoted prayer, her submission before (his) authority: all these made her special. He would often tell people, with an air of gravity, that his niece was "a wise maiden" (haec est virgo sapiens).[1] It was said that the marquis esteemed his niece so much that "he was already seeing her canonized."[2] Carvajal says she felt shame at his over-the-top praise, but surely his sentiments touched her. Even if she felt uncomfortable, she must also have felt chosen. After all, her uncle's insistent attention and his rigorous physical and spiritual demands succeeded in providing some measure of spiritual attainment, or, at the very least, whatever sparkle of divine proximity she experienced from her earliest years brightened with his help. Carvajal felt herself a sinner, but less so than many others. She gradually became more convinced of her salvation.

Over time, it dawned upon Carvajal that her family was deficient. Although, as we've seen, she sometimes made her uncle out to be a church-like authority, he was, in fact, not that. With experience, Carvajal "began to sense that there was a great discrepancy between his behavior, although it was so saintly, and his being a lay person."[3] Although he was her most immediate spiritual authority, he was not the ultimate one, because when push came to shove, he was imbued with earthly traits that excluded him from true sanctity. Carvajal came to this poignant awareness because of the occasional shortcomings of his counsel, his perhaps unintended direction away from purity. Most importantly, as mentioned in chapter 1, she interpreted her uncle's attempts to have her married off as a diversion from her spiritual calling. He also dissuaded her from modesty. Although

Carvajal is ambiguous about this, the marquis, while steering her from vanity, seems to have advised that she be more forthcoming (presumably to him) in her feelings and her performance of self-discipline, something that rubbed her the wrong way.[4]

Ultimately, despite true love and affection, only distance from her uncle could erase the stain of his worldliness. She could overcome dangers her own uncle posed because she was ultimately guided by her direct relationship to God: "Our Lord willed it from early on that I foresaw how wretched it was to place my trust in someone other than himself [God]."[5]

When the family moved to an imposing palace just off the very busy Calle Mayor in Madrid, Carvajal hid behind those thick walls. She chose to live in an apartment separate from the rest of the family, in as austere surroundings as her wealth and status allowed. Her decision to self-isolate, the deepening of her meditative practices, the profundity of her prayer, and the extension of her penitential suffering were means by which to approach true devotion, methods of self-purification, and activities meant to achieve a better understanding of the divine. Carvajal was trying to assume a form of detachment that most people could not, either because of their constitution or their social position, and she knew that. Her devotional efforts were thus articulations of difference and, most likely, superiority. Indeed, she became ever more convinced that God had spoken to her in special ways even before she came under her uncle's protection, and that after her uncle's death she became ever more aware of God's will.[6] She portrayed herself as effective in the arts of discernment. All her behaviors, all her actions, all the times that she seemed to perform things that were not pleasing to some, she would lean on this understanding and would claim that if she followed a certain path it was only because she knew that God willed it.[7]

### A BID FOR NOTORIETY

To be sure, Carvajal's decisions were not taken lightly. Had she not sought counsel, it would have been a clear indication of pride. Consequently, in contemplating her new life, she would have been expected and encouraged to seek the guidance of confessors. She did. However, Carvajal went one step further, reaching out to people beyond her immediate community. In 1586 or 1587, just a year or two before she went to Madrid, Carvajal decided to write a letter to an extraordinarily famous author of devotional books, Fray Luis de Granada, and his extraordinarily famous confessant

Maria da Visitaçao, a woman who would be dubbed the "nun of Lisbon." Since the 1570s Maria had demonstrated healing powers and prophetic acumen, and she had experienced ecstatic episodes and raptures in communion with God that culminated in the stigmata. Fray Luis promoted her across Europe as something like a new St. Catherine of Siena to combat the corruptions, sins, and heresies of the times. So, when Carvajal wrote to her, she was aiming very high.[8]

As Carvajal later recalled, the letter sought advice about her sacrificial designs. She explained to Maria that her devotion to Christ was such that she desperately wanted to give her life for Him. Specifically, she described her desire to go to England because the ongoing persecution there would allow her to "die for our lord and at least suffer very much for his sacred love."[9] As she wrestled with these desires, Carvajal wanted the nun to commend her to God and offer her opinion on the matter. As it happened, Maria never responded, something Carvajal's first biographer counted as a blessing—in 1588 the nun would confess to having feigned her spiritual experiences and painted on the stigmata.[10] Her punishment was seclusion and obsolescence.

But Carvajal didn't know any of that. The calculus of her missive was surely based on the respect and awe she felt for Maria's renowned spiritual gifts. But the fact that she felt compelled to communicate with such prominent figures, and that she expected to receive a response, indicates the plane on which Carvajal understood herself to be operating and the value (or potential value) of her spiritual mission. We can take Carvajal at her word that she was seeking to quell her internal struggles by talking to others, but she was doing more than that. Her primary interlocutor was Maria herself, but Carvajal also expected her to fill Fray Luis in, thus creating an inchoate audience of two. We have to imagine that Carvajal recognized that they might talk to others about her. Should she succeed in establishing a relationship with these figures, she would have inserted herself in a much more expansive network that would lead, at the very least, to greater name recognition among the holy and devout. She was trying to create an *audience* for her work.

Carvajal would not have been interested in fame as such, but she welcomed notoriety. This would not have been a strange penchant and, in fact, she would have been operating within a licit mode. A culture so immured in tradition, historical exempla, and tropological readings of scripture and nature allowed individuals to develop a strong sense of potential exemplarity. Although, as Brad Gregory argued long ago, the search for martyrdom was earnest in those days, there's little doubt that martyrs understood the pedagogical significance of what they were doing, something demonstrated by, for example, their performances at the gallows, where scripts were followed (and eluded) with various publics in mind.[11] These performances had resurged in Carvajal's lifetime within the context of confessional strife and religious warfare. Public acts of defiance were understood as continuations of efforts reaching back centuries, and they were construed through the lens of the *vitae* that were such an important part of Carvajal's spiritual diet. Indeed, it almost goes without saying that tales of saints and martyrs inspired holy behaviors and objectives. It is also worth underlining that sixteenth-century Christians were aware that the subjects of those *vitae* attained enduring relevance in their own times and were, of course, promoted by writers contemporary to the events described. As Juan Basilio Santoro says in the introduction to his massive compendium of saints—one of Carvajal's favorite books—their lives were originally written and preserved by "those present and who were witnesses to the saintly spectacles of the martyrs."[12]

Given the persona Carvajal would assume, we must notice the public import of her intimate choices. Aside from her reaching out to Luis de Granada, we can point to another example of this dynamic: her quest for martyrdom. Carvajal's goal of a holy death was instigated by a deep desire to satisfy God, to follow his "sweet steps," thus "uniting closely with him."[13] And yet this does not contradict the fact that her journey was not private, even before her departure for England. One contemporary recalled that of the several spiritual promises she made, martyrdom was the only one that she may have advertised or made public: she would carry her written vow in a little tin box.[14] Of course, martyrdom in itself is not a natural occurrence. In its most pristine form, it is a death accepted and sought to fulfill a holy cause, typically in sight of foes and friends alike. Indeed, piety can be private and objectives truly and honestly a reflection of spiritual goals embedded deep in the soul, but there can be, and almost must be, a public side to the whole business. We might ask, as Aviad Kleinberg does, "What was the point of behaving like a saint, if it was not recognized by others?"[15] Without that recognition, Carvajal would be completely uninteresting, an unnoticed absence in the historical record. It is both paradoxical and totally predictable that, as Christopher Henstock has noted, "though she claimed to be leaving the world, she was in a sense entering the world."[16]

## CORRUPTIONS OF THE CITY

The path toward public piety was by no means easy. When her uncle died, Carvajal was that much closer to leaving the shroud of nobility behind. But, as her confessor would tell it, the marquise (after her husband's death) forbade Carvajal's hard life outside of her home. Carvajal was, of course, disappointed, but she told her cousin that "today you see how my lady takes this away from me, pray to God that her excellency lives a long time, as I desire, but I think it certain that our lord will take away all impediments to achieve my vocation."[17] Her aunt died six months later, and we imagine it was ultimately a relief for Carvajal. Soon after the marquise's passing, the marquis's brother, who was a priest, tried to intervene. Since Carvajal sought neither marriage nor conventual removal but instead wanted to live a recollect life outside either state, he suggested that she live under his wing. Carvajal refused, saying (as her confessor reports), "God calls me for things different than living with a relative [deudo]."[18] Ultimately, the marquis of Almazán, her cousin, arranged for her to stay in a "very poor and uncomfortable" house close to the Jesuit college, where she would live with her servants, who would soon become her "sisters."[19] In the wake of Carvajal's decisions, this assistance might have been the last act of familial kindness for a long time. People would later claim that her family came to "detest and abandon [her] and did not recognize her [as family]."[20]

Carvajal may have ended up in a modest home, but it was a well-placed one. The proximity to the Jesuit college had extraordinarily important benefits for her spiritual growth, and she seems to have spent some time there, which means that she also spent a great deal of time near an important intellectual center and theater of international missionary (and political) activity. According to Walpole, her confessor, Carvajal had bought two chairs for her little house, one for herself and one for the Jesuits who would come to visit.[21] At first it seems that they were essentially the only ones welcome. Later, things became a little looser. Though Carvajal apparently scorned the time she had to spend with others, she nevertheless had built into her schedule two hours (from four to six) during which she would meet with visitors.[22]

Her encounter with Joan de Ceráin—a native of Madrid who played a role in Carvajal's secular affairs—can serve as an example of her pious interactions. As a young man, he had heard about "the laudable and saintly life lived by this virgin saint," and he, "in part out of devotion and in part because of youthful curiosity, wanted to see her, wishing to know her because she was a subject of such sanctity."[23] Carvajal made a point of concealing herself and remained elusive, but he eventually managed to make contact. It was an awkward exchange. When he came to call, Carvajal did not allow him up the stairs, something he initially found rude. Soon after being turned away, though, he recognized her aloofness as a sign of virtue and holiness. Later, he learned though Carvajal's confessor that she would have spent much more time with him, offering spiritual counsel, had he been a woman—proof, Ceráin claimed, of her great wisdom. Ceráin would spend some time with Carvajal on business but relatively little time in spiritual consultation. He was reluctant to take much of her time, instead sending his wife, who would die the good death, and his daughters, who would become nuns, largely thanks to Carvajal.[24] This engagement and nonengagement with Ceráin and his family reveals the relational thickets Carvajal established even in her removal from the world. Worldly interactions were nevertheless sites of spiritual edification. Perhaps most importantly, we can glean the way in which Carvajal's rich counsel to women—something that must have taken up a lot of her time—could be a means to bolster the piety of a male devotee as well.

Carvajal had many intimate encounters, but in the first years after choosing a life of public piety, Madrid was her main stage. Not only was she in a big city but she also lived in its center, within walking distance of the Plaza Mayor. A life of abnegation required Carvajal to scrounge for sustenance and, commensurate with her life of poverty, she became intent on living by seeking alms. For example, her confessor reveals that she sought charity at the Church of St. Francis in Madrid, where she stood among the beggars seeking food, waiting for alms and bread crusts. After receiving these gifts, she was said to have prayed until vespers inside the church, only moved from meditation by a companion who tugged her mantle.[25] Even when she was not begging—something she did ostentatiously—Carvajal always struck a humble pose; witnesses say she walked in the middle of the Calle de Toledo, one of the busiest thoroughfares of the city, with a basket on her head. More shockingly, she reveled in filth. People commented on how Carvajal would cross paths with her family when she shopped at the plaza, rejoicing in the dirt that splashed on her as their horses passed by.[26]

Sights and rumors of these spectacles surely led some among the upper classes to say she might be crazy. Others blamed the family for having let "such a young and important" woman go around as a mendicant. Among the commoners she was just a source of ridicule.[27] Carvajal's confessor reports that she took it all with rock-hard constancy. But for us, signs of her fortitude matter less than the very fact that both her performativity and the known context of her nobility rendered her noticeable within an urban landscape and, in a sense, legible to witnesses in Madrid. Carvajal was presumably aware of her role as a model, a visible manifestation of abnegation and devotion to God. People may have been too fleshly and corrupt to fully appreciate the embedded messages in her activities, but she certainly had a point to make.

If there was much talk about Carvajal, pro and con, behind her back, people talked to her directly as well. When this happened, she had the opportunity to sermonize. For instance, the duchess of Medina de Rioseco remembers seeing her at the plaza in Valladolid once Carvajal had moved there, carrying a little basket and buying some herbs to eat. The duchess stopped her carriage to ask, with some judgment in her tone, "Why are you walking around like this, with such mortification and self-scorn?" Carvajal quickly answered: "Your excellency mortifies herself much more in debasing her greatness by talking to me than I in what I do." Carvajal's response had at least a twofold meaning. She was underlining how lightly she wore her penitence and she implied something about the duchess, for whom the simple act of talking to a person of lower rank would have been felt as a sacrifice. Weak wine compared to Carvajal. The duchess claimed to have been deeply edified by the incident.[28]

Carvajal was creating something like an urban public. Hers was not a one-off show but a regular, and regularized, set of performative activities meant to galvanize an audience that would then comment on and assess why she lived the life that she did. Indeed, although it would be too much to say that she was bringing into existence a group of spectators with coherent interests, her confessor does intimate that there were types of discourses, types of readings of her, that were shared by social classes who all mingled but remained distinct in a city environment—thus all the rumors and judgments circulating behind her back and to her face. If, as some scholars have suggested, her acts of charity and such were not "successful" in terms of lives, or souls, saved, Carvajal succeeded at making people aware of her quasi-sanctity.[29]

This dynamic was a prerequisite and, indeed, a manifestation of her political presence in Spain.

Carvajal was a purifying element amid the muck of city life. Both Madrid and Valladolid pullulated with activity, much of it carnal and commercial.

Because both cities were epicenters of governance, they were overrun by political aspirants, people petitioning for court appointments, and people seeking just rewards from the king. Since visitors and inhabitants were finely attuned to the dangers posed by corruptions of all sorts, these spaces of worldly action inspired some to voice their concerns and outrages by many means: print, manuscript, rumor, and public exhortations. Although neither court nor king was the city itself, both the monarch and his household represented all the miseries and sins that afflicted the republic.

Thus monarchs did not escape harsh commentary. While critiques of Philip II's reign were not new, its last decade witnessed an upsurge of discontent. (The failed armada and stern tax policies did not help.) This period coincided with Carvajal's move toward independence. She, perhaps unsurprisingly, had unkind things to say about the king. When Philip III ascended to the throne, she argued that the previous regime had witnessed a time of "rack and ruin." Maybe there was something personal about her distaste: Carvajal thought Philip gave her uncle short shrift and rancorously said that Philip had not deserved the marquis.[30]

After Philip II's death, things scarcely had gotten better in Madrid and at court. Carvajal was willing to give Philip III a chance—he was not subject to her sharp pen and tongue—but she nevertheless hated the political scene in Madrid. Still, there was hope. By 1601 the regime left the capital behind for the more relaxed environment of Valladolid. It is unclear that any court setting could be cleansed of worldly desire, but Carvajal thought that the move, which upset so many courtiers, might be a kind of punishment for them, since "they were all very taken up and occupied with their business and moneymaking, their households and creature-comforts."[31]

There is no evidence that Carvajal's "fame" was ample enough to have interested or concerned Philip II, but she certainly caught his son's attention. Indeed, at least by some reports, news of her holiness had spread to such an extent that the king's entire family wanted to be in her company.[32] Philip III was so intrigued that he would eventually provide regular subventions. He did so out of piety and admiration, no doubt, but also surely because he wanted to be in the good graces of someone considered holy. Since some of Carvajal's spiritual energy might rub off on the almsgiver, support for the holy insinuated royal piety. To achieve notice from the monarch may not have been her primary intent, but it was indisputably a result of her performances of piety.

In a sense, monarchical attention was an extraordinary win if her intent was general reform. The precise dynamics between Carvajal and Philip's court are unclear, but one incident—which cannot be corroborated in Carvajal's extant letters—might provide insight into the semiotic possibilities afforded by the relationship. It seems that Carvajal was invited to court by Queen Margaret. Carvajal hesitated, only going at the behest of her confessors. (Again, her confessors both abetted and encouraged her public persona.) We can imagine Carvajal walking a sweaty walk past the Plaza Mayor toward the royal palace and making herself known there, an exotically humble sight within the most palatial of palatial walls. She was eventually greeted by the queen herself. The encounter might have begun with some nervous chitchat; at the very least, we know that there was some awkwardness and tension. Margaret recognized that "she [Carvajal] was not there willingly" and suspected that she would feel embarrassed meeting the king (who was out, but now approaching). Carvajal admitted as much and responded that the queen would be showing her "great mercy" if she let her leave. And so she did.[33]

There is more to the story. That an account of the event circulated in some detail suggests someone (or several people) felt it was useful, likely for several agendas. Incapable or unwilling to be flexible, Carvajal indulged her petulance to the extent that the queen noticed her inhibitions and could read the meaning of her disquiet—an allergy to the royal ambience. Not only did Carvajal come off as the saintly figure she longed to be but the queen came off well, too, for recognizing her sanctity. While it was not uncommon for holy women to be invited to court and take part in its political workings by means of their sage counsel, it is telling that at least in this case, Margaret was the one doing the summoning. Thus it was Margaret who enjoyed the fruits of Carvajal's piety. The queen's clemency could have been seen as a reflection of her own inhibitions, an important suggestion given the troubled situation at court. Margaret had an interest in supporting a trope of purification and embracing cutting critiques of court life because she was at the center of political discord, fighting for continued influence at court against the king's *privado*, the duke of Lerma. Part of the onslaught against his vile faction was a well-developed discourse about its insidious corruption.

It stands to reason that if Carvajal's fame reached the pinnacle of royal authority, her story would resonate among other powerful people in and around court. One witness for her beatification proceedings reports with admiration that "ecclesiastical and secular princes and the gravely learned" venerated her. He specifically mentions that Melchor de Molina—a member of the king's council who had also been Carvajal's lawyer in Valladolid—said that he took her "for the person [sujeto] of greatest sanctity that he knew, that he was certain that in the tribunals of the king, no one was seated with greater judgment or genius than this blessed lady."[34]

When Philip III moved the seat of government from Madrid to Valladolid, Carvajal moved as well, landing in another modest house not far from the palace and right next to the English College, a quasi-Jesuit institution that was a place of both piety and political intrigue. As I've suggested so far, such proximities are not incidental or aleatory. They testify to the fact that she wanted to be in the thick of things. This might have gone against her simplest instincts, but there were concrete reasons for which she remained, during much of her time before departing for England, with one foot firmly on the ground.

They had to do with money.

Carvajal's father expected and desired that she would develop into a young woman worthy of the family. He, and later her uncle, had assumed that she would be swept into a properly arranged marriage or that she would choose a conventual life. To help ensure these outcomes, her father left her an extraordinary inheritance that would be used for her spousal dowry and a smaller (but still substantial) amount should she decide to take the veil. Her father had not accounted for the strange limbo that Carvajal chose, a life of no institutionalized matrimony, wedded neither to Christ nor to man. When it was clear that she had chosen this different kind of situation, there was a question about what would happen to her inheritance. Her brother, Alonso de Carvajal, had a solution. To him, it seemed that she had chosen to live in an ersatz convent, and so she should receive just a small portion of the monies in his possession. His sister disagreed, and the conflict would take years to resolve. For us, the details of the case are not important, but the discourse surrounding it does matter for understanding how Carvajal situated herself within her social setting.

Carvajal insinuated that part of her mission was pious, even in worldly matters. At the time, as one contemporary put it, "people were scandalized to see her at court claiming properties [pretendiendo hazienda] while on the other hand living as a poor person, saying that she wanted nothing."[35] In response, Carvajal emphasized that she fought for her money at the recommendation of her confessors and that it would be used not for herself but for some act of piety. (Ultimately, she would fund the establishment of an English novitiate in Louvain.) But there was another, equally pious end that ultimately justified the tenacity with which she pursued her inheritance. As many people remembered it after her death—when bidding for her canonization, people had to grapple with the perceived money-grubbing affair—her conflict with her brother helped purify him. What might seem like something debased actually had didactic potential and might be a vehicle of salvation. It would later be said that her success ensured her brother "would participate in the merits of her good works."[36]

This configured charity was in line with the role she had arrogated to herself of quasi-confessor to her brother. A series of superficially courteous letters to him suggests a measure of disregard. When he suffered a period of sickness in 1602, Carvajal wrote to him expressing hopes for his full recovery. Even as she did, however, she seemed wary. In language that is far from comforting, she expresses a providential belief that God might save him—but then again, he might not. It seems as though salvation is, in part, left up to her brother. While she is certain of her own, she says she felt it "intolerable . . . to think that I was not going to see you in heaven's eternal glory." Consequently, she exhorts him to throw himself "confidently into His hands with genuine contrition for offences committed against Him and the firmest resolve you can summon to mend your ways." This kind of advice was, to an extent, expected for anyone in a fragile state of health. Everyone should aspire to spiritual betterment while in the throes of death. And yet Carvajal understands that she might have crossed some sort of line. She offers a mild apology: "I do not know what I am saying, dear brother."[37]

She knew what she was saying. In future correspondence, in the thick of their legal battles, Carvajal would unleash her temper. Her brother seems to have ignored her advice, at least in her judgment, so she warns that his soul is in danger and implores God to "deliver it from such great evil." She laments that her brother does not have adequate spiritual counsel at hand and insists that he go to confession, which would be a sign that he had chosen to follow the right path. She urges him to avoid the ways of the weak, who put off the proper worship of God to a later time. She berates him for his inconstancy, pointing out the deficiency of those who during an illness (wink, wink) ask for forgiveness only to return to their old ways when better. She begs him to change "so as to favor salvation." She damningly reminds her brother that "goodness ensures salvation as far as possible, and eternal and consummate evil will deprive you of it." We cannot know for sure what set Carvajal off in such a blunt way, but we can assume that, in general, she did not like what he had to say about their financial dispute.[38]

But there was a bigger issue at stake. In berating him for his worldliness, she also cautions her brother against political corruption. She reminds him that "there are no affairs of state or empire" more important than salvation. If such matters have any serious importance, "it is insofar as they relate to the salvation of souls and the pleasing of the Lord." Save for those imperatives, power and authority "have no weight or value."[39] Carvajal did not suggest that matters of state were unimportant or that they should be neglected but that they were secondary or subservient to God's will. We must assume she believed that the workings of politics, the everyday affairs implied in governance, were not inherently abhorrent unless they contravened that will.

Such cautioning is important because it serves as a reminder that a crucial part of Carvajal's "project," even in relatively private matters, had to do with redirecting the energies and occupations of the wealthy and powerful. This was not a marginal endeavor or a set of easily compartmentalized spiritual goals. Carvajal was out to right the wrongs of society. As mentioned in chapter 1, Carvajal's basic aims would be uninteresting were it not for the fact that they had particular force in a period during which tropes of faithlessness and decline seemed prevalent, ominous, and pertinent to "matters of state."

### VIRTUES OF THE COUNTRY

In this context, the court/country dichotomy seemed apt. The distinction was not a Spanish or early modern invention, but this dualism operated in early modern polemics looking to criticize regimes perceived as corrupt and, more broadly, the debauchery of cities. One of the most famous books along these lines was published in the 1530s by a Dominican friar, Antonio de Guevara, titled *Menosprecio de corte y alabança de aldea*.[40] In it, he describes life outside the hustle and bustle of big towns as peaceful, absent of psychological torments, simple, and safe. The countryside was no place for dissimulations, luxury, and sinfulness.

This sensibility colored the moral mindset of the age. Luis de León, an Augustinian friar whose works Carvajal knew well, rejected the ways of the world. In his ode *La vida retirada*, the protagonist seeks to remove himself from earthly strife in a world brimming with false flattery, pride, fame, and wealth. Instead, he seeks nature: the garden, the hill, the river, the fragrant breeze, and the singing birds. While others seek the ephemeral, he chooses to recline and sing in the placid shade.[41] In a more substantial work, *The Names of Christ*, León expands on these sentiments and occasionally speaks directly to the political nation. He laments the misguidance offered by the king's intimates, as "those who surround the king not only make mistakes but often try to deceive ... to further their own private purposes."[42] If the court is a den of deception and political corruptibility, the countryside provides the optimal context for moral rectitude. There, a life of quietude and security allows love to set deeper roots among the populace, facilitated "by the free spectacle of the sky, of the earth, and other elements, so that their life is a clear image or a school of pure love."[43] The pervasiveness of love in extra-urban spaces suggests that there, the republic flourishes; without that love, there could only be ruin.

It is no surprise that in times of political dislocation—amid factional disputes during the reign of Philip III, for example—the smear of urbanity and the potential of extra-courtly life would form the propagandistic theme of choice, especially against those who had attained outsized influence and power.[44] It is thus useful to consider this court/country dichotomy, a parallel of the division between body and soul, within the context of Carvajal's poetry.

Scholars have decided that Carvajal's poetic output was written and completed by 1600, during her time in Madrid.[45] They have pointed out the Ignatian qualities of her work and have insisted, because of her poems' autobiographical nature, that they should be used to understand her piety and her devotional practices.[46] This seems right. Indeed, Carvajal's poetry speaks to her own spiritual journey toward a union with Christ in at least two ways. First, it is descriptive of that union (and the struggles to achieve it). Second, the poems were her own meditative tools that would aid in achieving proximity to the divine.

Nevertheless, they also had public functions. As with all her writings, they were circulated in manuscript, a discreet medium thought appropriate for women (although utilized universally by men as well), suggesting a limited if not necessarily insignificant audience. The diffusion of her work was purposeful and reflects further self-fashioning efforts. Just as importantly, her writings reflect didactic interests, an obvious desire to nurture the spiritual life of others by any means possible.[47]

The choice of the pastoral mode in her poetry is rooted in generic influences of various, widely disseminated kinds of spiritual writing. As has been noted many times before, Teresa of Ávila and San Juan de la Cruz deeply affected her. These exemplars were, at least early on, mediated by her uncle, who also wrote spiritual poetry (now lost).[48]

Based on the eloquence and beauty of her work, an early biographer would insist that there could be "no heart so cold that will not feel some heat from such a blaze."[49] Carvajal's audience is hard to know, but we can assume two things. First, although not totally gendered, her poetry was most available to women who were the primary targets of the author's guidance and advice. Second, although we know that clergymen and nuns had access to her work, it seems likely that her output was also aimed at the nobility and those within circles of power.[50]

Carvajal was not unaware of the fact that aside from conforming to generic exigencies and assumptions of familiar spiritual writings, the genre she chose resonated with pastoralist discourses mentioned above. It is reasonable to assume that some of her poems relate to a critique of courtly culture.

This is not to say, however, that Carvajal's poetry was the same as the polemics that circulated in and around court. If much of that literature grappled with actual earthly geographies as sites of corruption, Carvajal is less attentive to actual places than to the rejection of this world more broadly in favor of Christ. The bucolic is more "placeable" in an ethereal realm, far from any actual field or orchard. Aside from depicting the countryside as a place for meeting with Christ, Carvajal portrays Christ himself as the manifestation and expression of nature. Thus, in her "Redondillas espirituales de Silva," Christ's complexion is likened to a "florid springtime," his skin to pure snow; he "seemed like the dawn." His presence allows the natural world around him to flourish. In highly eroticized language, Silva describes Christ entering her garden and how he enlivens it. In Christ's presence, flowers emit transcendent aromas and dried fruit trees sprout leaves—"everything green, dressed in freshness."[51] The garden is in this case a metaphor for the soul revived by Christ, but more than mere description, as Alberto Escalante Varona has emphasized, the poem is profoundly didactic. In it, Silva (Carvajal's alter ego) is speaking, or sermonizing, to a mysterious shepherdess, recounting the beauteous ends of true devotion, capping things off by exhorting her—and, by extension, the reader—to seek God out. Carvajal emphasizes that the experience of spiritual awakening requires a quest involving reflective practices and recollection.[52]

In another romance, we find Christ alone, sitting on the ground—his "green seat"—surrounded by fresh grass, leaning against an elm tree at sunset as "crystalline waters" lap against the shore. Christ is again figured here as one with nature. He casts his eyes upon what he has created: all his creatures, which he has dressed "with glory and beauty," and all the fields that he has "detailed with flowers." He listens to birds singing in harmony until the sun sets. The scene, as Carvajal's gloss points out, is meant to show "the tenderness of Christ's breast filled with love for nature, with which he talks, and with each and every soul in particular."[53] From this place of contemplation, Christ communicates with a disembodied woman (Silva? Carvajal?), crying thick, "oriental tears," asking how she could reproach "such a lover and husband that for you sorrows and sighs." He ultimately promises, "I will force you to love me / leaving you so wounded / from my love, that you will not rest / even one bit without me, my soul."[54] Although the scene ends with some erotic violence, its setting is one of earthly placidity. That place, even if painfully found, is the end of the journey where Christ is discovered and where the union between the individual (she) and Christ is achieved. Only in the fruitful and florid garden can one approach life's ultimate ends.

For the enforcement of divine will, Christ often had to conquer. Although a hoary trope, militant language is used to describe Christ's victories. In her "Romance a Cristo nuestro señor," when Silva sets out to look for Christ, she seeks the one who has pierced her with his arrow. As a sign of his victory, he has planted a flag. On this banner, there is a device with Christ's words: "Against the conceited I make bloody war, and I pardon the humble who follow my laws." The enemy and subject are both subjugated. There is something of a double conquest described: one involves annihilation of the prideful, and the other, the entrapment of the faithful. The result of such benign aggression is imprisonment and slavery, gifts given to tame the soul and to better worship the conqueror.[55] Christ is understood as an absolute ruler over a soul he can grab hold of—a fate that is sweet and uplifting, a reward for good men and women. God does not choose the cowardly, indiscreet, and tepid, and so their capture cannot be meek and mild.[56] Christ is not, of course, an earthly ruler, but he is most certainly *the* exemplary one. Thus, here we catch a glimpse of Carvajal's understanding of the social order, one in which the "monarch" can licitly use force and coercion for spiritual ends.

Those ends are what matter most. In suggesting this, Carvajal's poetry is eager to overturn the logics of this world in favor of the spirit. Even if this might not be her primary objective, she seems to subvert the authority of the state as falsely exerted in the name of terrestrial prudence. Further, Carvajal confirms what was admittedly a commonplace, that Christ is king over kings and that his is the true royal palace (Real Alcázar).[57] In a "Redondilla espiritual," amid a series of antitheses, she marvels that courts "of the supreme king / take place in a manger; / and the celestial Highness / is between a mule and an ox."[58] The humility of Christ's court contravenes common assumptions of regal grandeur, overturning a penchant for earthly delights among rulers of this world.

Carvajal's work also speaks of resistance. One poem recounts the battle of an individual against a "treacherous enemy," a "tyrant" to whom they would not bow. The individual has become detached from the "infamous kingdom" (reino infame) of worldliness and freed from its "rule" (gobierno). The protagonist stands up to the enemy, recognizing that his power was a sham: "You showed yourself to be giant / in vainglory and honor."[59] None of this is innovative or new, but it is nevertheless worth noting. The poem is about the brave and firm rejection of earthly entrapments that threaten to govern the lives of the weak. In its articulation of well-worn tropes, there is something insinuated about the entwinement of worldly comforts and bad governance that requires active rejection and even vengeance ("Cobrada tengo osadía / para vengar mis agravios").

As a confirmation of the "work" that Carvajal was doing, we can point to one telling poem. One of her "spiritual sonnets" directly refers to her cousin Isabel de Velasco y Mendoza—daughter of the marquis—under the guise of "Amari." It calls for reform and reorientation. In her gloss, Carvajal describes a "great woman, whom she loved very much and whom she wished to see very occupied in spiritual things." She did not want to see her brimming with "human occupations and interactions, even if with good intentions."[60] There must be something in particular that inspired Carvajal to contemplate her cousin's debilities, but we'll never know what. However, she is clearly reacting to what she saw as Isabel's loss of spiritual devotion. The poem asks Amari why she cares more for her "rustic herd" while forgetting he whom "with such love is loved." The poem asks if she has been "bought by vain occupation" or if she has been transformed by "black arts." Carvajal's accusation that her cousin had been "bought" might have more specific meanings but must allude, broadly, to an embeddedness in a world of exchange, perhaps of commerce. The reference to the black arts seems like a weightier accusation, a suggestion that her cousin's neglect of God has resulted from evil temptations. Carvajal goes on to exhort her to "fix yourself because you are losing love's way." The path she is following, according to the poem, might be "vast and delightful," but underneath "little flowers" and "fresh grass" it hides dangerous terrain. This is not the thick garden mentioned above but only a simulacrum. It is very unlikely that Carvajal was encouraging her cousin to remove herself from the world altogether—Isabel was, after all, a wife, and a wife to a powerful husband. Nevertheless, the poem expresses deep concern that, in Amari's mind, there was some haziness between the necessities of the world and those of the soul, or at least an unhealthy separation of the two. This problem is, in part, one of discernment, because although the path toward Jesus leads to a verdant place, here Amari does not recognize salubrious from insalubrious ground: she walks along an apparently beautiful pasture, but one that is thin and superficial.

If we understand politics as inherently opposed to or distinct from the devotional, then Carvajal's poetry has little place in this book. However, here and throughout I would like to question the simple dichotomy between devotion and politics. Undoubtedly, contemporaries understood there could be such a dichotomy, but it is also the case that, as elsewhere, devotional language was transferable into secular terrains. When Carvajal talks about Christ's governance, then, she might be working on a higher spiritual plane, but her language resonates with the platitudinous perceived truth that kings were supposed to follow Christ's example. It is not that Carvajal thought of her poetry as crassly political, but the lessons therein could just as well be used to understand the requisites of the right sort of ideals and behaviors becoming of a ruling class that read her work.

### BONDS BETWEEN COUSINS

Contemporaries seem to have thought that Carvajal's written efforts—not just her poetry—worked, or, at the very least, that she was deeply connected to the sanctity of Spanish nobility. In 1616, just two years after Carvajal's death, Fray Miguel Salón wrote a panegyric in remembrance of Carvajal's cousin, the aforementioned "Amari." According to Salón, Isabel was a prime argument against those who claimed that "devotion and recollection, and spiritual things are not for secular people, especially the most noble and illustrious, but only for people who are removed from society [retiradas] and locked in a religious order [encerradas en la religion]."[61] While the book is about the duchess's virtues, it is just as much about the exemplary people who would have instilled them in her, most importantly her mother (Carvajal's aunt) and her father (Carvajal's uncle). In this context, Salón somewhat awkwardly transitions from Isabel herself to a short biography of Carvajal. The contents of the book—though worthy of more extensive treatment—are less important at present than the fact that Carvajal and her cousin are mentioned in the same breath and that the latter's piety is interwoven with her cousin's. In fact, Salón includes full letters that Carvajal sent to Isabel (among many he could have published, he says) and some that Carvajal received from her.[62] These letters largely tell of tribulations and horrors experienced by Carvajal and English Catholics and thus reveal the spiritual sustenance Carvajal gave her cousin—a master class in suffering. More importantly for us, they are evidence of the contemporary sense that such written communications reflected the "spirit and so much Christian devotion [afición] and charity with which these two cousins, these two servants of God, wrote to each other."[63]

Presumably, this story of Carvajal's teacherly efforts and successes could have been replicated many times through countless anecdotes. We've already noted how Carvajal provided counsel to the high and mighty, but it is important to consider how these individual efforts amounted to larger reforms. Take, for example, the way in which Carvajal "used" Leonor de Quirós, a good friend and lady-in-waiting to the very important countess of Miranda in Valladolid. Through Quirós, Carvajal tried to ensure that the great lady's holy passion remained constant. In a letter from 1606 (when Carvajal was in England), she pressed Quirós to spend her time reading spiritual books so that through them she might achieve "perfection in your habits, victory over the passions and the death of the self in all that is not God, however painful that might be." Equally important—and here we can see the transformation of letter into action—she exhorts her to infiltrate the mind of her mistress. At bedtime, while she does the countess's hair or otherwise assists her, she should "inflame" her mind by speaking to her of God "in a natural way." For example, Quirós might suggest "how sad it is to see a beautiful rich canvas of gold, thrown on to a dung heap and landing amidst rubbish and filth." Quirós should pester the duchess to persevere in prayer, "even though this might go against the comforts and courtesy of visits." Here, Carvajal wants to instill the primacy of the soul over the body, but the effects—given the duchess's status—are not simply personal. Her (potentially) prayerful life might put some off, as it might appear to go against norms of hospitality. Nevertheless, Carvajal says that others will eventually recognize virtue in her neglect of social courtesies: "[S]ooner or later it [her prayer] will touch their hearts and cause confusion." Not everyone could be as exalted a spiritual figure as Carvajal, but she busied herself trying to purify the soul of other noblewomen, and by doing so she hoped to have a purifying effect on others, thus reproducing a spiritual orientation that would then be further reproduced—a chain of sanctity. Carvajal was interested in more than individual devotion. Through her efforts, she tried to spiritualize society.[64]

## CONCLUSION

So far, I've described how Carvajal inserted herself into a public sphere that she hoped to influence by example and through exhortatory efforts. It is crucial to emphasize that her work, mostly carried out in perceived centers of vice, attempted to reform the republic. She had her eye on Philip III's palatial life, but Carvajal sought to intervene with the nobility who constituted the most important stratum of the political nation. Carvajal's utterances resonated during her times because they were, implicitly, in conversation with dominant political discourses. Some learned elites—including men in the Society of Jesus she so cherished—concerned themselves with establishing, in ways that sometimes seem paradoxical, separate zones between church and state while contemplating the unity of a longed-for theocracy.[65] Carvajal's message is not expressly about such structural nuances, but she is all about diminishing earthly desires, something that could only be accomplished through the solitary work of exploring the capaciousness of the soul. There is little doubt that she esteemed the law and order imposed by the church, but its impositions could only function among those who lived with and in God. Moreover, the state could only function fruitfully and successfully—and it would only be able to help maintain the church—if its ruling class aspired to, and achieved, a manner of sanctity forged through hard devotional work.

CHAPTER 3

# On the Verge of England

In Madrid, Carvajal might have heard about a wounded sculpture. Martín de Padilla, navy general of Castile, and the countess of Santa Gadea, his wife, had come to own an image of the Virgin bereft of the baby Jesus.[1] Originally in a monastery in the coastal trading city of Cádiz, the sculpture fell victim to marauding Dutch and English troops who had raided the town, looting and destroying as they went. Later accounts reveal how the statue, then intact, was dragged out into the street, spit upon, rendered a spectacle of abuse in a public square, and left mutilated. The remains of this sacred image, an image made more sacred by its wounds, became a target of pious desire for members of the English College in Valladolid. It eventually went to rest there in 1600 after some prodding of its then owners. The sculpture would be dubbed the Vulnerata. If Carvajal had not heard of or seen the sacred statue when it was in the hands of the count and countess in Madrid, it would become an object of her profound and complete devotion once she moved to a humble house near the college in 1601.[2]

Although Marian devotion was normative in early modern (Spanish) Catholicism, the bruised image held special significance. As an account of the statue's entrance into the English College attests, the Vulnerata played at least three devotional functions. She represented Mary's nurturing maternity: the students were, it was said, nourished by her (metaphorical) milk. She was also an example of suffering—evidence of martyrdom exuded from her wounds. Finally, she was a warrior, out to slay the dragon of heresy. The seminarians would have been buoyed by the Virgin's protection as much as they would have been enraged by the vicious attack on her. They would have also been inspired by her display of valor, and she would enhance their own willingness to suffer and stiffen their will to stamp heretics underfoot. Although it might be tempting to describe Carvajal's devotion to the Vulnerata as something banal, she surely would have noticed the full range of meanings embedded in the image, especially given the fact that she *did* seek martyrdom and took up a life of combat against heresy.³

Carvajal's frequent devotion to the Vulnerata and her proximity to it surely helped crystallize her interest in, and concern for, English Catholic matters. It is hard to pinpoint when Carvajal decided that she would choose England as her field of spiritual battle—certainly not until sometime after 1601—but she was typical among so many in Spain who increasingly looked upon England with horror and took pity on those who suffered oppression under Elizabeth's tyrannical thumb.⁴ Because her uncle was enmeshed in various political networks, he received—and Carvajal became aware of—an early and very concise report of the Jesuit Edmund Campion's death at the hands of executioners during what was the first officially sanctioned mission to England from Rome. It would later be said that the news of Campion's demise focused Carvajal's intentions, although it does not seem to have been the main inspiration for her future efforts. Indeed, many more reports would follow, in letters and print, about new martyrs shedding blood, bathing the world in their sanctity. It is likely that the cumulative effect of these executions determined her fate, but we know with some certainty that the death of another Jesuit, Henry Walpole, in 1595 had a great impact.⁵

To an extent, there was nothing particularly special about Walpole relative to, say, Campion. Indeed, it seems that Walpole had been at most a tepid Catholic until the moment that Campion's blood splattered on him at his execution. Walpole would leave England by 1588 and make the rounds in northern France and Rome—he even spent some time in Spain at the English Colleges in Seville and Valladolid. In part because of the Valladolid connection, the English Catholic exile Joseph Creswell, a crotchety man who would become Carvajal's confidant, published a short book describing Walpole's plight for Spanish audiences: the *Historia de la vida y martyrio que padecio en Inglaterra, este año de 1595 el P Henrique Valpolo*. Carvajal slept with the book under her pillow every night.⁶

Carvajal's fascination with the *Historia* is evidence for the effectiveness of English Catholic polemics in Spain. As with most martyrological accounts, Creswell had his eye on powerful readers who could help the English cause. In February 1596, he reported to Rome that in Spain the book had been of "great comfort and of edification to His Royal Highness and the most important men of this kingdom."⁷ Walpole's life served as (further) evidence of Elizabeth's dastardly nature and the great sacrifices suffered by English priests. Such a story should inspire the requisite sacrifices (in men and treasure) of those with power to slay the evil queen. The carrot offered by martyrdom narratives was the promise of divine assistance to those who helped produce and support religious warriors and their objectives. Not coincidentally, the book was written at the very moment that English Catholics at court were lobbying for anti-Elizabethan naval action by Philip II's regime.

Creswell also suggests a set of objectives related to English Catholic priests themselves. He expresses his hope that Walpole's story might contribute to quelling dissensions among those at the English College in Rome.⁸ The book was meant to remind backbiting men (more on this below) in the college of how important the English mission was and the care that it required. Linked to this higher objective, the book provided guidance to seminarians who, apart from inspiration, needed to learn about how martyrs were treated before martyrdom and how they interacted with the Elizabethan authorities.

Although we can only extrapolate from Carvajal's later actions, the book surely inspired real devotion that would only increase for the English College and its priests. She must have taken to heart, too, the lessons meant for seminarians in preparing for her own holy mission.

Of course, the English Question had never been a purely internal matter. Because many of the most fervid English Catholic voices ended up exiled on the Continent, their efforts against English heresy involved the participation of foreign powers. They worked to ensure consistent and aggressive foreign intervention, and many came to believe that the most obvious and potentially effective allies for these efforts would have been the Spanish. Still, despite a record of intrigue and plotting, Philip II had been, to an extent, prudent and sometimes hesitant about anti-English action.⁹ As a result, even despite the Armada of 1588, he was subject to critique for lack of interest and misguided dithering. Some of the accusations from his own subjects and his English Catholic petitioners could be quite severe: failures on the English front could be, and were, often tightly woven into the fabric of anti-regime polemics in Spain itself.¹⁰

With the succession of Philip III to the throne, some English Catholics saw a door opening for the kind of concerted action against England that the previous regime had, on the whole, dropped. It seems that those who harbored such hopes were not altogether wrong and that the new king not only sympathized but was willing to make good on his promises of anti-heretical action. The results of his zeal were not positive, however. For example, the regime had taken a gamble in 1601 with assistance sent to Irish allies in their battle against perceived Elizabethan oppression at Kinsale, but those efforts failed.

If even the king's unsuccessful efforts would have pleased his English (and Irish) Catholic allies—at least he tried!—those allies were also aware of the changing geopolitical landscape that made Habsburg alliances and pugilistic assurances more complicated. Nothing about the Spanish Habsburg Empire had ever been simple. The "composite monarchy" that the king ruled over was a patchwork of polities and legal traditions that mitigated the extent of absolute monarchical rule. Things arguably became more turbid by the end of Philip II's reign, when the political landscape in his Burgundian territories changed. The king forwent claims to sovereignty in Flanders in favor of new, independent governors: his nephew, Archduke Albert, and his favored daughter, Archduchess Isabel Clara Eugenia. Although Madrid and Brussels were on the same page in terms of fundamental goals, such as the integrity of Habsburg and Catholic rule, cohesion was not absolute. A hawkish faction fantasized about total victory against Dutch and English Protestants as the most effective way to assure Spanish might and influence, but the archducal couple favored caution and careful talks with confessional enemies. Indeed, they were interested in feeling out potential paths of negotiation on relatively flexible terms well before this became a concrete policy radiating from Madrid. Brussels had started talks with London toward the end of Elizabeth's reign, leading to an ultimately fruitless conference between representatives in Boulogne in 1600. As a result of these diplomatic dalliances, from an English Catholic perspective, Flanders was at first the source of much greater concern. It is no surprise that—insofar as the sources attest—Carvajal's first foray into the realm of international politics focused on the situation in Brussels and began during the first half of 1600, once she started hearing rumors of peace negotiations with England in the lead-up to Boulogne.[11]

It is well known that one of the most important ways in which the Infanta established, solidified, and symbolized her authority was by means of patronage and, in particular, her funding of monastic institutions. In a letter to the marquis of Denia (later the duke of Lerma), she laments and fears how much money would be necessary to fix all the churches and monasteries that had been afflicted by drawn-out confessional conflict. She reveals that her most pressing goal was "collecting nuns that wander un-cloistered because they have no house for it."¹² The benefits of such efforts were myriad: she would stiffen the spine of Catholicism against heretical onslaughts, all the while signaling her charity and confirming Counter-Reformation credibility. She would also cement royal prestige. Further, she knew that patronage would establish and extend important interdependences. Especially in her endowment of female institutions, she helped create networks of women outside of court proper who would grease political wheels in matters both local and international.¹³

Once rumors started flying about attempts at entente between England and Flanders, Carvajal quickly tried to take advantage of the "ins" she had at her disposal in Brussels. Most importantly, she tried to make use of the Spanish nun Magdalena de San Jerónimo, one of her most important correspondents for years to come.

POLITICS AND FRIENDSHIP

Carvajal and Magdalena presumably met in Valladolid sometime around 1601. Not too much is known about Magdalena except that she took a habit and that she spent most of her energies working with "fallen women." She famously established the Casa Pia de Arrepentidas de Santa Maria Magdalena in Valladolid, an institution devoted to converted prostitutes, for which she would eventually obtain official royal support and subsidy in the early seventeenth century. Details about how she accomplished this and the precise nature of her relationship with those close to royal authority are not obvious, but we know for certain that she was well-connected and well-traveled. In an astute move, she journeyed from Spain to Flanders to gain proximity to none other than the Infanta. Indeed, Magdalena seems to have been an impetus for the archduchess's establishment of a discalced Carmelite convent in Brussels.¹⁴

Her tight bond with Carvajal resulted from things we cannot re-create today, but it must have been influenced by their shared sense of duty articulated through activism and public engagement. Both Magdalena and Carvajal had been counselors to prostitutes, for example. Like Carvajal, Magdalena was eager to maintain ties with the powerful while not shying away from pointed critique that might apply to those same authorities. So, in 1608, and in the context of a crusade against prostitution that had met timid support at court, she spoke broadly about Spain's social ills and the fact that "the greater part of the corruption [estrago] and damage that exist in the customs of these kingdoms of Spain were born of the liberty, dissolution, and the destruction [rotura] of many women."[15] Carvajal would have recognized the moral ills Magdalena mentioned. She would also have appreciated the admonitory spirit of her rhetoric.

Although Magdalena and Carvajal were already friends, their relationship needed to be cultivated for maximum success. To an extent, Carvajal had to reaffirm their amity by prodding Magdalena to maintain open and frequent communication. In a letter written from Madrid, she playfully complains to her that, while Carvajal knew she had received previous correspondence, Magdalena had not sent responses. Indeed, she knew that Magdalena had responded to another set of letters written by a priest that went in that packet. She jokingly suggests that perhaps Magdalena had come to own the memory-wiping ring that Josephus describes Moses as having sent to his wife, Tabaris.[16] Undeterred and insisting on a response, Carvajal sent her yet another letter, which Magdalena presumably could not ignore. Carvajal registers her dismay lightly and coaxes by humility: she asks how she might best serve Magdalena, which she was prepared to do with "great willingness and love."[17] Carvajal recognizes Magdalena's kindness and frequently asks her not to forget her in her prayers.[18] The intimation of servitude or inferiority—an important feature of most of her letters—is reinforced by strained verbal genuflections and with persistent formalities, such as references to Magdalena as "madam" along with varied apologetic asides.

The fashioning of an asymmetrical relationship was not only "useful" but reflects Carvajal's need for Magdalena. It seems that Carvajal did not have immediate contacts within the Flemish court. Indeed, Magdalena herself was knocking at the door in Brussels, still trying to attain full credit there. Because she was a novelty around the Infanta, Magdalena might have been more flexible than a more established fixture there; perhaps she could be convinced of the just cause Carvajal advocated and could inject new ideological and strategic blood into the Flemish scene. Of course, the goal was to reach the ears of Isabel herself, a childhood companion who had cut off those early entanglements in her role as princess and governor. What Carvajal sent Magdalena was by no means for her eyes only. Following contemporary norms, her letters were surely meant to be shared orally or through their manuscript circulation.

And so Carvajal's voice would have been amplified and might have resonated within a (semi-)public sphere. Or at least Carvajal wanted this to be the case. This explains her insistent encouragement that Magdalena say hello to other women at Isabel's court, including Juana of Jacincourt, an important lady-in-waiting and a potential future correspondent.

Success was not inevitable. To start, beyond gaining Magdalena's attentive ear, Carvajal needed to ensure that she would be a willing ally. That was a tall order, because Magdalena wanted to nurture and maintain archducal patronage and would want to avoid crossing or contradicting the sovereigns' policies and predilections. Indeed, Magdalena would gently, and eventually not so gently, push back against Carvajal's critiques of court, defending the regime's tactics and demonstrating ambivalence, followed by hostility, toward her friend's zealous letters.

Two years into their (known) correspondence, Carvajal is still cajoling. In a letter from the summer of 1602, she reports on her legal affairs. The inheritance problem keeps plodding along and uncertainties remain, but she claims to trust in God's will: He will lead her "through obstacles which . . . are like prisons and chains of Algiers." Carvajal's sense of imprisonment was rooted in both the ongoing threats to her claims and, more importantly, her understanding that the longer the trial, the more she would have to expend energies on things of this world. Carvajal's update on litigious affairs also served as a segue into Magdalena's current endeavors. Carvajal insists that Magdalena is a positive example and gestures at pious envy, observing that her prayers were not just "locked away in your heart like mine, fruitless through procrastination." Carvajal insinuates the perceived insufficiencies of purely private devotion and a longing for the active life afforded to Magdalena. She is bursting with admiration for her friend's opportunities—until Carvajal's letter enters an exhortatory mode. In Flanders, God has given Magdalena so many opportunities for good works and, she emphasizes, "there is so much cloth left for you to cut." In an intriguing phrase, Carvajal echoes Magdalena's sentiment that "Flanders is like a great Indies of the spirit," presumably a place for one's own spiritual nourishment but also, implicitly, a place ripe for spiritual conquest and expansion among heathens. This vast expanse of spiritual potential should help focus Magdalena's efforts at court and inspire her to tell the Infanta of "the great opportunity she likewise has, so that not even the smallest part of it can slip through her hands." Carvajal hopes that Magdalena could help the archduchess be her purest, most godly self. This, she insists, "is currently the gravest and most important business of state, and all the rest are defined in their quality and importance by the part they play in it." Everything is for naught if the glory of God is undermined by "reason of state." In reminding Magdalena of this, she is also providing a path for pious action, which Carvajal still sees as *in potentia*. Interestingly, Carvajal is saying that the path of piety relies on and culminates in worldly affairs that can only succeed with the guidance of true faith.[19] Carvajal is not simply telling her friend to enter the terrain of politics, despite its dirtiness—she is identifying politics as necessary for the effects of salvation.

Magdalena did not need convincing when it came to an "active" life, but clearly Carvajal thought she needed to ensure that her friend saw matters through the lens of good and evil, the holy and the satanic. This was true in 1600, when Carvajal started nagging Magdalena, but needed more emphatic articulation two years on, especially as Brussels experienced defeats at home and continued to explore peace with the Dutch. Although the heatedness of Carvajal's missives depended on the specific news she received at any given moment, her letters to Magdalena all have a familiar air. This is not only because Magdalena was not listening (at least from Carvajal's perspective). Carvajal was also providing Magdalena a script she could parrot in Flanders.

Carvajal states the obvious. Neither Magdalena nor most people at the Flemish court would have thought highly of Elizabeth. Carvajal wanted to take advantage of adversarial predispositions by emphasizing loudly and brashly those things her correspondents already believed: Elizabeth was, fundamentally, a monster. All English (Protestants) had "the devil in their souls and hearts, are bold and shameless, without faith or truth, [and] they will grow bolder still and will perhaps dare to do what otherwise they might not."[20] Among them, the queen was "the most wretched creature," and so Carvajal was sure that she could not do anything good "unless it were a miracle or a marvel."[21] As with Satan himself, her function on earth could only be a divinely ordained punishment for believers and nonbelievers alike. To be sure, Elizabeth would go down in flames: "Until now she has only served as an instrument of God in that He has allowed her to store up for herself never-ending and immense amounts of eternal damnation." On the other hand, in the same way that personal pain gained through sacrifice was ultimately a good thing, Elizabeth's violent tyranny led to the blessed spilling of martyrs' blood: "To her own great cost and against her wishes and desires, the wretch has adorned the crowns of so many glorious martyrs and people of faith."[22]

Elizabeth's most noxious qualities and her most heinous actions required a specific kind of "reading." Just as her savage violence implied divine favor (for Catholics), the topsy-turvy world resulting from devilish havoc ensured that nothing was as it seemed. Thus, while it might appear that Carvajal's penchant for seeing the devil in things makes her warnings and pleas irrational, in fact her discernment of demonic behaviors renders legible a kind of analysis centered on distrust. She argues that while it might appear that the queen was ready to come to the table for negotiations that might be mutually beneficial, this could not be the case. Carvajal reminds Magdalena and those around her that the queen is a liar—that she is willing to work under a "cloak of innocence," having her counterparts follow through with their agreements only to "do what she pleases, and whatever suits this wretched state of hers."[23] Of course, the queen would do this with some craft and cunning. She would find ways to claim a level of propriety even as she drank the blood of martyrs. She would kill, but she would not go too far, ensuring that "by subterfuge and gilded hypocrisy" she might gain some traction with otherwise good princes.[24] This would conform to a pattern: although Elizabeth had used her wiles to persecute Catholics in a way not seen for centuries, she had still managed to deceive Catholic princes "who trusted her somewhat, perhaps not being able to believe such evil in a woman."[25]

Mistaken goodwill or not, Carvajal wanted to emphasize that anything but resistance and combat against the queen would be insufficient. She insists to Magdalena that if she had been able to fling insults and scorn into the queen's face, she would have done it and would have considered herself lucky. Carvajal would not hesitate or feel much fear "because my spirit has always been dedicated to the defense and advancement of faith."[26] Aside from evidence of Carvajal's high self-regard, her suggestion of superior fortitude is meant to shame Magdalena into being a better Christian. She should be more like Carvajal in recognizing that compromise is intolerable and a sign of spiritual flaccidity. The confrontational stance Carvajal would take before the queen was, indeed, the only one truly available to the faithful.

Of course, Carvajal was perfectly capable of considering the earthly logics of diplomacy. For example, she does not hesitate to suggest that there were temporal advantages to having England turn Catholic, as Flanders would have a sure ally.[27] Moreover, she does not reject outright the worth of earthly contentment, admitting that "even that [temporal benefit] has its advantages, revealing courage and other virtues, and nurturing them anew in the soul."[28] She might consider, as Magdalena seems to have suggested, that there could be tactical logic in opening talks with England; it might allow some breathing space, and negotiation could at least temper or stall Elizabeth's worst instincts. But, ultimately, such short-term expedients would be futile and even dangerous.

The logic of Carvajal's staunchness is relatively simple. She cannot imagine a world in which any attempt at entente would not include an Elizabethan request to surrender English Catholics living in Habsburg territories. To contemplate—and much worse, to accede to—this point, regardless of "reason of state," would be "a serious provocation to our Lord." On the contrary, not ceding at all and rejecting "apparent reasons of state offered as sweeteners" will ultimately lead to success and God's rewards.[29]

To ensure the commingling of secular and spiritual matters, the very ends of diplomacy needed reconsideration. Although peace, tranquility, and territorial integrity might seem ideal, in fact, virtuous *struggle* was a sign of divine pleasure. Spiritual refinement could only be achieved in adversity. Paradoxically, from our perspective, Carvajal encourages avoidance of the dangers present in "the so-called safe and peaceful parts of the world." So-called, because that assessment is based on metrics of wealth, prosperity, and position, all of which pose more dangers than anything else "for there is no Scylla and Charybdis, or Flemish sandbank, that can match up to Him." She underlines that "great people who have been either on earth or in heaven made something of themselves and emerged victorious amid difficulties, travails, hardships, and enemies." When one discerns the truth, there is no other option than acting upon it. Only then will a state be rewarded with peace.[30] In sum, geopolitical travails provided the opportunity for Carvajal to offer a godly interpretation of misfortunes (at least as pertinent to the good): "[T]hey are useful means toward greater salvation, being above all an example of the closest friendships with the sovereign majesty of Our Lord God."[31]

Carvajal offered Magdalena a providential reading of the archduchess's political life that she could then pass on. She saw Isabel's role of governess as evidence of God's designs. She marvels at the fact that God "has taken her there [to Flanders] and has set her in circumstances so strange to her and so different from those in which she grew up." In Spain she had already shown "prudence" and "spirit," but the unfortunate context she was now in, away from Madrid, allowed her "to demonstrate her magnanimity of spirit, and constant, loyal faith in her God and the holy Catholic Church." She now had the opportunity to become "the bane and terror of heresy and infidelity." Unsurprisingly, Carvajal insisted that the difficulties the archduchess experienced would only make her stronger. God, she said, would ultimately grant her and her husband victory, "but He will also want this to cost endless cares and travails, in order to make them more glorious to his divine eyes and in the eyes of the whole world." In difficult moments, Albert and Isabel would need to take refuge in God and thus become closer to Him. In saying this, Carvajal personalizes and concretizes her general understanding of good governance and that which she hoped would motivate the archduke and archduchess in the future. She wanted to provide the Infanta and her court (through an intermediary, of course) a way of reading political realities in the mold discussed above. If prayers were to be said—themselves political, as a subset of devotional acts—they are so that the Infanta would recognize the opportunities she had been given and the divine logics she should employ.[32]

If Albert and Isabel avoided consorting with the demonic and instead fought Satan's minions tooth and nail, the spiritual benefits would be eternal. They would "become saints, fit for canonization, and brave monarchs of the Church."[33] In another letter she repeated this sentiment, imagining a time when the Infanta might be queen of England, having staked her reign on God's will. In this case, she might become "a holy queen and they might canonize her, as they have done other glorious queens throughout history."[34] The argument here is multi-vectored. As holy queen, Isabel would achieve a measure of exemplarity for others to follow, she would assure her salvation, and (in a gesture toward the royal ego) she would achieve true Christian glory, a potentially nefarious secular desire turned good and righteous by means of sanctity.

All this was the stuff of so much anti-Elizabethan polemic produced by certain kinds of aggressive English Catholics and their Spanish supporters. Nevertheless, that Carvajal participated in this discursive mudslinging is important; that she felt capable of taking part in it is also noteworthy. Her letters to Magdalena tell us something about what she thought was licit and important to do within the context of perceived threats of heresy. They also tell us something about how aware she was of contemporary polemics based, presumably, on her own reading of things as well as her interactions with English Catholic exiles in Spain—people like the aforementioned Jesuit Joseph Creswell in particular.

Creswell encouraged Carvajal's epistolary activities with Flemish circles for at least two reasons. First, she could, given certain specifically feminine networks, achieve direct or quasi-direct access to the Infanta. Second, Carvajal's words might carry a certain heft that even his own could not. Not only was she a noblewoman who, by virtue of this status, could talk to power, but the expanding awareness of her ascetism and holiness among the powerful potentially made her words and arguments much more effective. Her understanding of geopolitics and her conceptualization of proper behaviors that should be carried out had a particular force that only her years of accrued holiness could achieve.

This was certainly the judgment of Creswell and others around Carvajal, but it had clearly become fundamental to how she perceived herself as well. Carvajal had developed a spiritual persona, a level of spiritual understanding, and a proximity to Christ to such an extent that she came to believe that she could process things differently. As she condescendingly told Magdalena, "If you could see this from the point of view that Our Lord has given me, madam, you would soon feel the zeal that I showed in my letter."[35] This is an extraordinarily important statement because it makes clear that her political insights are not based on extravagant prophetic powers or gifts (a claim frequently made by contemporary "living saints") but on an interpretive filter provided by access to the divine, which might very well be prophetic by other political means. Again, this is a reminder that her devotional practices, while internally nourishing, could and were expected to produce a kind of wisdom not available to the uninitiated. As mentioned in chapter 1, this was precisely the reason why moralists like Juan de Ávila insisted that priests be intimate participants in political decision-making.

BUYING INTO ENGLISH POLITICS

Carvajal tried to establish relevance at the archducal court, but to no avail. Still, she would find ways to intervene in English affairs that were both more tangible and more successful, primarily through her efforts to establish English Catholic institutions on the Continent.

Educational institutions were an important part of the English Catholic "project" outside England. They produced missionaries who would return home to sustain Catholics living steadfastly in their faith and to fortify those who seemed more precarious.[36] Ultimately, as all involved in the colleges knew, martyrdom could be the price paid for their efforts, a possibility that was promoted within the seminaries and further inspired by those on a mission. From the Elizabethan perspective, the colleges were dens of sin, and legislation against seminarians only became harsher as time passed—to the point that their very presence in England was criminalized. On the other hand, across Catholic Europe, seminarians and the colleges garnered substantial support and sympathy from the elite, including the pope and Spanish monarchs as well as many nobles.

The road to security, however, was not simple. There were some, especially early on in Spain, who were not thrilled to have Englishmen at their doorstep, and other religious institutions were not happy about having to compete with these newcomers for resources.[37] Indeed, as an English presence expanded in places like Valladolid and Seville, ever more funds were needed to fight the good fight. Thus, a good deal of energy was spent ensuring an income and garnering royal and noble patronage.[38] The pitch made to potential donors and current benefactors—including Philip II and Philip III—was that the blood of English martyrs would soak them in holiness. But there was more to it than that. Often, especially in appeals to Habsburg rulers, calls for funds were made in the same breath as efforts to harden anti-Elizabethan stances. Such an approach meant that fundraising efforts could be assimilated into a realm of polemic far more complex than simple bids for institutional support. Backing for the colleges could be seen as one of a range of actions taken by the powerful in ongoing efforts against the Tudor and then Stuart regimes. Helping create an army of spiritual soldiers who took true faith with them to England sent a message that challenged English authority—despite claims of depoliticization. This was because the presence of missionaries was illegal and because many of the priests who went back to England encouraged resistance to the monarchy in spiritual matters, which were ultimately matters of state as well.[39]

Increasingly, English women also became a prominent presence in Europe. Most famously and dramatically, in the very years that the English Colleges in Valladolid and Seville were being instituted, a group of nuns made the arduous journey from England through (partly heretical) France and (pious) Spain to reach the new site of Syon Abbey in Portugal. There, or so contemporary accounts would say, the exhausted women essentially submitted themselves to Philip II (Philip I of Portugal), becoming subjects of the man who some believed should be king of England.[40]

Carvajal tried to support attempts to institutionalize an English presence in Spain. As far as we can tell, her first effort on this account was linked to the visit of another group of women on their journey to Lisbon in the early seventeenth century. As Carvajal reported to Magdalena, on the day that her visitors were preparing to leave, a woman, Doña María Cortés—the very wealthy widow of a onetime public receiver, Juan Bautista Gallo—stopped outside Carvajal's home. From a middle distance, she creepily watched. Carvajal wondered if Cortés was imbued with "great spirit" or just simply nosy. Later, Carvajal noted that someone had told someone (she didn't know who) that someone else was asking about the English women and why they were leaving. Carvajal (somehow) figured out that it must have been Cortés and asked her if she had been inquiring because she wanted to "set up some sort of convent" for Englishwomen. Later that same day, Cortés came to Carvajal's house, and as a result Carvajal became deeply immersed in a lobbying campaign for the new institution, despite the apparent tepidity of many in Valladolid. As soon as this possibility emerged, she wrote to the Jesuit Robert Persons, an important figure in Rome and head of the most zealous wing of English Catholics on the Continent. He was enthusiastic. Carvajal also tried to gain traction for the enterprise via Flanders. She asked Magdalena, on behalf of Doña Maria, "to ask her most serene highness, our Lady the Infanta, to favor this project in her invaluable letters to her brother, the king, and our lady the queen so that, over there, their majesties might move in such a way that no one should dare prevent it."[41]

Despite such efforts, the politics of setting up the new institution could not be overcome. Cortés seems to have gone cold on the idea, despite Carvajal's pleas that Magdalena continue to beseech her. The reasons are obscure, but her tepidity was entwined with intramural English Catholic conflicts. It seems that Augustinian monks were swaying her to endow an institution of that order to the detriment of the English College. These machinations occurred at precisely the same time as conflict had emerged between Jesuits and Benedictines in Valladolid. The latter had poached many English seminarians, a split that reflected different visions of how to deal with the Protestant problem in England. The Benedictines were no less interested in the return of Catholicism, but those who left the college wanted to distance themselves from an aggressive course of action endorsed by "jesuited" zealots, neck-deep in matters of state and various plots. As James Kelly has suggested, the Benedictines, free of Jesuit baggage, "were a fresh voice in what many English Catholics believed was to be an era of de facto toleration under the Stuarts."[42] Carvajal, clearly on the side of the college, reported on the internecine conflict to Magdalena and testily censured Augustinian meddling. With a huff, she threw her hands up, bemoaning Cortés's ignorance: "Because she knows nothing of this business with the Benedictines, as she pays no attention to it, no one can change her mind."[43] Cortés was still invested in supporting the English cause, but it seems clear that she had spun off to support (wittingly or unwittingly) a faction Carvajal considered inimical. Thus, even if it was not intended in this fashion, what seemed to be an anodyne push for patronage ended up muddied by Catholic turf wars and, more importantly in this context, a conflict about Catholic anti-Protestant approaches, one deemed more "political" than the other.

Carvajal would not have to wait long to take things into her own hands. As she became embroiled in the founding of a possible convent, she would soon receive news of her monetary windfall. After years of very worldly litigation, the time had finally come to put that longed-for cash to pious use. It is unclear that Carvajal had a definite notion of where her money would go, but after some lobbying and a growing sense of solidarity with the English Catholic cause, her money was invested in an English novitiate in Louvain.[44]

Right around the time Carvajal decided to make that investment, Robert Persons was busy at work, trying to ensure the establishment of a probatory house in Flanders. He was lobbying the Spanish monarchy, arguing that the lack of such an institution caused great inconveniences to English Jesuits on missions to their homeland. More specifically, Persons asked Madrid to encourage a commitment to the project from the archduke and archduchess, who would become partners with other benefactors in "Christian zeal."[45]

Not as a direct result of Persons's requests but certainly amid such pleading, Carvajal played benefactress. In so doing, she was complying with an expected role as a rich noblewoman, yet her actions seem particularly significant at a moment when such patronage was sought from royal coffers. Carvajal was showing up her superiors and, in a way that Cortés could not do, putting her money where her mouth was.

Carvajal surely expected a measure of recognition, but her charity was also personal. Probably as an unintended consequence (but of consequence nevertheless), her largesse meant something to her family. As mentioned above, her donation was a lesson for her brother, a goal that was part of the apologetic rationale for what might otherwise seem like sordid pecuniary desires.

In the long term, Carvajal surely saw her gift as a bid for permanence. Later in life, she would say that Louvain would be a fine resting place after death (a martyr's death). But even if she did not make it back to Louvain, Carvajal left the institution cherished objects that would be reminders of her. In her will, she provided the house with a crucifix that had been left to her by her uncle and a piece of the true cross that had been given to her uncle by the Holy Roman Emperor during his embassy there. This gesture fundamentally embedded her noble house within a broader pious mission and, because she entrusted prayers to her family in exchange for spiritual tokens, she sought to ensure the salvation of her forefathers.[46] In a way, by bequeathing such pious objects—both connected to the marquis and one specifically linked to the marquis's efforts in Germany—Carvajal was bringing her uncle's politico-religious efforts against heresy to a fit resolution.

The coup of receiving Carvajal's money must have inspired English Catholic support for her audacious decision to leave Spain.[47] She probably did not know for sure that she was fated to die in England, even though she fudged reality when she claimed her mission was a foregone conclusion. But there's little doubt, given her desire for martyrdom, that the thought would have crossed her mind well before she made the final decision to go. A cynical version of this story would underline the unlikely coincidence that once her inheritance was secured, English Catholics were more than willing to abet her escapades. Things are probably more complicated than that. Her extraordinarily generous gifts would have ensured support for what she wanted to do, but English Catholic allies genuinely saw virtue in her actions and motives. Moreover, her mission made sense given the then current situation. By almost universal account after her death, the immediate impetus for her decision to leave when she did (in early 1605) had to do with the peace negotiations and ultimate peace treaty between England and Spain (1604), a diplomatic arrangement not totally surprising but profoundly disheartening.

Newfound tolerance between England and Spain, though heinous from Carvajal's point of view, did provide new opportunities. Some would say that she went to England knowing she would live safely, impervious to English law, to a place where martyrdom would *not* be easy to come by. Although this might be a point of criticism—and, for some, evidence of Carvajal's hypocrisy—at least one supporter did not see any real contradiction between her claims of self-sacrifice and the relative security of her mission.[48] Hers was by no means some self-serving quest. Her efforts posed dangers; at the same time, they had definite benefits. Carvajal absolutely sought martyrdom, but her mission, as a public-facing one, depended on living long enough and in enough security to facilitate an apostolic role.

English Catholics had, to an extent, been pinned to the wall upon the accession of James VI and I. Hopes that Elizabeth would be succeeded by a Catholic had fizzled, and once the Scottish king settled in London,

Philip III would be a much less fortified Catholic ally. While he, from the very start of James's reign, had wanted to protect Catholics, he also knew that he had to tread carefully in his support and his contacts with them, lest they face more harm or have their heads chopped off as a result of passion and overheated aggression.[49] Instead of raising the temperature, the king wanted Catholics to cool off and avoid violent excesses.[50] He chose a wait-and-see policy, because after Elizabeth's death in 1603 the cards had been reshuffled. "Without the queen with whom we were at war," Philip told his ambassador, "the cause [of war] ends."[51] As a further blow to the desires of some English Catholics, the king signaled the demise of Spanish Habsburg claims to the English throne. Philip recognized those rights as legitimate but decided to lay off them (for the moment).[52]

English Catholics on the Continent were as punchy as ever, but, like the Spanish regime, they wanted to see if James was more pliable than Elizabeth. There were some who still harbored hopes that James might convert or, at least, that he could be guided toward leniency. Even Robert Persons, Joseph Creswell, and other hardcore Spanish Elizabethans like Lady Jane Dormer made appeals to the new king.[53]

This feeling-out period was also pursued because the English Catholic situation mitigated any aggressive instincts. English Catholics were then involved in crude and cruel polemics, not against "heretics" but against coreligionists in matters concerning ecclesiastical politics that quickly (and necessarily) became entangled with different views on Catholic loyalty to the state. Some, often aligned with the intransigent stance of so-called Spanish Elizabethans, were pitted against others who preferred a path of accommodation and had achieved some measure of opportunistic support from the English regime. Indeed, part of the Elizabethan establishment wanted to cultivate a clan of Catholic "moderates" to counteract what they viewed as the true Catholic enemy, a certain kind of zealous Catholic—read: Jesuit—who was a disloyal, wannabe usurper interested only in world domination. Given these accusations, the supposed evil and dangerous wing of Catholicism slung mud right back. However, on matters concerning allegiance to the crown, they had to be nimble. They did not want to come off as tyrannicides, even if many did, in fact, believe that extreme measures were licit against Protestant tyrants. Catholic "conservatives" were not eager to prove their enemies right, and so they had to make sure they performed loyalty convincingly.

Ultimately, whether they liked it or not, English Catholics in Spain (and elsewhere) could not blot out the fact of James's reign and his new relationship to Catholic powers. They were no fools, and they knew they could not continue to take a maximalist stance. Even the most fervent had to make the best of a bad situation. Along with his attempted rapprochement with James, Creswell tried his hand at backroom diplomacy in Valladolid by establishing an affinity with a Catholic-leaning English ambassador at the Spanish court.[54] This did not result from a change of ideological orientation or transformed instincts but from a strategic decision made in specific circumstances, which Creswell must have found somewhat galling but nonetheless necessary.

Carvajal felt no such constraints.

The precise timing of her departure was not coincidental. The aftermath of August 1604—when peace was ratified by English, Spanish, and Flemish signatories—must have been a period of angst and disillusionment, but things were about to get worse: by mid-1605, an English entourage would be coming to Valladolid. While many would participate in the pageantry of the ambassadorial entry into court, others would look on in absolute horror. Luis de Góngora would capture the grief and rage experienced by some in a sonnet: "The queen gave birth, the Lutheran came / with six hundred heretics and heresies; / we wasted a million in fifteen days / by giving jewels, lodging, and wine." He venomously refers to the English legation and its spies, who he says swore peace "on Calvin." The Spanish held "enchanting feasts" that left them impoverished while Luther became rich.[55]

Carvajal was spared the spectacle, but she could have predicted it and hated it well in advance. However, she left Spain not to avoid heretics on her soil but to seek them out where they lived. She assumed the role of chaos agent right when the entente was being solidified and even feted. Her hasty departure seems to have been, at least in part, an act of counter-diplomacy.

Her decision to sacrifice herself for a cause she believed in can be considered heroic, but her valor was predicated on fear. Like-minded people across Europe believed that amity across confessional lines—in fact, dealing with the devil—would lead nowhere good and that such overtures would have snowball effects, rolling everyone toward complacency. Heresy would spread from kingdom to kingdom, dooming all of Christendom. Carvajal was out to battle against the indifference that she understood to be the straight path to damnation.

If Carvajal was certain, plenty of onlookers were wary of her endeavors. She could not have pursued her aims without vehement English Catholic support, because many saw her designs as problematic. Perhaps most importantly, there was squeamishness about the fact that Carvajal, as a woman, was undertaking a masculine project. Although, as we shall see, she believed that the maintenance of Catholicism and women's work converged, most stories of missionary sacrifices concerned men who had been sent by their superiors to England and who were readied in seminaries for the arts of apostolic rigor. Carvajal's going off on her own was a novelty, and in those days novelties were not considered good.

Even the famed Jesuit Luis de la Puente, one of Carvajal's most important confessors in Valladolid, developed qualms. De la Puente was by no means against supporting and even exalting the voices of powerful women. Indeed, he was confessor to the paraplegic noblewoman Marina de Escobar, who, through her many prophetic utterances, also had much to say about Anglo-Spanish relations.[56] He was so devoted to her that he wrote a book, based on Marina's own writings, about her life and prophecies. From the book's introduction, we can see what de la Puente expected of a holy woman and the potential pitfalls of women who claimed something like sanctity. The true holy woman was fixated on purity, lacked pride, was completely focused on prayer, feared demonic deception, willingly faced tribulations, wanted to save souls, and submitted to her confessor.[57] To an extent, it seems that Carvajal would have checked all these boxes, but, on the other hand, it is easy to see how a confessor would have had doubts and why de la Puente would become (at best) ambivalent or (at worst) hostile toward her efforts.[58] Her definitiveness might have seemed to imply a kind of self-certainty verging on pride and devoid of the inner turmoil that de la Puente admired in Marina. He certainly felt more comfortable with an immobile Marina than a Carvajal on the move. One was more likely to be under the thumb of her confessor than the other. Still, while de la Puente was circumspect in his support of Carvajal's initiatives at first, he did end up supporting her initial voyage, a kindness not afforded to Carvajal's good friend Inés de la Encarnación, who wanted to travel with her.[59]

From the start, then, Carvajal had to carve out a place for herself amid myriad naysayers. Many voices would increasingly criticize Carvajal by questioning her motives. Some said that she was in it for immediate monetary ends. Some said her actions were prideful and rooted in a desire for glory. Some wrung their hands, wondering if she would be able to extricate herself from the muck of politics that had proved difficult for other Catholic missionaries to escape.[60] Some wondered whether her presence in England during such touchy times would do more harm than good.[61]

It is a testament to her grit—and connections—that she was able to overcome her critics' admonitions. Divine stirrings convinced her that her mission was appropriate and based on good instincts, but these were tempered and rendered legitimate through prudent analysis based on precedents. As mentioned at the start, her diet of martyrological literature both edified and inspired her.

Although Carvajal seems to have been assessing her options for a long time, her decision to go to England was also informed by a real-life encounter with those five English women, mentioned earlier, who had traveled from England through Flanders and France and stopped at Valladolid on their way to a conventual life in Lisbon. When Carvajal heard that this new crop of future nuns had arrived, she excitedly invited them into her home for ten days, during which we can assume she imbibed all that they had to offer in terms of their own experiences and a more profound understanding of the situation in England. Carvajal would say that her time with these English women was edifying because "they were like angels."[62] Soon, as a result of talks with her English visitors, she would also be involved in trying to secure the arrival of Margaret Walpole—sister of the martyred Walpole whom Carvajal so admired—to either join her own community in Valladolid or to travel on to Portugal.[63] Carvajal may have put these women in the same category as others she had never met: the Bridgettine nuns who first (re)established Syon Abbey in Portugal or Elizabeth Sander, Mary Champney, and Anne Stapleton, laywomen who had ventured back to England from exile in Flanders to support English Catholics at the risk of imprisonment and further exile.[64] It seems plausible that Carvajal believed she would be joining something like a league of fierce women unfazed by the heresies of their times and willing to move from here to there for the maintenance of true faith. Women, just as much as men, could lead kinetic lifestyles.

## POLITICAL ACTION

In this context we might consider Carvajal's first political act within an English political sphere: composing her life story. Here it is worth recognizing that the assumptions that follow will be critiqued by some readers for being tenuous or based on weak foundations, criticism that I will take in exchange for offering a very plausible understanding of Carvajal's autobiographical work as something more than a set of personal documents. Moreover, it is worth thinking about her work as something more than "spiritual" in any constricted sense. Such a narrow view of things undermines the fullness of texts that were intertwined with her English mission and thus "political" by nature.

Carvajal's efforts never stayed neatly within a feminine sphere, but she knew that her work would be particularly effective among women, especially women of her caste. Her correspondence bears witness to the female networks she maintained. And although Carvajal transgressed the limitations of her gender, she was not immune to social norms dictating that, even among "manly" women, female spheres were their natural fields of action. Five years after Carvajal's death, an anonymous commentator would suggest that her most potent service in England had been to provide a model for noble women. In a pitch for an Anglo-Spanish royal match, the commentator would insist that England was home to good Catholic women marked by "truly hard and solid virtue and ... enlightened by the study of perfection and disdain for human things." The most illustrious of them had been inspired to imitate "Doña Luisa de Carvajal ... to employ themselves firstly in their own perfection and then ... the health and perfection of others."[65]

If this was, or could be construed as, Carvajal's great accomplishment, it was an extraordinary one. By influencing women in England, she would have been contributing to a particularly important aspect of (English) Catholic culture. Scholarship has long acknowledged the pivotal role that women, especially women of status, played in maintaining Catholicism in England. They funded the work of missionaries, they hid them in priest holes, and they maintained kinship networks that even the grandest of men found difficult to maintain in their sometimes beleaguered recusancy. Though it would be inaccurate to consider the work women did as purely domestic, wives were meant to be sustaining members of society in keeping their families on the right spiritual path.[66]

Carvajal was probably more well-versed about English women on the Continent, but even while she was in Spain, she was undoubtedly kept informed about women in England. As would be expected, given realities across the Channel, news of Catholic women and their efforts was sent regularly through, among other means, correspondence and formal reports known as *avisos*. To take one *aviso* at random (housed at the English College in Valladolid), there was a story about a group of women in Winchester who had been picked up at the same time as soon-to-be martyrs Ralph Milner and Roger Dickenson. Authorities believed that the women would be frightened and weakened by the mere idea of stern punishment, but when they saw that the prisoners were constant and even heartened by the idea of imminent execution, authorities had to regroup. As the report explains, when the women realized that Milner and Dickenson had been sentenced to death and that they would not meet that same immediate fate, they started to cry and plead with the judges "because they too had been condemned for the same crimes."[67] In this sort of report, Carvajal would have gathered that women actively sought the same ends as men and transcended the expectations of their society. (She might have also noticed that women were treated differently by an Elizabethan regime squeamish about executing women for religious reasons.)

We have very limited knowledge of what reports Carvajal read, except for one (to us) mysterious case. In two letters written in 1602, she says she received a manuscript, apparently in Magdalena de San Jerónimo's own hand, about "the martyrdom of the saintly Marta." Although Marta is not quite Margaret or Margarita, it was used as a nickname for those names. A detail in her letter suggests that the Margaret in question was Margaret Gage. Carvajal mentions that the subject of the manuscript had a brother in Spain—Gage's brother, William Copley, was there as a pensioner of Philip II. But if Margaret Gage was "Marta," it is curious, because she was never actually martyred. Still, an *aviso* at the English College in Valladolid attests that news from England reported that she had been executed, despite the fact that she had been pardoned at the last minute. Indeed, when Magdalena sent her the account, Gage was in trouble again with the authorities, suffering loss of property, not life.

Nevertheless, even if she received an erroneous report, the lessons it contained were clear. Should she have known Gage's story—or at least some then outdated version—she would have been made aware of the subject's constancy. It was the story of a noblewoman who, despite her youth, had given a priest shelter in an affront to the Elizabethan regime. When it came time to confront the state, she did so with no hesitation, thwarting the wiles of a regime that tried to coax her with the promise of clemency.[68] This was a consequence of the strong ties that she, her husband, and the rest of her family had maintained with the church and its most vocal elements.[69] Such an account of suffering would have had a powerful effect on Carvajal, both because of the fortitude it displayed and also because it was displayed by a woman of a rank and standing not too removed from her own.

Though to my mind less likely, at least one scholar has speculated that the Marta in question was Margaret Clitherow.[70] Clitherow had been crushed to death by Elizabethan authorities in York, and her story became something of a cause célèbre. A formal vita, written by her confessor John Mush, circulated liberally in manuscript, though all extant copies are in English. While she had a brother-in-law who was Catholic, there is no evidence that she had family in Spain. Be that as it may, Carvajal surely knew of her story, as shorter printed accounts by Richard Versteghen and Diego de Yepes would have been readily available to her.[71] Indeed, it would be hard to imagine that she would not have had access to more substantial accounts of her life, either in writing or by word of mouth.

Clitherow's story was somewhat more complex than Gage's. As recent research has shown, her life and death enlivened and amplified tensions among different interest groups, most obviously Protestant authorities and Catholic subjects but also among different kinds of Catholics who approached the business of Catholic survival from varying strategic perspectives. Indeed, as John Mush explains, if Clitherow was slandered by "heretics," she experienced little better from coreligionists. He witnessed how she was persecuted by confessional enemies as well as for "her true virtue, by someone or other emulous Catholic."[72] The latter were discomfited by the pushy and open way in which she practiced her faith, potentially bringing danger upon the community. There was also a sense that she undermined established social propriety. Clitherow's husband was not (openly?) Catholic, and her behaviors put the family in danger while overturning the proper domestic hierarchy. Indeed, one Catholic man, in the wake of tightening anti-Catholic legislation, counseled her to lay low, stop her protection of priests, and moderate her proselytizing impulses. He insisted that she should not continue in her ways "without license of her husband."[73] Her more intransigent Catholic advisors, on the other hand, said that at least in matters of religion, she should not fear diverging from him. These kinds of social and familial tensions would have suggested the difficulties of everyday Catholics.

To Spanish observers in England, the chasm within families defined a crucial aspect of the religious disarray there. As the Spanish ambassador to England, the count of Gondomar, would describe it, in "many houses only the wife is Catholic and in others the husband." This reality ensured that competing confessions existed, uneasily, side by side, usually to the detriment of Catholics who—owing to the heretical state of England—would have to worship in the shadows.[74]

Carvajal would encounter such familial problems firsthand throughout her time in England. Although priests were bulwarks of the true faith and although English martyrs were largely men, she had a strong sense that the Elizabethan and Stuart regimes had succeeded in thwarting their best efforts. Because priests were so muzzled by statute and popular inhibitions about them, she came to understand that "the conversion of these people falls to such insignificant people as myself and others" (read: other women). To the extent that there was any success in coaxing heretics or schismatics toward a godly path, the burden fell on unexpected people, including "a woman who was a neighbor, a serving girl, a daughter of the house."[75]

Carvajal would become a careful observer of women in action. For example, she followed closely the case of Mary Neville, who had turned toward Catholicism to the consternation of her family. Both her husband and father were distressed, she reported, even if she did not "think that in their hearts they are out and out heretics."[76] Just as tepid Catholics or cool Protestants were a source of annoyance and anger, no doubt it was precisely those kinds of waverers who could be worked over.

Because Carvajal was conscious of her image and what it would express to society at large, because she took seriously her role as an exemplar, and because she well knew that her presence would be important to women in England (and Spain, for that matter), she must have considered ways in which her life would resonate there. But before we mention her life writings from this point of view, it is worth underlining why it makes sense to discuss Carvajal's autobiographical work as part of her incipient English endeavors.

All that survives of Carvajal's formal autobiography, in her own hand, is fragmentary. We have a partial clean copy concerning her childhood and further sketches through the age of twenty. Scholars simply do not know why more of her life was not written (if indeed a more extended version was not written), and they are not in agreement about when Carvajal sat down to write. Of the most recent commentators, Anne Cruz suggests that the autobiography was written relatively early during her stay in England, against Camilo Abad's older suggestion that it was put together toward the end.[77] Elizabeth Rhodes suggests that it might have been written in Spain, leading up to her voyage. She suggests that the documents can be seen as a way of pitching her missionary goals to her confessor, something that merits more consideration.[78] Christopher Henstock, in the most sensible discussion of the issue, says that the text must have been written after 1599 and that it was likely written while she was still in Spain.[79] If at the very least we can assume that her writings emerged from a 1604–5 context, it is important to think about how Carvajal projected her persona forward to the English experience.

If "when" and "where" leave some room for debate, the question of "why" seems more straightforward. Early in her manuscript, Carvajal somewhat apologetically says that she feels compelled to talk about childish things ("niñerias") at the insistence of "your grace" ("v.m"), who had asked that she write everything she remembered.[80] Spiritual autobiographies were typically requested of potentially holy women to understand those who displayed keen spirituality and to discern the roots of exalted experiences. Were they gifts from God or demonic stratagems? As Jodi Bilinkoff has demonstrated, just as the relationship between confessor and (female) confessant varied in terms of the power dynamic, so did authorial control.[81] Part of this had to do with the spiritual qualities of the confessant, but there was a social element as well: those with more wealth and social capital may have wielded more influence in the manufacturing of their own lives. In Carvajal's case, she struck the subservient pose, but in fact she had some leverage because of her noble status and her declared right to choose a confessor.[82]

"Confessional" life writings would also serve the practical purpose of providing confessors with materials to write proper "lives" that might, in the most important of cases, be used as evidence for canonization or, more informally, as raw materials for books meant to edify a broad readership. This facet was well known to confessant and confessor, not least because published lives of holy women speak in no ambiguous terms about how autobiographical texts were crucial for composing subsequent official narratives. Indeed, the closeness of the coauthors was a trope used to legitimate the authorial voice of the confessor. Given Carvajal's understanding of the genre, we must assume that she confected a version of herself concordant with literary patterns and with readerly expectations. She surely emphasized those parts of her life that proved her orthodoxy, including her childhood instincts toward charity and her severe mortifications.

It is unlikely that Carvajal expected her life writings to be circulated, but she must have assumed that a mediated version of her writings or, more specifically, her story would circulate orally and ultimately by means of a formal book, as it did soon after her death. To judge by the extent to which those who testified for her canonization were in the know, many aspects of her life were indeed public before her death, and many stories were heard from her own mouth.

Given the familial clefts that divided English Catholics and even would-be Catholics, not to mention the broader societal rifts between Catholics and Protestants, Carvajal knew that her own travails would be "useful" stories to tell, either directly to her intimates or circuitously through rumor and other informal means. Carvajal did not lean on the uniqueness of her experience, nor could she. Although she knew she was extraordinary, her life was easily legible in its exemplarity. It reads as broadly similar to narratives that came before her, in part because its legitimacy depended on justification by tradition.

But Carvajal's life functioned differently from those that had been legitimated by the church, by antiquity, and by the printing press. She had the virtue of being alive and present and, to an extent, in the world. Especially within the English context, where many Catholics had to be prudent, Carvajal's story would have resonated in special ways because, barring martyrs themselves, it was tricky to be a hardcore, public Catholic. The story of her fearlessness would have been of interest because it underlined the difficulties of choosing a pious life at odds with domestic expectations.

Carvajal described the difficulties of achieving detachment. Hagiographic literature often portrayed the family as a site of contention and a roadblock to spiritual fulfillment. Carvajal's story exemplified this. As we've seen, she became allergic to her family's unholy ways but could barely escape. Indeed, she described how her family actively tried to stunt her. This could be by means of her aunt's abasements, but it could also take on more physical forms. Carvajal tells of a time when her cousin was trying to beat her to a pulp and she just took it, later chiding her assailant: "Are you happy now that you've lost it? What a lovely thing you've done!"[83] As already noted, she also described how, over time, her uncle was something of a hindrance, especially in his efforts to marry her off, immuring her into a world she wanted to escape.

In Carvajal's story, tensions between her desires and those of her uncle speak to ambiguities between personal assurance and the spiritual direction of her superiors. Although Carvajal became disillusioned with her uncle, she would not dare cross him. She was "willing to do anything, yielding completely." But this came with a warning. Carvajal recounts telling him that he should heed the duty the Lord had given him "to watch out for what was best for my soul."[84] Carvajal suggests that she was the best judge of his success, an intimation that conforms with her will to choose her confessors based on an assessment of their quality. Over time, while she loved her uncle, she grew to love God even more and could not bear to divide her affections.[85]

Throughout her life writings, Carvajal emphasizes a constant desire for privacy. She says that from her childhood, she was wary of promiscuous socialization. She recalls that even at the tender age of five, she judged her mother for being surrounded by people. In her squeaky, childish voice, she proclaimed: "When I grow up, I should not let so many people visit me."[86] When Carvajal was at the Descalzas, she remembers much frolic and play, but she was already exemplary in the intensity of her private prayer. Similarly, when she came to live at her uncle's home she could not partake in her cousins' cavorting; instead, she chose to pull back and pursue her spiritual edification. On a regular basis, as she describes it, she would spend her days alone in an oratory or in her own bedroom, removed from everyone else, so that her "dealings and conversation with earthly creatures be exchanged for that of angels and celestial saints."[87] In particularly harsh language, she describes finding only her uncle, confessors, and "very spiritual people" worthy of her time, while everyone else, "even though they were cousins, relatives and friends, tired me and I felt a natural disgust and difficulty in their conversation and dealings with them, regardless of how decorous it was."[88]

This longing for removal went hand in hand with her discretion. Time and again, she reflects on the secrecy of her penitential activities, even as a girl. Being a devotee of discalced friars, she would occasionally walk barefoot, even in, or especially in, the most unpleasant circumstances, without anyone seeing her. She tells of "walking around some room alone, and in very cold weather, delighted to see my bare feet on the floor." Should anyone appear, she would "stoop down so that my dress covered my feet, and once the person left, I would start walking about again."[89]

As a teenager, her concealments became less innocent. We've already touched on the descriptions she gave of the traumatic times when her uncle had her beaten by a maidservant and the many times she thrashed herself raw until she bled, a suffering she hoped no one would see. In her autobiography, she tells of a time she beat herself and improvised a way to hide her blood. She put a folded towel on her back so that her servants would not notice. Nevertheless, the next day, when she tried to remove it, "it was so stuck to me that I had to leave it like that." She ultimately succumbed to her pain, giving a loud cry, but told no one why. Carvajal only confided to the woman who assisted in her disciplines, and she helped by discreetly asking a doctor "in a roundabout and secret way" about how to deal with such wounds. She got some patches and salves to deal with the infected skin.[90]

Ultimately, while Carvajal does not for a second deny the necessary submission to superiors, she describes more intimate paths toward spiritual ascension. Devotion could achieve its most advanced stages only through worldly separation and private ("mental") prayer that her uncle encouraged. She speaks of how her meditative trances focused intensely on "death, sins, judgment, and hell." Such lugubrious thoughts were meant to stir emotions and in so doing elicit "love or fear." Achieving this state of emotional awareness was hard. She was in constant battle with distractions and temptations, including "vague thoughts" and an often-overwhelming sleepiness.[91]

Carvajal reveals that her spiritual exercises taught her to long for martyrdom. She describes how at the age of seventeen, during a bout of prayer, she started to consider "dying for the sweet Lord who died for me." Sometimes she lost herself in wishful thinking about being torn to pieces for the true faith, something that made her soul feel "the greatest satisfaction and greatest joy that can be imagined."[92] Her story, as she configured it, was a path toward this realization, a long road of prayer, pain, and detachment that necessarily wound toward the realization that the sacrifice of her life would be a joyous gift.

These aspects of her story, and probably others, seem pertinent to the English situation. In everyday life, English Catholics had to overcome various constrictions. As in Carvajal's case, these could be broadly social and/or specifically domestic. The antidote to these challenges required a turn inward. To be sure, many would have enjoyed the spiritual benefits of harboring a priest, but English Catholic spirituality could not depend on priestly or confessorial hounding that was typical in Spain and elsewhere. While, for example, the issue of private prayer could be polemical within Catholicism at large, evidence suggests that there was a pronounced receptivity and a concerted effort to promote it as an essential aspect of English Catholic spirituality.[93] Moreover, although public and outward confessional allegiances within a Protestant setting were much lauded, Carvajal's story also allows a space for prudent behaviors. She would never countenance the fainthearted, but her story reveals a sensitivity to the challenges posed to elevated piety in terms of its achievement and its concrete manifestation within a range of social experiences. Discretion was, of course, fundamental to the very survival of the English Catholic community and its spiritual uplift.

Still, Carvajal's story plainly argued that despite subtleties, there was ultimately a prevailing truth: individuals should be willing to die for their faith. A private life of the spirit, achieved by private prayer, could lead to a proximity to Christ, which in turn could—or would—inspire a willingness to suffer the most severe consequences for that pleasure. Not all (English) Catholics would have seen things in this maximalist light, but Carvajal wanted to plant the seed of such martyrological aspirations.

To be clear: Carvajal's life was not unique. Nor was it relevant solely to an English audience. In a sense, her trajectory could be universally significant in a Counter-Reformation context. But the fact is that when Carvajal wrote a version of her life, she was or planned to be in England. The soul-searching and self-fashioning must have been written within the context of her mental, emotional, and spiritual preparation for the journey ahead.

If Carvajal promised to give herself and her experiences to England, those gifts were not and could not be "purely" spiritual. As she knew, the kind of fortitude she peddled there was not only a matter of individual salvation but, in its ultimate consequence, the salvation of the republic (a favored word in the Spanish context). Consequently, the internal movements of the soul could ultimately serve a public function that was contrary to the desires of the monarchy and local governments as well. Hers was, first of all, a mission of civil disobedience.

## CONCLUSION

Carvajal's efforts were not provincial. There was something alluring and exciting about experiencing the kind of life that ancient spiritual warriors experienced, but there was a present vitality to the English predicament as well. England's fate exemplified the horrors of spiritual looseness and heretical tyranny, thus offering all Catholic realms a negative exemplar. But England was more than a "myth." Its cruelties had ramifications, because the English abetted heresy writ large and, more concretely, coddled different forms of Calvinist refuse. Destroying the English hinge of pan-European Calvinism was dreadfully important. As Carvajal contemplated all this, she must have felt the growing weight of her pious desires. For her, the heavier the better.

Nevertheless, on the eve of her journey to England, Carvajal was worried. She was concerned about the threats of heresy and the health of

Christendom and was trying to figure out how she could be productive in God's plan. Her decisions would have derived from premises assimilated in her youth: first, that she could and should be a purifying element in society; second, that just as for the individual, matters of state required conforming to God's will. There is no evidence that she had set out to be a player on the stage of international relations or on any other political front, but her aims and ends were dictated by realities and opportunities. Information she received through her extensive networks in places of power—and, perhaps most importantly, among her English Catholic informants—helped her realize that Christendom was in peril not only because Protestants were a threat but also because engagement with the enemy seemed to be increasingly dictated by secular logics. Once she recognized this as a central problem and realized that Anglo-Flemish amity had become a real possibility at the start of the seventeenth century, she decided to intervene using the tools at her disposal: feminine networks and binding correspondence.

Although her first try at diplomatic engagement started in a Flemish sphere, the English Question proper—the evils of the monarchy and the sufferings of Catholics—seeped deeper into her mind, again largely because of English Catholic books and friends. It is not surprising, then, that she would become engrossed by English Catholic needs and desires and that, given those purported needs, she would work toward upholding and even funding a certain brand of English Catholic project with unambiguously anti-Elizabethan ends. Indeed, as we've seen, the fact that she went for the more "radical" wing of the English Catholic spectrum in itself reveals a decision to support a version of English Catholicism that was unafraid of certain kinds of political maneuverings that went against the diplomatic niceties of the time.

This sensibility was redoubled at the moment when England and Spain made peace. Once again, a more developed interest in high diplomacy and a feeling of hatred for the confessional enemy coalesced and nudged her to find a way to make a positive intervention. This time, letter-writing would not do, at least not on its own. She decided—surely with encouragement from English Catholic supporters—that she herself, her own body, would be the weapon used to fight off the devil. She had already developed this sensibility, especially after she started living away from her family. But before she moved her "operation" to England, she had to navigate the power dynamics dictated by patriarchy. After successfully peeling away from the Spanish scene, and based on her claims of spiritual exaltation, Carvajal started finding a way to make her *story* a potentially disruptive force and started imagining how her eschewal of personal satisfaction, performances of devotion, and ultimate death could hinder an Anglo-Spanish peace that posed dire threats to the viability of the church.

CHAPTER 4

# An English Life

Carvajal's voyage to England was rough, but there were probably moments of satisfaction along the way. She first passed through France, stopping gloomily in Bordeaux and eventually arriving in Paris. There, just a year earlier (in 1604), a group of Spanish nuns had established a Carmelite convent that would become an important center of Catholic spirituality. She probably enjoyed hearing her native Castilian again and listening to stories about how her compatriots—fellow travelers, willingly displaced—had navigated through different cultural and political landscapes to serve God's cause. Carvajal had much to learn. However, the nuns would have only offered a partial education. France was home to many Protestants, but it was a Catholic kingdom, and none of her host nuns had suffered any real threat to life and limb. Moreover, no matter how much she admired the cloistered life, there was a chasm between what she hoped to do as a laywoman in the world and a nun's more (though certainly not completely) enclosed life. Moreover, unlike the Carmelites, not only was she traveling to different lands but she hoped to travel into a different time as well. She had longed to find herself in the age of the primitive church.[1] Carvajal expected to find a similar environment to that of the ancient martyrs, a land rich in pain.

The person who understood the contours of Carvajal's spiritual journey most was not a fellow Spaniard but a notable Parisienne, Barbe Acarie. In future years she would take the habit and become known as Marie de l'Incarnation, but in the early seventeenth century she was still married and concerned with the everyday needs of her family. Acarie had also been a vocal figure in the heated politico-spiritual world of late sixteenth-century Paris. Her husband, Pierre Acarie, was affiliated with the so-called Holy

League, a network of men (and, by association, women) intent on defeating the threat of Protestantism and, in the 1580s and 1590s, ensuring that secular authorities would not stand in the way. Most importantly, they led a prolonged battle against the succession of Henry IV, a known Protestant, to the throne. Those were heady times in Paris, with fire-breathing preachers, weapon-wielding monks, and many other performances of piety, ecstatic and militant. Acarie stayed close to her husband's view of affairs and was just as active as he was in the streets of Paris by providing aid to poor neighbors, attending to sick soldiers, and participating in public acts of faith in order to help "appease the wrath of God and avert the great misfortunes with which the state was menaced."[2] She also carried out more pedestrian tasks, such as facilitating funding schemes for the war on behalf of her husband.[3] Both she and Carvajal were women of a certain status, and both were willing to wade in the muck of their times—out in streets and alleys—to fight the confessional enemy.

When they met, she and Carvajal might have turned to discussing the English situation.[4] Barbe and her husband were supporters of the English clergy in Paris and so would have had plenty to say about the plight of exiles and the horrors Catholics experienced across the Channel.[5]

Despite shared interests and objectives, they would have sensed incipient divergences. In Carvajal, Barbe saw something of the life she had started to leave behind, one of hard-nosed rebellion in exchange for one of charity that would ultimately lead to conventual walls. In Barbe, Carvajal would have found a source of inspiration, but also something of a warning. Ultimately, Barbe and her like-minded allies "lost." Their most feared claimant to the crown did succeed after saying, according to rumor, that Paris was worth a mass.

Carvajal left Barbe and the other women she met in Paris for the lion's den.

The final leg of her journey was miserable. She had, according to her biographer, an "extraordinary aversion" to seafaring, which made travel in choppy waters and hurling gusts that much more of a sacrifice. However, fervent prayer had made it so that the weather turned benevolent and calm. The skies were serene, the moon shone clearly, and the night air stood still.[6]

Carvajal was welcomed to England by a miracle. When she was close enough to the shore, she stumbled from excitement. A young boy happily greeted her, reaching out to help. She jumped off the vessel without trouble. When Carvajal's companions joined her, they asked who had gotten her out of the boat—they had not seen the boy, and Carvajal no longer saw him either. He had disappeared. This was a sure sign of divine approval, so she got on her knees to thank God, who had favored her.[7]

English Catholic exiles had already established the groundwork for her, so Carvajal quickly made her way into a noble household where she would ease into her new situation, in a comfort she disliked. After tumbling from one place to another, she ultimately upgraded to quarters in the Spanish embassy, partly because English Catholics were not excited about harboring a Spanish woman, especially in the aftermath of a failed terrorist attack organized by Catholic radicals against Parliament: the Gunpowder Plot. Don Pedro de Zúñiga, then Spanish ambassador to England, insisted on protecting her. She did not like the idea of hiding away in a protected embassy; doing so kept her from facing the dangers imposed by a heretical regime.

Her desire was selfish. Only Carvajal would have benefited from the threats and punishments of the authorities. If she had continued hopping from one English home to another, her hosts would have (mostly unwillingly) suffered the consequences.

And yet things were complicated. Carvajal has not left traces of her inner turmoil, but we can imagine her feelings were consistently mixed. From the start, she would have appreciated the protections afforded by the diplomatic corps, even though she lamented the time spent in the safe enclosure. On the other hand, when she managed to go it alone, she was content to use her diplomatic connections to save her skin. This is not to claim that Carvajal was disingenuous but simply to note that she was human, subject to conflicts that even saints were said to have felt as they ascended above the clatter of the world. She ultimately left Don Pedro's household to live in the company of a small group of women, presumably to fulfill a life of more austerity and to inch closer to her bloody fate.

A MANUAL FOR ENGLAND

Since martyrdom was her goal, it is worth trying to imagine what she thought that path would look like. Her desired future would have been influenced by the hagiographical stories she had heard in Spain and during her first years in England. No book would have made more of an impression than that about Henry Walpole's holy end. After all, as mentioned above, she slept with it every night.

If Creswell's rendering of Walpole's martyrdom was crucial to Carvajal's life, then we can assume it imparted to Carvajal a possible script.

Although we can construe the book to be a kind of devotional text, or understand its functioning as such, that was, as we've seen, only part of its "use." Creswell did not expect a Spanish noblewoman to read it with an eye toward her own mission, but we must assume she did, and if she did, she would have registered a range of concerns that were not what one would expect from a (female) reader crying herself to sleep with visions of spattered blood. Creswell's account of Walpole's march toward death certainly contains moments of high drama aiming to meet the rhetorical demands of murder, but these theatrical heights are not pervasive and are most effective because they are retold in sharp contrast with the preceding narrative.

The book is largely a description of the less salacious aspects of Walpole's experience, partly because the book was meant to be, aside from a fundraising pitch, a handbook for how a missionary should engage with the Elizabethan regime. If martyrdom was the goal, the path there required specific kinds of public performances and engagements that would give meaning and greater resonance to what could be the simple story of an individual being drawn and quartered. Much scholarship has shown that the gallows was a site of contestation; the confrontation of the Elizabethan regime and its Catholic nemeses gave both sides an opportunity to fashion the meaning of the proceedings.[8] This being such an important part of the spectacle of punishment and holy death, it is no surprise that Creswell's account would linger on how events played out concretely, on how the state and the martyr interacted and why. Carvajal's cherished book thus contains a great deal about Walpole's "public protestations" that were meant to "return Catholicism not only to the whole public, but even more the queen herself."[9] Walpole intervened in contemporary polemics by writing learned books that hinged on theological niceties, but he also made public speeches when he faced off with the regime.[10] In his spoken performances, Walpole warned his accusers and assailants of God's looming punishment.[11] Further, the book describes how the soon-to-be martyr enunciated a central challenge to Elizabethan authority when he insisted that the regime had no right to punish him because he was a priest.[12] Carvajal would have thus learned that the martyr's struggle depended on the composition of books, spicy discussions with assailants, public proclamations, and demonstrations of stoicism at the very end. An understanding of the period's dynamics as they pertained to the confrontation between the English Catholic community and the Elizabethan authorities was important because, as much as a book might inspire tears, some readers also needed to understand the ways in which heresy should be fought and how these divinely selected holy men went about their business.

Creswell's book would have also hinted at a central problem or tension related to the whole endeavor. It would have been hard to miss that the spiritual/secular, state/ecclesiastical elements of English affairs could not be easily disentangled. English turmoil was fundamentally defined by the erosion of such boundaries, if only (from the English Catholic perspective) because the state was perpetrating evils.

English Catholics had to make this point abundantly clear because the Elizabethan regime insisted that it was only interested in punishing treason, not religious beliefs. English Catholics had to insist otherwise, but in doing so they understood that their polemical efforts could not be extricated from the fray of politics—despite claims that they were interested in spiritual matters alone. Robert Persons, an exile on the Continent and the most effective and influential (and controversial) politico-religious English Catholic figure during Carvajal's life, put it this way to his Jesuit superior Claudio Acquaviva, a man sometimes timid in his approach to secular matters: "[T]hings concerning the Catholic religion in England are so bound and mixed with those of the State, that one cannot treat one without dealing with the other, as there is no other state in England than a heretical one, and everything that we do in favor of religion is against their state."[13] It did not take a political mastermind to figure this out. It was more or less explicitly stated in so much English Catholic polemic and propaganda. Indeed, the lives of people like the abovementioned Margaret Clitherow, according to her biographer, mattered because they shed light on the "[e]cclesiastical authority of God's church," which could not be usurped by "any temporal prince" or any "civil magistrate."[14]

Such a reading of things could not have escaped Carvajal, and she had no reservations about it. In a letter where she considers Elizabeth's claims of treason against her English Catholic subjects, Carvajal embraces the kind of rhetoric that Elizabeth took to be treasonous. The queen accused Catholics of wanting to kill her, and Carvajal does not disagree; she just sees it from a different point of view. Those whom Elizabeth accused only wanted to preserve Catholicism from what was worse than Turkish heresy. And, yes, if they wanted to kill her, it was not because they hoped to subvert the proper running of the state but because they did "not want her as pope and head of the church of their kingdoms."[15] This statement carries with it a set of assumptions about the queen's illegitimacy, the powers of church over state, and the (monarchomachic) duties of subjects in the face of tyranny. Carvajal was thus expressing, quite liberally, things a certain kind of English Catholic exile would have said behind closed doors but very rarely on paper. Like many despondent and (of necessity) meek English Catholics in moments of quiet rage, she fantasized about unhinged confrontations that would reveal both her steadfastness and the evils of her enemies.

CATHOLIC SINS

Aside from the different ways English Catholics engaged with heretics, there were concerns about how Catholics dealt with one another. There were squabbles, and sometimes outright fights, among different factions within the "community." The central problem: there was no agreement about how English Catholics should interact with the state. This had always been an undercurrent of martyrological literature, which meant to focus the rays of self-sacrifice among all English Catholics, many of whom were perceived as waverers. As Peter Holmes defined the dynamic, the relationship between Catholics and Protestant authorities often fluctuated between resistance and compromise.[16] The divergence between flexible and stubborn tactics divided many into intransigent camps that led to long-lasting fractures.

In comments well after Carvajal's death, her confidant Isabel de la Cruz recalled how Creswell griped about those in England who had given up the fight. Some said they simply wanted to live in tranquility regardless of who ruled, and many feared poverty and the hand of the law. According to Creswell, Carvajal helped reprimand (by example) dissimulators and waverers. Priests came to recognize that "this woman has come to admonish [repreender] our tepidity and to shame our little spirit and valor, which she showed in confessing our holy faith and the great desire she had to give her life for it." This message was redoubled by the fact that "a lady so loved and esteemed in her kingdom left it and traded peace for persecution."[17] Carvajal took seriously her role as exemplar, insisting that the English needed "religious people of perfection after the manner practiced in Spain."[18]

When Carvajal arrived in England, she had missed the most brutal episode in intra-Catholic warfare, the Archpriest Controversy—at its core a bare-knuckle fight about differing visions of Catholic ecclesiastical hierarchies in England. Some urged the establishment of a new ecclesiastical model of governance through the creation of an archpriest, while others argued for the establishment of a traditional episcopal model. Many saw institutional innovations as a front for Jesuits, who were in favor of an archpriest, to expand their influence outside of their order; in this argument's most extreme formulation, some ranted that the Jesuits aimed to take over the world. As Peter Lake and Michael Questier have shown in detail, the debates occasioned by such conflicts, far from being marginal or provincial, contained within them a whole range of larger issues, including the place of Catholicism in England and concerns about the social order writ large.[19] Technically, the matter was resolved by papal fiat in 1603, when George Blackwell was confirmed as the first archpriest.

Carvajal inserted herself squarely in the middle of remnant squabbles. In October 1607 she decided to pay Archpriest Blackwell a visit. In the recent past he had decided to take the Oath of Allegiance required by James I. Worse still, he had publicly encouraged others to do the same. Carvajal must have recoiled in horror because now, given Blackwell's mistakes, weak and wavering Catholics could comfort their consciences and justify their actions (or inactions). If Blackwell could bend to the regime, why not them? The regime's chicanery would thus be legitimized and the war against heresy would become that much more difficult.

When Carvajal met with Blackwell, they talked for hours. He was holed up in the Clink prison, where no doubt the pressures of enclosure inspired his change of heart regarding the Oath. Since both parties knew why they were meeting face to face, there was likely little need for niceties. Carvajal would have cut to the chase and started berating him about his descent into dirty schism. Blackwell had come to believe that the Catholic plight would be relieved by a show of loyalty, and he justified such demonstrations by providing a particular reading of papal authority within the context of secular rule. To allay his conscience and recruit others to his position, he tied himself into knots, trying to have it both ways: he did not want to reject papal authority in things spiritual, but, despite the fact that the Oath declared those who supported papal deposing powers to be heretical, he wanted to emphasize that taking the Oath did not contravene beliefs in (a version of) papal supremacy. Carvajal says that they went around and around on the topic, but Blackwell ultimately argued that the pope's powers of excommunication were thoroughly restricted to cases when he wanted to "set an example, and there will be no need to go down that route in England." Overall, he stayed true to his general approach of circumscribing papal authority, except on rare occasions, while rejecting any practical utility of following an aggressive course in England.[20]

Carvajal scoffed. His arguments "were utter nonsense with no rhyme or reason."[21] As suggested in chapter 1, she did have a nuanced understanding of the quandaries posed by tensions between church and state, but she ultimately favored God's supremacy (as she conceived it) over the world of man. Put simply: there is no doubt that she supported direct papal authority over state matters, especially when they affected the soul.

Blackwell laughed it all off. Carvajal thought it was a nervous laugh, but she also acknowledged that he stood firm in his erroneous convictions. She would continue to say that Blackwell felt himself backed into a corner by his own miscalculations, but even if that were the case, his intransigence against papal entreaties suggested that his qualms were not as disturbing as she imagined. Maybe Blackwell was laughing *at* Carvajal, this woman who could stride into jail, impervious to the law, trying to encourage the martyrdom of others. Blackwell also likely smelled the sulfurous odor of Spain. From his perspective, the bellicosity of Spanish kings was part of the reason English Catholics were in this mess. His recent entente with James's regime came with a rejection of any Spanish ties. Carvajal likely knew this, and it probably drove her crazy.

It is unclear what exactly Carvajal sought from her visit. Perhaps she was trying to change Blackwell's mind; perhaps when she visited, the door still seemed open. But if this had been the case, she would have been at variance with some of her most important Catholic allies, like Robert Persons, who from September 1607 had given up and lobbied the pope to take away Blackwell's title.[22]

As ever, there was more than a little theatricality involved. The moment was ripe for such a show, given, as Kathryn Marshalek has pointed out, that a papal brief condemning the Oath was bound to arrive any minute.[23] Carvajal was drawing a line in the sand between those who accepted and those who rejected James's decree. Aside from the welfare of Blackwell's soul, she was fighting for the greater community and in doing so was acting as the living, breathing mouthpiece for her "party." This was an important function because other (male) Catholics did not have the ability to confront the likes of Blackwell. Of course, debates among imprisoned Catholics within England happened frequently and bitterly—the so-called Wisbech Stirs among secular and Jesuit priests is a famous example—but in this case, the Clink was home to many compromisers. As Michael Questier has suggested, the place was akin to a seminary, though from Carvajal's perspective, it was a school for the weak and sinful. Through her visit, she was penetrating enemy territory to give the "seminarians" a good talking-to and to report the position of their opponents in an intimate way impossible to re-create in print.²⁴ Carvajal's was not (exclusively) a paper war.

Carvajal's visit was also a confrontation with the Jacobean regime. After all, for years, elements within it had been developing relations of convenience with certain kinds of tractable Catholics to whom they even offered outright support. Her visit was thus charged, and that much more so because she was a woman. The whole spectacle was an exercise in shaming. These wilting men needed to be shown that a woman had more guts than they did.

## THE POLITICS OF SPIRITUAL DIRECTION

As Carvajal's encounter with Blackwell shows, prisons were porous in those days. Confined Catholics did not want to be there—many escaped—but such enclosed spaces became epicenters of Catholic activity, places where teams were formed for further battle. A discreet or not-so-discreet payment provided intimate access to prisoners. Outsiders could easily come in to see their favorite would-be martyr. More broadly, unlike the hidden oratories of Catholic households, prisons could be sites of public ritual—masses were said there and, if contemporary reports are accurate, very large groups sometimes attended. Carvajal mentions her visits to prison casually, suggesting the ease with which she did so.

If Carvajal had to hold her nose with Blackwell, she detected sanctity elsewhere. The idea that she might be in the proximity of soon-to-be martyrs was part of what inspired her frequent prison visits. But not every occasion was equally important; some encounters with "good" Catholics could have a special charge, depending on the circumstances. A cluster of encounters in 1610 took place at the very height of tensions between ecclesiastical authorities and English Catholics. Carvajal had become invested in the imminent deaths of Thomas Somers and John Roberts, both of whom she had spoken to prior to their formal sentencing, a moment of high drama during which the regime had one last chance to make the accused succumb to the desires of the regime. As Roberts left his cell, Carvajal recalls how he told her, in the spirit of self-criticism, that he trembled. Carvajal was reassuring, reminding him of the "Great Captain, who used to tremble greatly when putting on his armor and would say that his flesh was afraid of his heart."²⁵ This supportive gesture reminded Roberts of the battle ahead and the defenses necessary to keep earthly concerns from overcoming spiritual ones. As far as Carvajal was concerned, the steel of his armor was intended to stave off not physical assaults but attacks to the spirit, which his executioners intended to be fatal.

The call to fortitude was not novel, but her performance surrounding the whole affair was extraordinary. It had started the day before, when she sent the men a pear pie. Ecclesiastical authorities made much ado about the gift; they claimed that she was tending to bodies, not souls. Carvajal, on the other hand, played it off as an anodyne move, an insufficient gesture of appreciation by a woman who had nothing better to offer. The act of feeding, however, was not innocent. It was a sign of largesse. Indeed, as a child, when she played queen, she would distribute pears to display her charity. More importantly, Carvajal became the sustainer of the English Catholic cause by helping "manufacture" future saints. The next night, she exploited performed commensality when she convened a "last supper." She brought together around twenty priests and sat at the head of the table, with Somers and Roberts at either side.[26]

Importantly, the meal brought Catholics of different stripes together, thus reflecting unity in the face of persecution. This was especially true since Somers was a secular priest and Roberts a Benedictine monk, both members of factions increasingly associated with anti-Jesuit sentiments. Thus, Carvajal's place at the head of the table is that much more important because she stood in for the "radical" Jesuit wing of the English Catholic community.

In its most immediate context, the spectacle of eating was intended for the other prisoners who had to be readied for their own encounters with the law. The butterfly effect of those sweet deaths would have been felt outside of the jail cell as well and could have warmed the coldness of intransigent hearts. Moreover, Somers's and Roberts's demise would provide further evidence of the regime's rot and the glory of the true church.

Outside of Catholic circles, Carvajal's efforts intended to rack up a victory against ecclesiastical and state authorities. Indeed, while holy deaths were important in the long term, the drama of the scaffold was also a defensive measure in the short term. Ecclesiastical authorities worked hard to dampen Catholic fervor, hoping to bring many to their side or at least to cultivate a conformist kind of Catholicism.

Carvajal's success in helping ensure bloodshed stung. Upon hearing about her visit, James was incensed. He could countenance various forms of support for prisoners, but he seems to have been particularly put off by the "public" nature of her visit, especially on the night before an execution.[27] Three years after these events, members of James's regime recalled, in a diatribe against her, that Carvajal had aided and abetted Somers and Roberts in order to relitigate church/state matters and to reject Protestant insistence that the men in question were executed "not because of their faith but for treason and lèse Majesté."[28]

TAKING BACK CATHOLIC BODIES

Carvajal's hand in producing martyrs was evident after their deaths, too. With every execution, the state wanted to assert its control over treasonous bodies and so, apart from killing individuals, authorities carried out a series of fleshly rituals. Aside from quartering bodies, they could place heads high above on pikes and, as Carvajal described it, they would take remains and bury them in large pits covered by the bodies of common criminals and thieves. This was done to desacralize bodies that were seen as holy from a certain Catholic perspective. However, according to Carvajal, the brutal treatment of corpses, which was meant to signal a particularly odious level of criminality, ended up being beneficial to Catholics, because the common criminal would be buried whole: the holy could thus be easily distinguished from the profane. Carvajal was eager to have these quasi-saints in her possession, so she would coordinate the retrieval of dead bodies—pieces of death that were, she said, "our treasure and not theirs."[29]

On one occasion, she got a group of armed men to go to the gallows very early in the morning. Carvajal waited. It was six and they still had not arrived. Carvajal was on edge, so she hired a coach to go pick up the grave diggers and the freshly exhumed bodies. When the bodies finally arrived, the women in Carvajal's house formed a procession, all of them holding two candles. But on that day, they would have scant time to enjoy the full spiritual riches now in their possession. As (bad) luck would have it, Protestants came knocking at the door throughout the day, much to Carvajal's annoyance. In light of these unwanted visitors, she decided to dress the body parts quickly and hide them away in a lead casket. Thus, they became a sacred feature of her home, if just for a little while. Neatly packaged, the body parts were ready for dispersal among good Catholics.[30] It was by no means strange that Carvajal should want these holy remnants, because relics were highly prized spiritual commodities. Still, the investment in time and manpower, together with the risks involved, made her efforts truly extraordinary.

It is hard to fathom the kind of elation Carvajal and her intimates felt during their encounters with such present sanctity. Once their joy came back to earth, there must have been some satisfaction in knowing that a furtive victory against the crown had been achieved. Protestants had not won the definitional war. They had not succeeded in their desacralizing efforts. At least in terms of the holy dead whom Carvajal helped collect, Catholics were having the last word.

A MARKET SCENE

Carvajal did not just want to live among martyrs. She felt nudged a little further in the direction of her own demise when in shackles.

Her first experience as a prisoner occurred in the aftermath of a somewhat ridiculous (if seriously orchestrated) spectacle in June 1608. As she tells it, one day she went shopping at Cheapside market for an altar cloth. She describes Cheapside as the main street in London and the one "most full of people mired about the faith and with hatred for the pope, in which it exceeds the rest of the city."[31] For reasons that go unexplained, she asked a young man if a girl standing near him was his sister. He responded that "she was in Christ." Carvajal thought that such a pious response suggested he was Catholic, so she inquired. He was aghast. Shortly thereafter she started talking—presumably ranting—about religion. And soon after this, the young man's boss, other shopkeepers, and neighbors came. Carvajal inspired boisterous conversation. Was that her plan? Maybe the verbal fight was not premeditated but only the result of a foolish question. It's more likely that she was raring for a fight. Even if the young man had been Catholic, would she have reasonably thought that he would start flouting his allegiances in public? I don't think so. After all, by her own account she was walking through a den of sin, where Catholics would be outnumbered. She knew, as she would explain later, that Cheapside was "abundant in opportunities to rebuke their [heretics'] blasphemies."[32]

The conversation, she said, lasted for something like two hours. Carvajal was interrogated on many things, including "the mass, priesthood, confession and similar points, but most of the time was spent discussing whether the pope was head of the church, whether the keys of St Peter had remained continuously within it and with the popes up to this day."[33] Presumably, Carvajal had taken control of the conversation, expatiating on the truths she had aimed to impart to "heretics." That the conversation turned to the papacy signals her (and her nemeses') will to fight about matters at the center of politico-religious conflict: the aforementioned controversies about whether Catholics could, or should, take an oath to the king that rejected papal authority. The content of Carvajal's defense of the papacy was predictable, but it matters that she was going on about the issue in a very public forum. Although English Catholics often did not follow the regime's intended scripts during and just prior to their executions, their spoken and performed intransigence was carried out within the rhetorical field allowed by the state.[34] Carvajal snatched such control away from local authorities by picking a fight and vociferously articulating a series of strident Catholic stances in such a way that most others could have only gotten away with as they neared death, and only momentarily, before the state would have its final word.

Aside from the ecclesiastical and strictly religious, Carvajal did not fear entering minefields that cannot be considered anything but political. Apparently, an older member of the ad hoc audience asked whether Carvajal thought James I was unwise in supporting forms of Protestantism. Carvajal chose prudence in her response. She knew how sensitive and potentially dangerous her comments might be. Anything she said could be construed as anti-royal and might provide ammunition to those present. Perhaps unsurprisingly, she conformed to a stance favored by the Spanish monarchy to deflect direct criticisms from the king. She excused him because he had been an orphan lacking guidance, except from "puritans."[35] The choice of the word "puritan" might be important, because it could have specific resonances in post-Reformation England. The term could be used as a blanket pejorative by Catholics *and* certain kinds of Protestants, and so, while expressing typical bigoted vitriol, Carvajal (in theory) steers clear of poking too hard at James's own (explicitly non-Puritan) ecclesiastical establishment.

As soon as she could, Carvajal chose to pivot away from the king. In the spirit of prudence, but also because she believed it, she admitted that James was much more legitimate and agreeable than Elizabeth. Her tactic was successful: it changed the topic, all the while revving up her audience for further combat. She reckoned they cared more about Elizabeth because they were profoundly ambivalent about the king—so in her talk of the dead queen, she was goading her audience. Soon, a debate started that had been going on for decades about the succession—that old warhorse. Carvajal rehearsed a tried (and tired) Catholic line that Elizabeth had been born while the legitimate queen, Catherine of Aragon, was still alive, implying, as one audience member exclaimed in horror, that Elizabeth was a "bastard."[36] On the other hand, James descended from Henry VIII's sister. (Carvajal is careful not to mention James's mother, Mary Stuart, who had been executed by the Elizabethan regime.) Again, we see Carvajal's acumen on display. The legitimization of the king was tentatively supported, even though she hoped that one day the Infanta Isabel would take over the crown, based largely on French lineage.

Talk returned to a more recent and raw controversy. In April 1608, George Gervase had been executed for treason. One member of the audience brought the topic up and Carvajal quickly articulated the Catholic line that he had died a martyr, an incendiary assertion. Carvajal explained her case by asking a simple question of the perturbed man: "You tell me. What did he die for?" He quickly responded: "For being a papist priest and wanting to protect his religion." Carvajal pounced by proclaiming that if there was no other reason, "do not be surprised that he is called a martyr in the holy church." The man, she says, "seemed to take this well."[37] As mentioned above, from the regime's point of view, authorities punished priests not because of their beliefs but because of their treasonous activities, including the defense of a foreign ruler—the pope. Here we have insight into the "normal" man's take on the situation: either a specific kind of reading of executionary logic in tension with, but not in opposition to, the official line, or the response of a man who somehow, perhaps unwittingly, ended up (or had always been) in sympathy with aspects of the Catholic position.

Carvajal had a less successful exchange on the topic with the judge who questioned her. He did not concede her point. He insisted that Gervase had not died for his religion; rather, he died because he was crazed.[38] In a clumsy way, the judge wanted to deal with the dangers of what seemed to be a religiously motivated execution. Carvajal's claim that he offered a weak alternative to religious persecution—an inexact accusation of madness—was surely meant to underline her take on the regime's supposedly mendacious claims. Regardless, her exchanges with both men show how her efforts allowed for this central issue of the regime's motivations to become public. Indeed, given the fact that Gervase had been executed just a couple of months prior to the events described here, it is as if she were taking advantage of the polemically charged moment.

With darkness upon them, Carvajal headed home.

About two weeks later, she went back to the scene of the commotion. Again, the decision does not seem innocent. If her previous visit had stirred so many, it is hard to believe that she felt she would pass unnoticed. Intriguingly, in her correspondence about the event, she seems aware that people might wonder why on earth she would go back. She insists that she "did not trust anybody less careful than myself to do this [go shopping] because our poverty and lack of money demanded caution." She is sure to emphasize how she hated any excursions, and then she claims a certain naiveté: she walked through the fair and passed the notorious shop without thinking about the shopkeepers she had offended. This seems implausible. Carvajal wanted to stir up more trouble, and she did. Her enemies were soon on the prowl. A group followed her around, spying to see if she was doing her version of preaching and proselytizing elsewhere. Ultimately, they encircled Carvajal's house and looked at her like basilisks, with murderous eyes. They brought a constable, and he duly arrested her.[39]

Soon she found herself before a judge. He asked where she lived and she responded, quickly pointing out that she was next door to the Spanish ambassador. Then the proceedings followed a predictable line that had her repeating much of what she had said before, this time to another audience that, aside from the magistrate, included another ballooning, perhaps impromptu, crowd. Although by most accounts the back-and-forth followed certain scripts expected of both sides—Carvajal defends papal authority, the judge rejects it, the judge rejects the martyrdom case for Gervase, she defends it, and so on—one question seems to have stumped her. The judge asked if she knew that in Spain "they took the lives of English people who refused to follow the Roman religion, and whether it would not be just to take the lives in England of Spaniards who refused to follow the English religion."[40] Carvajal looked at him but did not say anything because, as she (most likely speciously) suggests, she felt unwell and so could not deal with subtleties in English. For much of her testimony, her quasi-miraculous ability to deal with various points of political/theological controversy had been just fine, but the judge's argument did not really follow a script for which Carvajal had been prepared. She was packed off to jail.

It is unlikely that Carvajal's plans had gone as expected. Although she sought martyrdom, she also had her "companions," the English women (whom Carvajal admired as "little angels" or "solid gold") who had chosen to live with her and exhibited "real virtue more than is usually the case."[41] Unlike Carvajal, they did not have quasi-diplomatic immunity and did not have the unique benefit of being Spanish. They were incurring the greater danger, but like their leader, they remained unfazed and seem to have been quite vocal in arguing with "heretics." Still, Carvajal was probably banking on covering them with her diplomatic mantle and/or "benefitting" from the relative restraint the authorities had regarding women. If that was the calculus, it had obviously failed, and so at their arraignment, Carvajal had to find ways to protect them. When asked if they attended mass and other compromising questions, she responded that she would not utter "a single word in reply to anything that might be damaging to others."[42] In saying this, Carvajal was conforming to her principles, but she was also acting out an ideal sort of behavior for those under the law's thumb: within a Catholic context, it was very important not to snitch.

Carvajal's gender became a point of contention in these proceedings. In the crowd, some had started murmuring that she was not a woman but a priest dressed in a woman's clothes. They also started saying that because she spoke oddly, she must be Scottish. Both claims, as Marshalek has pointed out, countered the tepidity with which the law might treat Carvajal and her companions, something that would have not been tempered had she been a man and a foreigner.[43] It seems unlikely that this would have been a strategic move; it would have been an almost "natural" effect of the discourses that defined "otherness" at the time. The cross-dressing accusation in particular allowed the audience, or parts of it, to indulge in the most rabid anti-Catholic fantasies. She was the object of horror, an almost monstrous creature, who allowed the audience to savor their prejudices against priests and the whole belief complex that painted Jesuits as destroyers of social norms, as sexually depraved, and as plain liars, too.

Although the judge himself did not subscribe to such accusations, he ultimately did hold her looks against her. When she was being set up to go to jail, she requested that she not be sent anywhere near men, but the judge only laughed. He said she was too ugly to attract attention.[44]

Ultimately, her first stint in jail was short. The diplomatic situation certainly helped, though the ambassador, Don Pedro de Zúñiga, took a prudent approach. He sent word that he would not be pushing too hard for her release, betting that the authorities would think twice about abusing a Spanish woman attached to him. He assumed that diplomatic niceties would prevail. They did. The judge sent her file to the royal council, where the treasurer intervened on her behalf because, Carvajal posits, he wanted to play nice with Don Pedro, especially in the context of looming Irish rebellion, in which the English were anxious that the Spanish might get involved.[45]

It is possible that Carvajal liked being in jail—the suffering and all that—but it is equally plausible that she *expected* diplomatic intervention and that she even welcomed it. It is not simply that she assumed safety out of self-interest; she surely understood that the performances leading up to her release would be valuable. Provoking a diplomatic incident meant an Anglo-Spanish face-off that would corner the English into some form of moderation while forcing the Spanish to take a confrontational stance.

The results were not great. The regime had to continue the farce that she had been arrested for purely secular reasons, perhaps unwittingly allowing room for the legitimacy of her spiritual mission (for sympathetic audiences, of course). But the claim that Carvajal was primarily contravening secular law had important drawbacks, especially when news of the whole affair was projected abroad. If the legitimacy of her actions in England were based on pious grounds, rumblings about her political work might rouse suspicions. Indeed, when news of her problems traveled to the Continent, some would say she only got into trouble because of the things she said about Elizabeth.[46] Further, if her plan had been to act as a diplomatic agitator, the outcome was suboptimal. Don Pedro extemporized while the Jacobean regime was able to signal moderation and good faith toward Spain, a stance that would be useful for prolonging a fragile Anglo-Spanish peace.

Beyond geopolitics, Carvajal intended to influence "real" people on the ground. While the whole affair ended up being a mess, the gist is probably what mattered most. Within the context of relative immunity, Carvajal could be an exemplar by following—without the deadly consequences—a general theatrical script that was often reserved for martyrs. She stood up unflinchingly for the church and the pope, she refused to further incriminate her partners, and she embraced imprisonment. This would have appealed to a "hardcore" Catholic audience and would, in theory, have fortified them.

But she hoped to preach beyond the choir as well. Carvajal did not expect any sort of immediate conversion to her point of view but thought that she could plant a seed of true faith in some hearts. She came to believe that even among those who were put off by her arguments, there might be a little room for persuasion. She opined that "a few of these truths remain stuck in their minds, along with some reasons to ponder them, which is a great open door for God's holy inspiration."[47] Presumably, she was pitching not at the most zealous Protestants but at those who were already somewhat malleable. Among these, there were some who had never been exposed to such truths; they did not even know where to find a priest. Indeed, they were disserved even by Catholic neighbors who had relinquished their duty to teach and inform. There were those who purported to understand the true faith but did not "know how or wish to spread the word, given the great danger to themselves, without a more definite outcome."[48] If Protestants were bereft of direct exposure to Catholic messaging, there was no hope, so a person like Carvajal proved essential.

We'll never know if she changed minds in any significant way, but we can assume some measure of success insofar as she was galvanizing a varied public to grapple with matters of immediate import.

A CONVENT IN ENGLAND

Carvajal's final encounter with English authorities would be a result of what we might think of as private acts of publicity.

In 1612, Carvajal established a second residence just outside London's city walls, in Spitalfields. As she described it, it was a brick house with little round towers adjacent to a small square with a pulpit topped by a cross. She took care that this space was assiduously protected—more so than her other residences up to that point. The entrance was made of double doors, of which only one was ever opened at a time. Inside, the chapel was well hidden on the upper floor, and the house was strewn with locks and grilles. Although she clearly considered her home something like a convent, it was not exactly that. In the tradition of the *beaterio* in Spain, she did not seek to have her group linked to any (existing) religious order, and the cohabitants were technically laywomen, although Carvajal had written "rules" that institutionalized their mode of life. They were to be called the "Company of the Sovereign Virgin Mary, Our Lady."

A group of laywomen living communally, organized around a regimen of prayer and work, was by no means radical in Catholic culture, but the English context made Carvajal's foundation audacious. Following the example of the Society of Jesus, Carvajal envisioned an active life, with the explicit goal of serving an English community for the "salvation of the souls of your fatherland [patria], which is so in need of spiritual assistance."[49] To this end, she encouraged, indeed exhorted, her companions to live a tightly bonded life of love. They were to live as "one heart." This desire is both anodyne and significant. Calls to unity are pro forma, but this is uttered in the same breath as a call to exemplarity: their pious living should serve as edification for Catholics in England. As we've noted several times, such unity was more aspirational than real, and so such a public image was absolutely crucial for the mission as a whole.[50]

Carvajal argued that the sisters, like all Catholics in England, should relish living beneath the cross and aspire to martyrdom, "a violent and happy death for the holy Catholic faith." As she had desired for herself on many occasions, they would be part of and serve Catholics who lived as in the times of the "primitive church" in terms of "persecution for the faith." This, again, is not a strange desire per se, but even a surface-level consideration of the claim and intention should serve as a reminder that, as Carvajal conceptualized it, the endeavor was an act of resistance. After all, by and large, the story of the early martyrs was the story of fervent opposition to the state (including vocal forms of intransigence by women).[51]

This pugilistic sentiment is borne out further by Carvajal's decision to add a vow to the typical triad of obedience, poverty, and chastity. She wanted her companions to promise "special obedience and reverence" to the pope. In this, she was imitating her beloved Jesuits, both in their desires and in their spirit of defiance. She explained that such articulated subservience to Rome was important in the current climate: "It is good to make greater effort and resistance against the heresies of our time, in those places where they work hardest to raze the walls of the holy Catholic church." Aside from a trite statement of anti-heretical sentiment, the extra vow clearly meant to take a swing at *the* ideological battle at the core of confessional and intra-Catholic conflict—debates about the Oath.[52]

Carvajal's "rule" did not provide much guidance about public engagement. In part, we must accept that a good deal of her sisters' everyday life would be enclosed. Their piety in itself, in the form of prayers and good works, would be transformative, so that "the softest scent of your fervent desires and holy works rise to heaven, and ask for mercy against so much heretical abominations and other evils that are committed every day and incite His Divine Majesty to take revenge."[53] However, despite everyday rituals and devotions, her spiritual instructions allowed (very limited) time of formal interaction with the outside world. Carvajal says that after a period of silence, at five o'clock, and with permission of the superior, visitors would be welcome, but there were strict time limits on individual visits. Importantly, no visits could be private, even if the visitors were women or family. That said, we know from Carvajal's own life and example that while a cloistered life was an ideal, outside encounters could be regular and very meaningful. As mentioned above, Carvajal's ill-fated market visit was made with women from her house, who had also landed in hot water when the law arrived.[54]

Proselytizing receives short shrift in her "rule." However, we know, according to witnesses in her canonization inquiry and her own reports, that it was part of the enterprise. One important example circulated among contemporaries: a woman of somewhere between eighty and one hundred was walking by and Carvajal felt compelled to insult her, spewing a warning that she would go to hell if she did not change her ways. Carvajal offered to help her get on the right path, but the old woman demurred. Three weeks later, however, she came back. She had dreams intimating that salvation required a return to the true church. Further, God communicated that she should go to see Carvajal. It's unclear that Carvajal believed in the old woman's visions, but she took the chance to help her by, among other things, calling priests to take her confession. Thereafter the woman was a daily visitor, coming to recite the rosary.[55] Carvajal and her companions helped her die a good death, standing around her bed as she expired with "rare faith and devotion."[56]

This is precisely the kind of activity that enraged George Abbot, then bishop of London. Aside from his constitutional hatred of Catholics, he had been particularly incensed because of Carvajal's showy support of Somers and Roberts. But just about everything about her seemed reprehensible. As he reported to William Trumbull, the English ambassador to Brussels, she had first come with a "desire to see and yet to ease the persecution in England." This is an intriguing claim, perhaps suggesting that hypocrisy lay at the core of her mission or even that her motivation was partly voyeuristic. Whatever the case, Abbot was troubled by her support for priests and her boisterous presence in London. In the aftermath of her first arrest, Carvajal had laid low, but now (in 1613) she had started to cross lines again, reaching out and coaxing English "ladies and gentlewomen" to attend mass at the ambassadorial quarters. She then "catechized" them to the end of setting up a nunnery, "gathering young women unto her and using them as in a monastery." He describes her and her "disciples" as all Jesuitesses. Abbot considered their communal institution (and, one imagines, everything else about Carvajal) to be "a great scorn to the justice of the State."[57] Thus, as ever, although the presence of a Catholic institution posed spiritual troubles, the central fear and justification for concern was directly linked to the preservation of the commonwealth.

From the state's perspective, Carvajal's "convent" posed several challenges. The fact that she was persuading young women to join her reflected the persistent threat of an expanding Catholic base. Though this would have been disturbing enough, there was no way to understand Carvajal's efforts as anything but a power grab—the institution seemed to be a fifth column in plain sight. Linking Carvajal's home to Jesuits proved as much. It was assumed by like-minded people that Jesuits posed an existential threat, that they were far worse than run-of-the-mill Catholics, and that the order had imperial pretensions. Hence the lengths to which even the more moderate authorities would go to weed them out. To give Carvajal her way was akin to allowing all the Jesuitical terrors through the front door.

More generally, allowing Carvajal's convent to thrive would mean authorizing a freestanding, de facto Roman institution. Of course, there were plenty of Catholic spaces in England, some of them quite public. As noted above, ambassadorial homes were places of scarcely hidden Catholic worship, much to the consternation of many officials. Protestant authorities tried to constrain Catholic ritual for those outside the ambassadorial corps, but their success was limited. Allowing Carvajal to carry on outside of the exceptional allowances offered to official foreign representatives would be to open a Pandora's box. Thus, if there might be normative protections for some foreigners, there was by no means assured protection for someone overstepping—by a mile—the expectations of the host country.

Carvajal justified her living arrangements by referencing antiquity. She explained that back then, Christians had used houses for churches and that the public took them for parishes.[58] *Plus ça change.* In England, Catholic houses were much the same, and she placed her own within that context. The comparison is specious. Unlike, for example, Catholic proprietors of great noble households, she was a foreigner and a Spaniard to boot. The private homes of Catholics were part of a greater, multifaceted domestic scene. To be sure, hers was a home, but its primary defining characteristic was conventual. Thus, it was an independent sphere of Catholic activity and, in essence, a toehold for the Roman church. Moreover, the space's spiritual charge was defined not by Carvajal herself (though that is part of it) but also, and increasingly, by the holy dead. In this way, the house became a place of subversion and inversion, where the state's criminals were redefined as saints in a grossly public affront to the regime.

The house's existence collided with long-standing hatreds amid a set of circumstances that allowed the possibility of action. As Marshalek describes it, Abbot's concern about Catholics was boiling over out of fear. During the latter part of 1613, a group of hispanophilic and Catholic sympathizers had entered the inner sanctum at court and had increasing access to the king's ear. Added to this, the king's close relationship with the Spanish ambassador, Gondomar, had showed no sign of abating. But regardless of how close James had become to Abbot's natural enemies, the king's memory was not so short. It seems that nearly a year after he first heard of it, he continued to harbor strong feelings about the *Defensio fidei*, a book by the scholastic theologian Francisco Suárez. It had been a bold attack on the Oath and a thorough argument for the limited authority of the king, especially in religious matters. Its arguments did not become less combustible with time, and the regime surely knew that Suárez had infiltrated the minds of rebellious subjects. For example, Gondomar tells of a time when Irish representatives, who had long been on a quest for Habsburg aid, came around to ask him about the *Defensio*, especially the parts concerning whether regicide was licit.[59] Carvajal was certainly sympathetic to this "radical" Irish sentiment and would, not surprisingly, speak openly in favor of Spanish support for these needy and desperate Irishmen.[60] So when Abbot whispered in the king's ear about Suárez, he calculated that it would make a difference. In the same vein, as Marshalek has pointed out, when Abbot captured Carvajal, it was a means to expose "that the Spanish peace had allowed the dangers of international Catholicism to come home to roost."[61]

Carvajal's arrest was brutal. Because she had taken safety so seriously, the easiest way to enter her home was through the garden. It seems that assailants climbed the outside wall to get in and headed straight to the bedrooms. They destroyed locks, tore down doors, and forcefully apprehended Carvajal and her companions.

This was not a covert activity, nor was it done in the shadows of night. It was meant to be a public affair. One account testifies that there were at least fifty halberdiers and many more with weapons. Surely the scene invited spectators—and there were reportedly many.[62] Abbot clearly wanted to create an urban spectacle to galvanize the public and its hispanophobic tendencies. More specifically, he must have been trying to take advantage of an audience that would have already been knowledgeable about Carvajal, a reminder of the extent to which she had succeeded in making herself part of the urban landscape with the adverse effect of becoming a stand-in for the evils of Spain in the English imagination. If this had not been the case, then there would have been no point to Abbot's parading his fresh catch down the streets of London. It was said that she was transported by carriage, purposefully leaving the window uncovered to ensure that people knew who was on the road to punishment. People cried out, as if spewing a curse: "English nuns! English nuns!"[63]

Abbot might have wanted blood, but he knew it would not be shed. Diplomacy would prevail; Gondomar secured Carvajal's release. The king was willing to show clemency, but only if she left the kingdom promptly. In an extensive letter on the affair, Gondomar describes taking umbrage at the request that she be removed within eight days. It was something, he said, "that I should never offer nor fulfill, for I considered this lady a good and exemplary woman and so it would not be good that she be exiled by my hand when innocent, so that fabrications and charges which they laid against her would be supported."[64] Abbot would insist to the ambassador in Brussels that, against whatever rumors had been swirling, Carvajal was in fact released under the condition that she would remain under the ambassador's custody—no nunnery for her!—and that her departure would be expedited. Negotiations continued, each party ignorant of the fact that it was all about to end.

CONCLUSION

Much as in Madrid or Valladolid, Carvajal made her presence felt in London. When it comes to her English life, two things are certain. First, she time and again went out of her way to be seen, be it in prison, in the market, and even in and around her house. Second, authorities did not like her. Carvajal would have recognized such dislike as her great success. While the authorities may have wanted to control the narrative and use Carvajal as a tool for further degrading English Catholics and revealing their schemes, they were at the same time playing into her hands, because they helped magnify her persona. To be sure, Carvajal's temerity had to do with the fact that she did not care about suffering—indeed, she wanted to suffer—the most dire consequences. At the same time, for as long as it lasted, she knew that her life, audaciously lived, would benefit good Catholics and perhaps tepid ones as well. And this is the point. This chapter has not offered a blow-by-blow account of Carvajal's activities in England, but I've given enough to show that her performances mattered.

CHAPTER 5

# Carvajal's Spanish Diplomacy

TEMPERANCE AND DECORUM

Carvajal had never felt so Spanish as during her years in England. She missed her homeland and all its familiarities. But aside from those tugging human instincts, she loved Spain more from afar because she thought of it in relative terms. Her letters are sprinkled with gripes about England: the climate was terrible, the food was bad, everything was too expensive, and, of course, heretics lurked everywhere.[1] There was only one benefit: It was a good place to suffer. Of course, she was never blind to Spain's imperfections—an important part of her pro-(English) Catholic efforts had to do with ensuring that these coreligionists would receive proper support from lukewarm Spaniards, many of whom thought that things were not so bad in England after all. Nevertheless, if she recognized the faults of her compatriots, these needed to be glossed over in public, especially amid constant Protestant attacks. Fierce English animosity toward Spain required her to conform to an apologetic and chauvinistic script.

As we've seen throughout, despite her aura of saintliness in life, not everyone would have agreed with such unalloyed praise. From Carvajal's perspective, this would have signaled the faults of others. Indeed, doubting her was likely considered a manifestation of spiritual weakness and, in the worst of cases, demonic trickery. So she waged a multifront battle. Aside from combating English heresy where it lived, she had to deal with both potential supporters and (potential) enemies back home. Configuring, reconfiguring, and cementing appropriate responses to these audiences were crucial to her politico-religious goals.

Especially at diplomatically sensitive moments, Carvajal had to justify her presence in England. Again, from the earliest days of her mission, she had many critics; rumors swirled about her intentions. Was it pride? Did she have some financial motive? Were her intentions merely political? And so on. From the start, these concerns aligned with geopolitical considerations. For those who believed in negotiation and accommodation with England, she was a glaring liability. Carvajal consistently responded to critiques by refuting suggestions of self-interest or terrestrial concerns. She increasingly affirmed that her desire for martyrdom in England had sprouted at a very young age—something that does not seem to be strictly true—and that her decision to stay there was based on the advice of wise men and, just as importantly, her discernment of God's will. Carvajal fought fiercely from afar against critics at court who argued for her removal, in part because of her desire for self-sacrifice but also because she had developed a set of assumptions about her crucial role in ensuring the viability of English Catholicism. The promotion of Catholicism and the protection of Catholics cohered, in theory, with Spanish diplomatic efforts, but she alone could pursue these goals openly and, frankly, undiplomatically.

In her letters to grandees and politicos, Carvajal reported her accomplishments. She described the rigors of everyday life as signs of her humility, her proselytizing efforts as signs of her utility, and her open conflicts with heretical authorities as evidence of her true desire for martyrdom. Explaining the latter was tricky because, as we've seen, its accomplishment required a confrontational stance that would inevitably cause diplomatic discomforts. As a result, aside from providing facts, it almost goes without saying that she wanted to provide, through her letters, a version of the facts that shielded her from opprobrium. Indeed, the viability of her goals, which were not moderate, depended on her (occasional) claims of moderation.

In this context, it is telling that Carvajal would be eager to disseminate broadly an account of the events, discussed in chapter 4, that led up to her first imprisonment. She had no choice, considering the scandal that it unleashed and the extent to which it had irritated even her closest associates. Her critics would have seen the whole affair as evidence of the dangers she posed and perhaps the impropriety of her seeking out a fight. In this light, it makes sense that in one account—she wrote several—Carvajal would claim that her public debate with heretics happened by chance.

She avoided details about her first salvos, saying that "somehow or other" she felt inspired to ask the aforementioned young man if the girl nearby was his sister (and then if he was Catholic). While this question set off heated discussion, Carvajal emphasized that she did not promote acrimony. The shopkeeper and his neighbors started things. It was they who asked questions about the "mass, the priesthood, and confession" together with the nature of papal authority. Carvajal was anxious that her eagerness to teach heretics a thing or two might suggest that she was overstepping boundaries: lest she be seen as usurping a priestly role, Carvajal says she only touched on matters that "are well known and very basic" and used simple arguments "to make war upon error when the opportunity arises." While she took the opportunities as they came, heretics were the aggressors and, indeed, they were the ones who made this a public affair. She averred that the "*shopkeeper's wife* tried to turn everyone against me" (my emphasis). Carvajal suggests that though they fanned the flames, after a couple of hours, she put an end to the commotion and went home.[2]

In her recounting of less controversial events, Carvajal still seems to soft-pedal. As discussed above, she played a crucial role in fortifying would-be martyrs, but even this had to be treated carefully. Although, in retrospect, it is easy to see that she was in control of the prison spectacles she orchestrated, her letters hedge a little. She does not shy away from describing the Christological symbolism present (and fabricated) for important jailhouse performances, but she simultaneously holds back. In part because she undoubtedly thought that the martyrs' sanctity was their own, she minimized the high stakes of her prison visits and the insecurity she must have felt about the determination of the priests she counseled. Hers is merely a supportive role, and her efforts are subtle. As mentioned above, Roberts tells Carvajal, with a measure of self-criticism, that he trembled. She reassures him. He later worries about feeling too much joy at the prospect of death. She reassures him. While we know Carvajal was there to provide spiritual nourishment, her accounts bring things back to an earthly plane: she made them a pear pie, a plausibly anodyne, feminine, and domestic gesture.[3]

As we've seen, authorities in England did not buy her meekness; they wanted to portray her as an instigator.[4] Her correspondents would have looked kindly upon her support of martyrs, but she clearly aims to deny her accusers' assertion that she was inappropriately intrusive, that she was adding fuel to the flame. Though she would not have put it this way, Carvajal was, in fact, trying to remove herself from the *politics* of martyrdom.

This is not the same as saying that her actions were not "political." To the contrary, her diffidence is proof that she understood the consequences of her actions within a contested political matrix. Indeed, her self-protection is an attempt to ensure that her brand of Catholic politicking would be preserved.

THE SIGNIFICANCE OF MARTYRS

Active or passive, Carvajal basked in the reflected glory of martyrdom. This was implied by her physical proximity to martyrs and objects related to them. She talks of the good fortune she had of kissing the necklace of one of the unjustly slain. On another occasion she tells of having received a gift from one. Roberts, she says, had given her "a crucifix lovingly painted on parchment."[5] Importantly, she did not keep this precious object (the relic) to herself but almost immediately sent it to Creswell in Valladolid.

We've already seen that corpse-hunting was an important part of Carvajal's efforts against the English state; it also served her well on the Continent and anywhere she looked to flex her spiritual credentials. For example, she delights in pointing out biblical resonances. Carvajal explains how, when confronted with martyrs' bodies, she could not help but think of Christ. On one occasion, after placing linens on one freshly dead body, she soon found that they were drenched in blood, forcing her to replace them with a clean sheet. Especially because she mentions Jesus, Carvajal is, to an extent, positioning herself as another Joseph of Arimathea, who cared for Christ's body, as described in scripture.[6]

On a much broader level, the circulation of martyrs was part of a complex politico-religious economy. Scholars have shown that the dispersal of body parts was crucial for the construction of confessional identities and, among other things, for cementing the authority of individual rulers.[7] The bloodstained shirt and the occasional femur were not necessarily intended to be, nor were they in fact, crass political tools, and Carvajal did not consider them as such. But she was no fool, nor was she deviating from post- (and pre-) Reformation norms when she gifted them strategically. The dead were catalyzing agents for support from the wealthy and powerful, who would be eager to help a worthy cause and would be moved by the salvific energies of the fallen few. On several occasions, Carvajal told her supporters that their help allowed her to preserve holy bodies. For example, she reminds the marquise of Caracena that she wrapped a martyr with cloth that she had provided—"they have not had a stitch placed upon them that was not mine"—as a way to demonstrate the good use to which Carvajal put donations from abroad. She emphasized that all pious alms went toward the care of martyrs and their burial, "in one way or another."[8] The alms were, of course, a means to salvation. She told Rodrigo Calderón—as we shall see, an important benefactor—that his charity was a good work being "recorded in the book of account which your lordship will one day have to submit to Him."[9]

These activities do not imply the commodification of sacred objects— or at least they signify more than that. The whole system worked because of the relics' extraordinary spiritual charge; it is hard to imagine the emotional impact experienced by those who touched them. Relics were important identitarian objects for individuals as well as for regions and kingdoms, and consequently the logic of their "uses" hinged on their power over the imaginary and the soul. Within a Spanish context, there was a certain vitality to these sacred objects so that, aside from being venerated, they revealed the extraordinary spiritual opportunities present in England and the superior spiritual mettle of the best Englishmen.

For bones to work, they need a proper context. For the dead to have the effect that Carvajal wanted them to have, they needed stories. Although Carvajal leaned on tropes in her retelling of the demise of would-be saints, those narratives could nevertheless have specific ends.

Carvajal had the (un)fortunate need to promote the martyr's cause the same year she got to England. As noted above, in the fall of 1605, a group of intransigent Catholics had plotted to blow Parliament to pieces—a foiled effort known as the Gunpowder Plot. In the extant correspondence, Carvajal is curt about the whole affair, dismissing it as a mad plot and little else. (In this she did what all like-minded Catholics did: looked up, whistled, and said, "Not much to see here.") Letters that may have been burned at the time of reading perhaps delved more deeply into the topic, but too much talk of the sordid event with her correspondents could have been counterproductive. This was exactly the kind of crazed escapade that some critics of "radical" English Catholic factions feared.

Carvajal's explanatory efforts were spent not on rebellious riffraff but on the murdered, especially Henry Garnet.[10] He had facilitated Carvajal's entry into English society upon her arrival, so she had a special affection for him. To an extent, the "opportunities" offered by a devout Jesuit who died for the faith seem obvious, at least from a Catholic perspective. But the martyr is inherently polemical, a figure meant to deepen and accentuate the ideological and religious gulf that exists between combating parties.

As ever, things are more complicated than any dualistic model allows. We've already seen that within a divided Catholic "community," the significance of a death could be controversial. The fact that individuals might identify as Catholics did not guarantee a universal response to the death of a priest. Further afield, in Spain, Carvajal knew that she had to do a certain amount of hand-holding. Especially in the aftermath of such a troubling scheme as the Plot, her readers needed to be assured that the participants in the terrorist attack should be distinguished from the holy and pious. Without this context, we cannot fully understand her carefully constructed account of Garnet's demise.

Carvajal was deeply moved by the event and truly stricken, to the extent that she could not bear to see Garnet's quartered body. She had no doubt that she stood before a saint, but there is an apologetic tone to her description of events for people back home. For example, Carvajal undermines Garnet's confrontational stance. To start with, she deals with the fact that at his execution, Garnet voiced a definite opinion on papal authority. Asked if he would support strong papal action against England—an explosive topic at any time, but especially in those days—he unequivocally said he would, that "the pope can do this whenever he wants." Carvajal then explains, "One must remember that the intention of father Garnet in saying this was to explain that, supposing that the king had been brought up in heresy and remained in this state throughout his life, the pope would not wish to use such severe methods with him as the queen, without having first used gentle words in order to procure his conversion."[11] Carvajal is using contemporary versions of events in an attempt to soften the edges of Garnet's response. Her gloss foreshadows the kinds of arguments that priests like George Blackwell would make a few years later, much to her disgust. Indeed, this is a fascinating effort at temperance by a woman who had previously claimed that she would feel free to say anything in the face of English oppression.

Later, Carvajal described Garnet's own squirming about his (non) involvement in the Plot. Although he was privy to the wild efforts of a few Catholics, he did not believe they would act on their plans. His unwillingness to reveal the scheme was not a matter of support for any untoward and lethal action but simply a matter of confessional seal, which was unbound at his execution. Moreover, he claimed that when he heard about the nefarious plan, "he took every possible step to prevent it, assuming that it would not go ahead."[12] This needed to be described by Carvajal against efforts to paint Garnet as a snitch and to erase any suggestion that he was a coconspirator, thus removing any taint from him and his virtuous death.

Carvajal's account was clearly not the only one, and it was surely a distillation of others that circulated at the time. Indeed, she would have had immediate access to those versions collected by the Spanish ambassador, Don Pedro de Zúñiga, who would send quickly translated Spanish retellings for distribution in Spain. Garnet's story was soon well known. As the English ambassador to Spain explained, after Garnet's execution, "their preachers [in Spain] usually helped out their sermons with declarations against the cruelties of England, some of them affirming how much easier it was for the Christians in the days of Diocletian." Interestingly, in response to ambassadorial protestations, governments in Madrid and Brussels did their best, or claimed to do their best, to suppress any stories about Garnet that might be prejudicial to England.[13] This is a reminder of just how choppy the waters were when Carvajal packaged news from England. Her role in disseminating Garnet's end was a preventative measure against efforts to suppress important and spiritually edifying events. The very fact of her account showed how she did her bit against the earthly prudence that would inhibit the spread of (good) bad news while bowing to the complex world in which her story would be inserted.

If part of the trick was to ensure that the saintliness of martyrs was maintained among "good" Catholics despite compromising situations, Carvajal also had to deal with "bad" Catholics. In a letter to Creswell, she huffily reports that while Protestants spoke poorly of Spain, Catholics could be just as bad. Indeed, "sometimes the worst offenders are those who are brought up in Spain."[14] In a bid to offer an edifying story that might be circulated to students, she followed her complaint about ungrateful Catholics with an account of the death of Blackwell, the onetime archpriest. As we saw earlier, Carvajal had a serious debate with him about the Oath, so she must have felt a certain schadenfreude in telling the story. She reveals—based on the most recent account—that he perished without a last confession. In fact, he had been feeling fine when, all of a sudden, he keeled over. This was clearly a punishment. However, according to Carvajal, in a moment of redemption, with his last breaths, he claimed that "as for the oath he had believed that he was following what was best for his conscience, but that if this was not the case he was sorry for it." Carvajal goes further. She says the jailer at the Clink reported that before his death, Blackwell repented: "[H]e was sorry for having held that opinion [about the Oath] since truly it was false and against all conscience, and for this he was most remorseful." The jailer claimed that Blackwell called upon four witnesses to say this in their presence. The archbishop of Canterbury later called the chosen four for questioning, but knowing that the archbishop didn't want to hear about Blackwell's repentance, the supposed witnesses told him they knew nothing about it.[15] There is profound ambiguity here, as it is unclear whether Carvajal believes the story or not. (She certainly did not like Blackwell.) But just by mentioning it, Carvajal adopts a restrained tone, especially when compared to English accounts that could be much harsher.[16] For example, George Birkhead, the archpriest who replaced him, reported that Blackwell died with no remorse.[17] Carvajal, on the other hand, chose to treat Blackwell not as a negative exemplar but as one of conciliation, which she likely thought beneficial considering the extended audience of seminarians (and others in Spain). Those who insisted on a course of moderation should take heed of that man who had been so foolish in life and who realized it too late.

Within the English context, the deaths of Thomas Somers and John Roberts were macabre publicity coups—blows to the Jacobean regime's schemes and to the designs of "schismatics" as well. These holy deaths would also have resonated within a Spanish context, where Carvajal's account would be added to a catalogue of bravery and fortitude. Moreover, they could function as parables of political corruption of the sort that marked England and, to a lesser degree, Spain. The show of unity also mattered on both sides of the Channel. It is not by chance that Carvajal mentioned Roberts's affiliation with the Benedictine order. Indeed, in her account of the whole affair to Creswell, she emphasizes how in his last days Roberts talked to her about being a Benedictine monk and how, at the same time, he loved the Jesuit Creswell. This intra-religious affection was indicative of a desire to mend fissures among different religious orders. According to Carvajal, Roberts "was most anxious that there should be great unity and love between the fathers of the Company and Benedictine monks."[18] This would have mattered within a Spanish context because, as mentioned in chapter 2, there was a toxic relationship between Jesuits and Benedictines in and around Valladolid. This might have been Carvajal's pitch for comity or her effort to suggest its possibility. Not only would such messages edify seminarians in Spain but they might assuage Spanish onlookers wary of internecine English squabbles. These stories helped ensure support for the English cause.

## AMBASSADORS AND DIPLOMACY

Carvajal's most direct interventions in Spanish matters were on the diplomatic front.

If, as suggested above, Carvajal went to England to help shatter the newly minted Anglo-Spanish détente, her enterprise depended on Philip III's representatives to James's court. Not only did the king's ambassadors offer bodily protection but they also facilitated the payment of her royal stipend and provided their own cash when necessary. In the best of cases, the ambassador would also be a partner in defending Catholicism and offering comfort to Catholics. The ambassadorial home, then, protected as it was by ambassadorial privileges, could be a place of worship for Catholics and provide all-important spiritual sustenance. In a way that Carvajal could not, the ambassador lobbied for gentle treatment of Catholics and tried to save those whom the regime had condemned to death. Indeed, the ambassador provided access to the English crown and its council; if she was savvy and he perceptive, her discussions with him could be very influential. This prevailing dynamic explains why Carvajal was so mindful of ambassadorial politics.

Carvajal's relationship with Don Pedro de Zúñiga was, overall, a good one, and he had bestowed upon her many gifts and services. It is no surprise that news of his departure would cause some trepidation. In a letter to Creswell, she is blunt: "[S]peaking on a human level, we shall be left in dire poverty and very exposed." Having said this, she cleans up by insisting that, ultimately, these are worldly concerns and that her discomfort will be compensated by providence. Carvajal was sure that "our creator, the most generous Lord of heaven and earth, will still be with us, everywhere and at all times, as powerful as He is good."[19]

In another letter to Creswell, Carvajal, "out of gratitude and loyalty," expresses respect for the ambassador and registers support for his decision to leave. She underscores the general laments of Catholics who saw him as a dependable ally and competent in the turbid waters of English politics. Indeed, she says that "the Catholics love him, and influential heretics seem to love him, or at least they respect him greatly."[20] In later correspondence, she would speak glowingly about how Don Pedro's likability in England had positive consequences. His capacity to create lines of amity between England and Spain "has resulted in their moderating the atrocious things that they usually want to and do commit against the Catholics." She would go on about the "richness of his compassion" and his religious zeal.[21]

As evidence, Carvajal wrote to Mariana de San José about a recent episode of hurried kindness. She reports that Don Pedro had come early in the morning to call on her. He uncharacteristically looked agitated and was solicitous about finding a place for her to live, insisting that he did not want to leave her homeless. He suggested a house near the Venetian ambassador so that she would have access to the mass, and Carvajal agreed. When she asked why he was so desperate to make arrangements, he intimated that he might have to leave in a rush but clammed up when she asked for more details. The end was near, and she had no clue how it would go.[22]

Unsurprisingly, Carvajal was eager to help select the next ambassador. At the time, she had developed few relatively close connections that could help amplify her voice in Spain, but at least one of them was invaluable. Creswell, at the English College, was as good a contact as most she might have had, since he would have been involved in discussions about Don Pedro's replacement. Moreover, she could be certain that they were largely on the same page. Her suggested prerequisites are unsurprising, but important, given the context. Carvajal imagined someone on par with Don Pedro. He must be a "God-fearing" man who would be able to provide a good example of "honest living." He should be "generous and honorable" not only with his household but even among heretics in "affairs of state." His religiosity is, naturally, the most important quality: "He must be zealous for the Catholic religion and show great respect for it." Carvajal completely understands that diplomacy cannot be brash or strident, and so she acknowledges that a future ambassador should be tactful—but he should also be "brave and show resolve and be prepared to show his teeth when circumstances dictate it."[23] Thus, in counterbalance to her role on the English scene, she allows for diplomatic subtleties and suggests a certain flexibility in worldly things, so long as they do not touch religion. Perhaps time in England had given her a sense of how finicky diplomacy could be, softening her somewhat. Of course, her advice is more about choosing battles than submission to a heretical regime, especially given the extent to which, under other circumstances, she was quick to point out the malevolent Machiavellian core of diplomatic behavior.

Don Pedro's successor, Don Alonso de Velasco, proved a disappointment. She was disposed to think him acceptable, at first, but soon after his arrival she was quick to tell her brother that he had started off poorly. It is hard to say exactly what she means, but it is likely that he had not signaled feistiness against the regime, and his limpness suggested little benefit to English Catholics. Part of her sourness must have also been personal.

He had been cold to Carvajal, but she petulantly reports that she did not expect help from him anyway. In reality, she must have been spurned when it became clear that the dynamics had changed radically since the time of Don Pedro's embassy. Later, as his stay went on, she would grumble about his stinginess.[24] She reported with muted rancor that he was willing to let her stay in his quarters for only a couple of weeks.[25] Worse, he simply had no feel for how to proceed; he was credulous and, perhaps most damning, he simply would not work to ensure Catholics' best interests. He was not their defender in times of strife, and he would not jump into action when the regime seemed set to tighten screws.[26] Things would only decline as her complaints grew more cutting over time, especially toward the end of his assignment (1613), when everything spiraled out of control.

Don Alonso saw things from a different perspective. In fact, he did not lack empathy or care for English Catholics, but he wanted to act prudently, as the king himself had instructed. At the outset of Don Alonso's ambassadorial mission, Philip III had secretly commanded him to proceed with the "modesty and dissimulation that is convenient because I very much want to see them [English Catholics] free of the labor and oppression that Queen Elizabeth placed on them."[27] The moment was particularly sensitive, given the fragility of a new ambassadorial team—and the fact that during its early days the king of France had just been murdered by a Jesuit, to the horror of many, including James I. Discretion mattered more than usual.

It seems that, in fact, Don Alonso did work behind the scenes, not wishing his most sensitive pro-Catholic efforts to be revealed publicly. He knew, however, that some disliked his discreet approach. Moreover, he communicated both sorrow and displeasure at the fact that so many wanted to have a voice in his affairs. All these would-be advisors felt snubbed if he did not heed them and would whine that "everything has gone awry." He admired their zeal but not their judgment. As a result, he kept the cloak on. He did not think it "proper to inform them of the reason which moves me to make a decision different from what they would like."[28]

Thus, Don Alonso purposefully refused to establish a friendship with Carvajal. It was a strategic decision as much as it was personal animus toward her. Carvajal, although accepting of diplomatic realities, did not work in a diplomatic mode and was thus a liability. She had become a hindrance to the delicate balance Don Alonso wanted to maintain, and his almost theatrical distancing was a way to signal his own moderation.

Paradoxically, Don Alonso's avoidance of her was a sign of Carvajal's success. She had come to *mean* something within an English context and within the milieu of (ever-fragile) Anglo-Spanish diplomacy. In other words, from Don Alonso's perspective, Carvajal's stench was so potent that it could easily rub off on him.

When she had officially lost the direct ambassadorial ear, Carvajal, undeterred, continued to assert influence by means of correspondence with Don Pedro. She did not let up on trying to mold the future. In April 1611 she wrote a letter in what Glyn Redworth has pointed out to be a very formal style.[29] This was part of an extensive correspondence between Carvajal and Don Pedro that surely had many facets, both public and private. The formality here might simply be their mode of communication, but perhaps it also signifies a kind of official pitch for his assistance. Aside from comments concerning his impending marriage, the rest is meant to elicit his sympathy and horror. For example, when she reports on the deaths of Somers and Roberts, Carvajal intentionally emphasizes the close relationship Don Pedro had with both: Somers had administered the sacraments to English Catholics in his service, and Roberts was someone he "knew very well."[30] Carvajal is also sure to reveal how the persecutions of Catholics had increased since he had left, so much so that if she went into too much detail, she would need "a few extra packets of letters on top of this one."[31] Women, she claims, had faced pointed and more intense persecution, a perceived reality but also a powerful and striking sign of the regime's tyranny—in theory, women were meant to experience less rigorous persecution.[32] It is possible that she was implying her own danger, because her discussion of women's troubles in general took place not long before she revealed how she had, again, aroused the interest of local authorities.

Carvajal continued her assault on Don Alonso. For example, she reports that he insisted on great prudence regarding her upcoming meeting with the bishop of London, who hated her and had summoned her for questioning. He wanted her to avoid the meeting altogether, not necessarily for her own safety but because he did not think she would help the Spanish cause. He told her that subtlety should prevail, because the bishop "was a person of some consequence here, and in spiritual matters it was not helpful to be flippant or discourteous."[33] To an extent, she knew that Don Pedro would have understood Don Alonso's concern, but her critique was bundled with Carvajal's personal displeasure. She reports that Don Alonso and his family had been kind to her during a recent illness but points out that this was not the norm. She had tried to offer her expertise, but they refused to take it and seemed to be irritated by her. The relationship had soured, she continues, to the extent that they barely saw each other. This fractured dynamic was in contrast to her friendship with Don Pedro, which she recalls to elicit his pity (and charity).[34]

Carvajal is explicit in her frustration on a geopolitical level as well. This is done circuitously; she first mentions the work of the French and Savoyard ambassadors who had recently left England without tending to the safety of English Catholics. She devilishly tells Don Pedro that she hopes that they "not be guests at Herod's feast, with St John in prison." This blurted disapproval is followed by a general discussion of matters of state. The ambassadors "seek to be at peace with the whole world and under the guise of being gentle and pious, make Catholic princes forget the intolerable distress which those who are Catholic suffer here in this country, or else draw them in with their cunning to weaken their resolve." She was exasperated by the skewed logic that had led to such disregard for important and holy matters. Diplomats and other proponents of peace with heretics privileged the maintenance of the state above all else and censured those who indulged in "imprudent fervor." Carvajal, as always, rejects such logic, claiming that it was they who lacked both prudence and reason by ignoring God's will, without which states do not prosper. Then, in what functions as criticism of Don Alonso as well, she exclaims: "What great things ambassadors could achieve here, if only they had zeal and discretion."[35]

It is unlikely that Carvajal thought she could miraculously transport Don Pedro to his previous post (although he would, indeed, be sent on a special embassy a year later). Still, it is a reminder of how crucial she considered diplomats as facilitators of true zeal and the protection of Catholics.

For Carvajal, the exposition of horrors to a like-minded functionary of state was a means to influence those at the center of governance with whom Don Pedro was still very close. In complex ways, her relationships with ambassadors and the messages she sent them were, as ever, means by which to emphasize the importance of politics infused with Christian values.

### BY MEANS OF CALDERÓN

Before she got to England, Carvajal had tried (unsuccessfully) to use her female networks in Flanders, but once she arrived she increasingly focused on getting closer to the men at her disposal.

Carvajal seems to have used her brother, Alonso de Carvajal (of the lawsuit), as a further "in." Their sibling relationship went through several ups and downs and, predictably, she framed these different moments in moral terms. As mentioned in chapter 3, she had been concerned about her brother's soul—his failure to live up to godly standards. Aside from wanting to "save" her brother, now his spiritual attainments (or potential attainments) mattered in more public ways. As early as 1609, she reminded him that she had been working on his spiritual health for years. In tones of what can only be feigned humility, she took ownership of his failure: her inability to help signaled her own weaknesses. Saying this, she then jumped in to more (perhaps unwanted) advice. She wanted to know if he had done a general confession in which he recounted his whole life. She was eager to find out if he was taking communion and if he was praying daily. She admonished him: "I am begging your honor [to do so] ... because life hurries along to reach its end."[36]

After what she must have considered several lapses, and in time (surely not coincidentally) to establish firmer ties with people at the center of governance, she came to believe that her brother had finally undergone something like honest reform. Nevertheless, her reservations persisted. Indeed, she would not support his bid for the ambassadorial position in England; it would have been uncomfortable because of their relationship and perhaps damaging because of his inconstancy.[37]

Carvajal's brother facilitated her connection with Rodrigo Calderón, her cousin-in-law.[38] Calderón had become an important presence in Madrid during the reign of Philip II, and his star would remain ascendant during Philip III's reign. He would go on to have a very close relationship with the duke of Lerma, the king's *valido* (and for a while the number two figure in Spanish governance, behind the king himself). Carvajal clearly used Calderón to gain access to the court, sending messages she believed would be relayed to his superiors.[39]

Carvajal's brilliance as a political actor is manifest in her dealings with him. As with all her relationships, this one was facilitated by connections inherent to her nobility and the reception of her extraordinary piety. The latter gave her notable latitude in terms of what she could say to those who were technically her superiors. In a role she had assumed in many contexts before, she established herself as an arbiter of virtue and good governance. Indeed, she suggested that the primary justification for contact was not mere kinship but a spiritual connection.[40] In what appears to be one of her first letters to Calderón, she begs him "to think hard about your debt to God, to love him with all your heart, and to glorify Him." She encourages him to find God and realize that nothing is "preferable to fulfilling

His law." She continues by asking Calderón to take advantage of the gifts that God has given him and insists that should he do so, he would have no reason to fear going to hell.[41]

That this theme is a recurrent one in her correspondence suggests that she saw herself as a sculptor molding clay. Although, as scholars have pointed out, Carvajal latches on to contemporary political discourses to coax Calderón, she is primarily interested in using godly arguments.[42] Thus she exhorts him to take heed of the important place he has at court and to see it as a divine gift.[43]

The fact that she would go on in this way, and that Calderón would actively seek out her advice, is a testament to their reciprocal relationship, which flourished over time. She needed him to support her and her causes, while he sought in her a confidant and a mentor. He could provide cash and political connections, and in return she offered virtue. Just as importantly, she offered prayers that God might give Calderón "a perfect understanding of the richness and consummate happiness which is locked away in the fulfillment of His most holy will."[44] She excuses herself for her "old and well-rehearsed arguments," but "so sweet is their marrow and substance when they are carefully broken open that you come across their peaceful, pleasing novelty."[45]

All the effort spent on Calderón would, to an extent, come to naught if he ceased being a powerful politico. At the time that they first started corresponding, Calderón was in Flanders, and he found himself at a crossroads. He was close to Lerma, but court seemed teeming with enemies. He considered choosing a life away from it, possibly in a diplomatic post to Germany, which would be safer. Tellingly, Calderón asked for Carvajal's advice. At first, she seems ambivalent, but there is little doubt that she wanted him to remain within circles of power. She suggests that it might be a good idea to leave the tussle of court, but, in concert with Don Pedro, she ultimately favored his return to Madrid. Carvajal explains that she had been told that there is no one who could fill the vacuum he left behind. She continues, explaining that to "everyone who has commended this to Our Lord, sir, it has always appeared that you should return to your position if it is offered you by our lord the king or the duke, and without further ado."[46] In the end, the decision could only be made by him, but as always, it had to be made advisedly, with an eye fixed on God's glory. Should he be able to serve Him best at court, then he should go there, knowing that his enemies could not harm a man devoted to God.[47]

Carvajal may have thought of Calderón as a (potentially) purifying element at court, but her immediate interests were English. All the trite exhortations were in the context of what she perceived to be enfeebled support for English Catholics and a perceived (and unbecoming) tepidity toward James I's regime. It is in this context that Carvajal spends a good deal of time underscoring the sufferings of Catholics and, in turn, the duty to care for them. It is no surprise that she would insist that Calderón should offer "protection to the religious and the poor."[48] Exasperated, she blurts out that if "the great counsellors of state" understood how bad things had gotten, "I wonder if they would still be telling me that the peace was worth it!"[49] Predictably, while she critiqued others, she also wanted to advise the correspondent who had clearly not done enough and who might, owing to political prudence, fail to do so.

Carvajal consulted Calderón extensively about ambassadorial matters, especially considering Don Alonso's removal. Calderón was well-versed in Carvajal's antipathy, which, by the end of his embassy, turned into plain meanness. Her caustic comments were intended to ensure that the regime avoided the mistake committed in selecting such a mediocre representative.

Sometimes she approached the topic from an oblique perspective. Her criticism frequently took the form of praise for Don Pedro, who in 1612 was back in England on a special mission and who was firmly within Calderón's circle. For example, in one letter, she recalls how "on one dreadful occasion the matter of the Catholic religion was broached with him, he became terribly enraged, like a hedgehog with all spines," in contrast with Don Alonso.[50] Elsewhere, Carvajal returns to his leonine qualities. He appeared to her as "a great lion in his cave, showing courage without rushing about or talking."[51] As ever, there is an edge to what she is saying. By describing Don Pedro's forced restraint, she is condemning Spanish geopolitical strategy. If Don Pedro is in his cave, it is in conformity with Philip III's will: only "the obedience and respect due to our lord the king holds him back."[52] In these letters, Carvajal suggests several ideals at once: loyalty, submission, (Christian) prudence, and inherent wrath against heretics. Unfortunately, the latter is being diluted by royal desires. This suggestion cannot be seen as anything but a critique of the monarchy.

She does more of the same, from yet another angle. In a move very typical of the times, Carvajal gives Calderón a blend of exhortation and critique of Philip III by way of smearing the memory of Philip II. She is certain that the current king would be much more successful than his father, who was deficient in virtue and goodness. She says with palpable disgust that Philip II, for "reasons of state," had made a fatal error in (at first) showing kindness to Elizabeth and thus allowing her to take a crown that was not hers. He did this as a move against France, because the proper title belonged to Mary Stuart, who was then married to the French prince and thus stood to inherit both kingdoms. Though she allows that reasons of state matter, in fact—and here we return to an old warhorse—God's will cannot be overcome. It turned out that despite Philip II's scheming, the dauphin died young and Mary Stuart ended up imprisoned in England. The only one left standing was Elizabeth.[53]

Once again, the context of these tired tropes is what matters most. Her anti-Philip screed was written at the same moment as her reflections on the situation in the Netherlands. As in England—and these issues had long been seen as of a piece—Carvajal sniffed out the dangers of détente. Spain had made a limited truce with the Dutch in 1609, something profoundly problematic from Carvajal's perspective. As a result, she applauds efforts to crack down on corruption in Flanders. A lot of money was being used to the detriment of the Catholic cause; palm-greasing was endemic, as was the purchase of offices by "people who are no use in peacetime and even less so in war." She berates those inveterate sinners who have attained some measure of power and has no less damning things to say about those who should know better but fail to do anything about it. She says that now is the time for true reforms, because the breathing room provided by the truce should be used to positive ends—"otherwise it serves no purpose whatsoever." She makes sure to exclaim how insolent and arrogant the Dutch had been and proclaims her joy at the thought that they might ultimately be humiliated at the hands of Philip III.[54]

This basic messaging is also present in what would be among her last geopolitical interventions. In 1612, James I's son Henry died. As with any royal death, the political scene had to be rebooted and, in this light, trepidation spread broadly and quickly about what would come next. As ever, questions about succession arose, with new attention placed on Henry's sister Elizabeth, who stood to inherit the crown. Almost immediately there were rumors about a Spanish match, which, as expected, disturbed Carvajal—and she unsurprisingly spoke forthrightly about the situation. Carvajal reports that schismatics think that a Spanish match would make James look more kindly upon Catholics, something that Carvajal predictably balks at as "folly." If the English claimed to be interested in negotiations with Spain, it was simply an attempt to secure self-interested comfort with no regard for the "honor of our lord the king and the cause of the holy church." They were mendacious; rumor had it that James's court was waiting for a marriage proposal from Philip III only so they could embarrass him with a refusal. Moreover, as further proof of the regime's Machiavellian schemes, she describes the extent to which the Spanish are hated in England and how heretics are repulsed by the idea.[55]

Although she never does it directly, the whole diplomatic affair gives her an opening to advise Calderón and the regime about modes of proper behavior and diplomatic approaches. On the other side of the rumor mill, there was a lot of chatter about a possible match with the duke of Savoy. In this, Carvajal could speak freely about the wrong way for a good Catholic prince to behave. Carvajal thus pivots from Spain to the Savoyard morass intentionally, and, as usual, she gets to the heart of greater matters than the machinations of one individual. In telling Calderón about Savoy's potential negotiations with James, she is horrified about news that he had offered, via his ambassador, to have a Protestant marriage ceremony in a bid to facilitate the dealings. Carvajal uses this bit of gossip to comment on ambassadorial issues: "What a horrendous utterance to come from the mouth of such a prince [Savoy], and I can see, sir, that even in worldly respects there is little to be gained from weak-willed Catholic ambassadors. They become so swollen with arrogance and enthusiasm that one becomes inclined more to despise them than respect them."[56] She says this in the same breath that she commends Don Pedro's stiff back against heretics.

Her description of the duke of Savoy's own actions performs the function of a quasi-warning. He is shown to be a Machiavellian prince who is willing to place self-interest above God's will. He would negotiate with James to the extent that he simply failed to act as defender of the church. He had implicitly and at times explicitly rejected papal authority and was willing to abide and take part in heretical rituals, which was akin to embracing heresy itself. When his own betrothal failed, he expressed his lust for power by attempting to match his daughter with the young prince, Charles. In these wrangles he proved himself to be rudderless; he had "stooped so low that nowhere in the negotiations has there been a single word that would lead you to believe he is a good Christian and Catholic man."[57] The effects of the proposed marriage would be profound. She argues that submission to heretical imperatives would be to the detriment of Catholic morale and set a terrible example.

While Carvajal suggests that James was truly considering this marriage agreement for the monetary windfall it might allow, she pretends to assume that Philip III's purity of faith would not allow him "to get caught up in anything so vile and repugnant to the Holy Church's honor, not even by parting with a solitary *escudo*."[58] Of course, Carvajal said this because Spain was considering precisely this.

And so on. Carvajal was extraordinarily capable of multitasking. She could see the broad geopolitical picture, the local emanations of those larger trends, and the role that individuals could and did have in causing or rectifying troubles. Thus Calderón was crucial. The whole point of her correspondence and the political analysis therein was to influence a man of influence, to guide him toward a form of political analysis that would then infiltrate the highest levels of government. It is hard to say if she impacted actual geopolitical decisions, but what matters is that she worked hard to be in the middle of things.

Just like so many others, Calderón was not convinced that Carvajal lived the right (even if perhaps a good) life. He started posing the idea that she might come to his newly endowed convent of Porta Coeli in Valladolid. This seemed like an elegant solution to the Carvajal problem. It got her out of everyone's hair in England while providing a solid foundation to his endowed institution. Her presence would have reflected well on him, and her counsel would have been close by.

Carvajal predictably demurred. She remained a dependable troublemaker, someone who forced those around her to consider the holy means to secular success, something that they might accept even as they tried to muzzle her based on reason of state.

### TOWARD THE END

During her last imprisonment (see chapter 4), Carvajal put Philip III and his regime in an awkward situation. The Spanish would be painted with the same brush as Carvajal, and it was possible that she might take Spain's official representative, the count of Gondomar, down with her. The ambassador was willing to risk failure. Without the desire and skill Don Pedro showed in supporting while not supporting Carvajal during her first arrest, Gondomar was blatantly on her side—to the extent that his wife, who Carvajal suggests was not particularly zealous on other occasions,[59] was sent to make a public show of support for Carvajal by standing with her in prison. She did so, as Gondomar reported back to Spain, so that Carvajal would be "with the authority and accompaniment of a Spanish ambassador [embaxadora]."[60]

Philip III was upset; Gondomar proved too zealous. The whole affair thus became a spectacle and, from the king's point of view, a public relations and diplomatic disaster, pitting Spain against England.

Madrid reprimanded Gondomar harshly, and the indignant ambassador had to account for himself.[61] He reported, correctly, that the English had decided to make an example out of Carvajal—"it was decided that they would make some great demonstration with this woman"—so inaction would have been a public defeat. Digging in his heels, he complained that while some believed that he could have been more moderate ("mas templado"), he swore "to your lordship, to God and to this cross + that when they took her I saw things in such a state that I felt all we did was not enough."[62]

Carvajal would be released and, as with her first time in jail, she was likely pleased by the disquiet she caused and the way in which her situation had forced people to draw hard lines. Don Pedro had chosen the route of discretion years before, but this time, she had enabled Gondomar to take a public stance against heresy, even despite diplomatic pressures. She had created circumstances and had developed a persona that made his support controversial and thus significant.

For Gondomar, this was a welcome opportunity to send a message of Catholic solidarity and animosity toward a regime that he had come to distrust. The same year as Carvajal's death he wrote a gloomy report to Philip III, reminding him that the maintenance of peace with England was primarily about protecting English Catholics. But things were simply not improving. The possibility of freedom of conscience or toleration was completely up to James, but Gondomar confesses to having "less confidence every day after making considerable efforts to understand it [the king's good will]."[63]

Carvajal had been wrong about Gondomar. Having been burned by Don Alonso, she had been wary of the new ambassador at the start of his embassy. She could not have imagined that he would become her staunchest supporter and a true defender of Catholicism in barbaric lands. Gondomar was not always brash, and he ultimately sought to maintain Anglo-Spanish peace, but time and again he had proved himself worthy of Carvajal's respect.

Carvajal's exit from prison was no less spectacular than her entrance (see chapter 4). Carvajal was paraded in Gondomar's coach, passing the royal palace, among other places, supposedly this time with expressions of joy from the public. Carvajal's body, both enclosed and exposed by Gondomar (and Abbot), became a means by which different players could create meaning.

If Gondomar had tried to make "use" of Carvajal to positive ends on her "radical" terms, he was the exception to the rule. In general, she found herself demeaned by her compatriots; nearly a decade into her mission, she had to defend herself against naysayers. Tellingly, she took the leap of appealing to the duke of Lerma. She needed to go straight to the most important man at court. Her letter is short, with predictable genuflections, but she also takes the opportunity to defend herself. As she had been doing for years, Carvajal insists that "the vocation to come to England which I had since I was a young girl, in accordance with the teaching of the holy church, has been most clear and likely a vocation from God." He did not have to take her word for it because providential signs were clear. She would not have survived in England had it not been God's will. The will of the divine is key to her plea that the duke not be swayed by errant counsel to remove her from England. In telling the duke to avoid intervening with the providential, she is carving out a special place for herself as a stand-in for exemplary, virtuous behavior. In doing so she uses herself—her controversial efforts—as an argument against more milquetoast approaches to Anglo-Spanish engagements. To the extent that she could, just as she had done before, she was trying to back the Spanish court into a corner and establish herself at the root of Anglo-Spanish contention, the source of a beautiful disarray.

Lerma had little interest in playing Carvajal's game.

Carvajal had expected to leave England, but only after she died, preferably after her martyrdom. She had once told Calderón that she wanted something simple, that perhaps her body should be sent to Louvain, home of the novitiate she helped fund. If quiet simplicity was her inclination, she would not get her wish. She died peacefully in January 1614 after a short illness in ambassadorial quarters, but her body would become the object of one last dramatic scene in England. She ended up on view in Gondomar's chapel, festooned by flowers and pristine white candles. Some visitors took what relics they could, and others tried to request them because, as her first biographer says, "generally among Catholics she was taken to be a saint."[64] Carvajal would leave in due time, but not before good Catholics could come to contemplate the ideals of Catholic devotion that she had wanted to embody. James I, for his part, miffed though he might be about the extravagance of it all, could turn a blind eye. He had wanted her out, and now she was gone.

CONCLUSION

As we've seen throughout, letters were Carvajal's main means of self-preservation and relevance, especially in various Spanish contexts where they were lifelines. Missives were tools to justify her presence in England, or at least to ensure that her own activities and, importantly, those of English Catholics were not deemed detrimental to what should have been Spanish objectives and desires. However, she did not assume a tame posture. During her stay in England, she continued to promote—sometimes in the context of diplomatic wrangles—a kind of pious politics. Not only did she try to cultivate the interior spirituality of those who were in the center of political action—itself a crucial political move—but she also tried to underline that the solution to diplomatic quagmires rested in what we might in retrospect call a Christian reason of state. Although hers was just one voice in the wind, it speaks to a set of ideals that should not be ignored. Carvajal's was an embrace of pious politics that she tried to inject into Anglo-Spanish relations through the long-distance cleansing of men like Calderón, who, in turn, seems to have been a willing listener.

# Conclusion

For centuries after her death, Carvajal drifted mostly out of sight and out of mind, but that had not been the plan. Gondomar wanted to keep Carvajal's body in England, probably because to James and his regime, doing so would have been something like a slap in the face. It would have communicated the ambassador's continued devotion to a woman who was broadly disliked among confessional enemies and among those who were allergic to "radical" Catholic schemes more generally. Her body would have been more than a sign of Gondomar's spiritual grit. Just as in life, she would have continued to be (in theory) a galvanizing force among the "good sort" of English Catholics.

As we've already seen, Philip III's regime did not benefit from keeping Carvajal in England and disapproved of rigid defenses of her that jeopardized Anglo-Spanish decorum. The Spanish crown had much to lose in England and—with her prompt removal—much to gain in Spain. Her death rid the monarchy of a diplomatic nuisance, while her arrival in Spain under the king's auspices would have reflected his own piety and devotion and would have suggested some of his animus toward England amid critiques of unseemly royal tepidity. Far from hiding her away as an embarrassing feature of international diplomacy, he wanted, at least in the short term, to bring the Luisa spectacle back home.

Carvajal's body traveled to Spain in a lead box. It had been loaded onto an English ship—a tricky business, rendered even more complicated by contrary winds not far off the Spanish coast that swept the vessel back toward England. The body's custodians managed, by divine intervention, to arrive on Spanish shores, where further evidence of the miraculous came to light. Sailors noticed that the ship's hull had a big hole. Clearly, it had been there for days: it was hard to fathom how the vessel did not sink altogether. The state of the body upon arrival was also an assault to reason. Once in Madrid, at the convent of the Encarnación, her body was removed from its casket. When the casket was opened, a flood of dirty seawater poured out that must have been sitting stagnant for months. And yet Carvajal's body remained uncorrupted. Its survival in such unlikely circumstances served to confirm what many had already come to believe: that she was a de facto saint.[1]

No wonder, then, that there were clashes about who could claim the body. Upon arriving in Valladolid, Rodrigo Calderón, then marquis of Siete Iglesias, was upset that Carvajal's remains had returned to such fanfare. He had hoped to steal her away secretly to the convent of Porta Coeli, which he had helped found not too long before. A silly scheme, considering that the king himself wanted her for his convent in Madrid. Still, the marquis persisted, putting her in a family tomb close to her brother, Alonso de Carvajal. Meanwhile, the duke of Uceda wanted the body to rest in the recollect convent where Magdalena de San Jerónimo resided, and English Catholics both in England and in Flanders grumbled about their own wishes. None of these claimants had a chance. She was destined for royal protection and "use."

After Carvajal's death, a Latin version of her life was composed by Giraldo Orano (Gerardo van den Berghe) for presentation to Philip III (and for further dissemination as well, by print and manuscript). From the first page, it ostentatiously appealed to and revealed the king's self-regard. Under his name, written in large letters, the author wrote: "Virtue, majesty, power / and the ornament of all kingdoms / monarch second to none / Spanish Catholic king of Spain." Beneath this, someone has written a note, instructing that on the bottom half of the page there should be an image of the royal crown or something similar.[2] In an equally laudatory tone, the dedication emphasizes how the king has maintained the faith. Interestingly, and of necessity, the author does not provide a list of martial exploits but instead focuses on the quieter means by which Philip has sustained Catholics under duress. Indeed, the dedication insists that kings are not glorified for their military exploits alone but for their virtue and protection of the church. This protection took many forms, but among them, the maintenance of seminarians was key. The author thus thought that the book might be published under royal auspices, as the king had been a protector of the English cause. The book was worthy of the king because it represented royal sensibilities and because it, in the place of the living, breathing Carvajal, would be a vehicle by which to absorb her exemplarity.³

Later, during the reign of Philip IV, Carvajal would again rise to prominence in royal circles. With a concerted push by various interested parties, including the nuns of the Encarnación, the crown decided to support a bid for her beatification. Undoubtedly, royal blessings were based on true faith and the spiritual benefits that would come from such a holy quest. The queen wrote to the duke of Pastrana that she "wanted to take part in the merit of such pious work."⁴ Presumably, this would be another case of politics and religion intermixing, as it had, famously, with Teresa of Avila's canonization and with others, including the archbishop of Valencia, Juan de Ribera—another scourge of heathen evil.⁵ (In fact, we might say that Ribera and Carvajal were nearly twin cases: one esteemed for his anti-Morisco credentials and the other for her anti-heretical actions in England. They both reflected royal imperatives, yet they both failed.)

The beatification process offered opportunities beyond the recognition of sanctity. Muñoz's life of Carvajal, published (not coincidentally) amid the hullabaloo of the proceedings, was an appeal to Philip IV, a tool by which to inspire more devotion to Carvajal "so that better knowledge of the life and virtues of this servant of God might increase the devotion that Your Majesty has and the favor you give."⁶ He connects her to Philip III's piety, suggesting that, after the peace he made with England, he supported Carvajal as a means to prop up English Catholics and convert heretics. It was now Philip IV's turn, he insisted, to partake in his father's "virtue and zeal" by helping to extend Carvajal's memory and fame. He should do this for the sake of the church and to the benefit of Spain for being the "mother of such a heroic woman."⁷ Again, we have a potentially double meaning, a predictable exercise in compliment and exhortation. The author subtly yet palpably suggests that the king *live up to* his father's purported piety, support the English Catholic cause, and take up Carvajal's zealous efforts to nourish and chastise Englishmen of different stripes.

Although English Catholics in Spain could not claim Carvajal as their own in the same way Spanish monarchs could, they tried to capitalize on her death. She was celebrated at the English Colleges, even in those that had not benefited from her presence or her spiritual/monetary benefactions. Indeed, the most readily available description of funerary celebrations comes from Seville in 1614. That year saw the publication of various texts aiming to underline the lessons she left behind. Juan de Pineda, rector of the Sevillian college, went so far as to say in a sermon that even though she had been like a "precious pearl" in life, she only gained full value after her death.⁸ As he explained, her exemplarity benefited the good as much as it did the faithless. Consequently, Seville was an important site for Carvajal's commemoration, given its sinful cosmopolitanism. Not surprisingly, her story was aimed at the grandees as much as anyone else. He reminded them how a woman of their own caste trampled the flesh, relinquishing nobility in favor of "chastity and Christian laws."⁹ This was of a piece with sempiternal English Catholic imperatives. Pineda wanted to remind people, especially among the wealthy, that they should adopt the English cause. Carvajal was a symbol of what the Spanish could and should do: help protect England by supporting the sacrifices of missionaries (like Carvajal).¹⁰

In sum, during the first couple of decades after her death, Carvajal became valuable currency for many designs in Spain. She represented Spanish piety and (in theory) enhanced the good name of the crown. At the same time she was a means by which some tried to purify the crown, perhaps with the intent of disrupting the amity between England and Spain. English Catholics, who had long been implied in such projects, looked on with hope—no doubt dimming—that England could be saved from damnation through the efforts of Spaniards at court or outside it, by diplomatic or even martial means or, at the very least, by supporting martyrs.

In England, after the drama surrounding her death, both English and Spanish politicos wanted Carvajal's memory erased. In life, she was a thorn in everyone's side, and any efforts to enshrine her sanctity in an English sphere proper would have been counterproductive. Without institutional support, there was no hope for Carvajal's cultural or political permanence. And yet it was impossible for her imprint to simply wash away once she left English shores. Although we know very little about their fate, her English companions remained, dispersed, in their homelands, walking archives conserving the stories of their superior. Perhaps they made sure that, as some said, Catholic noblewomen would continue to absorb Carvajal's exemplary piety.¹¹

Such a controversial figure would not have been easily dismissed by those who took names. Carvajal's memory could have been used against intransigent Catholics. Like the Spanish, many at the English court did not want to risk diplomatic ties by bashing a dead woman—but not all politics took place at court. It is not surprising that Carvajal, ten years after her death, would appear on the London stage. In 1624, the King's Men performed Thomas Middleton's *A Game at Chess* for nine days straight, to the delight of most viewers but the consternation of some.¹² The conceit was a battle between black and white chess pieces. The dark side represented the hispano-Catholic team; the side of (relative) light, James I's regime. The play set London abuzz and sent diplomatic representatives into a tizzy. It was shut down by authorities, surely agitated by its undiplomatic tone and, perhaps more importantly, by its flouting of rules against the representation of living monarchs on stage. Philip IV of Spain and James himself would have been recognizable as the Black and White Kings.

It is possible that the Black Queen's Pawn was modeled after Carvajal. The direct equivalence is not as simple as that, of course. We are probably dealing with a composite character who shares some traits with, for example, Mary Ward (who did, in fact, share important traits with the real Carvajal). Still, it is hard to imagine that the resonances with the Spanish noblewoman would have been missed, especially considering that the play was, in large measure, an anti-Spanish hack job.

In the play, the Black Queen's Pawn is crucial to a plot involving the Black Bishop's Pawn (a Jesuit) and the White Queen's Pawn. The play starts with the Black Queen's Pawn coming upon the White Queen's Pawn, lamenting that such a delightful creature is a heretic. The White Queen's Pawn has the spark of what the Black Queen's Pawn considers true faith, and so she tries to coax her, to no avail, until the Black Bishop's Pawn appears. She encourages her to heed his words, betting that he will be able to take advantage of a woman's weakness. The Black Queen's Pawn explains to her how the Black Bishop's Pawn nurtures "[a]ll his young tractable sweet obedient daughters" (1.39). She reveals that she herself is a "Jesuitess," as are, she continues, many women "of wealth and worth" (1.41–42). The play continues: "He finds 'em all true labourers in the work / Of the universal monarchy, which he / And his disciples principally aim at" (1.50–52). Later in the play, the Black Queen's Pawn involves herself in more scandalous ways with the Black Bishop Pawn's carnal desires for the White Queen's Pawn, though ultimately the Black Queen's Pawn tricks him into sleeping with her.

While the play descends into the ribald and salacious, this description of the Carvajal-like figure is revealing. It is a testament to how a version of her could be deployed to articulate the more hysterical aspects of anti-hispano-Catholic prejudice. For the play's audience, the Black Queen's Pawn's sexual desires and fraudulence would have reeked of Catholicism through and through, with its deceits and its preference for pleasure. If she is a masterful manipulator, she is also beholden to, and in complex dialogue with, Jesuit malefactors whose objective was world conquest. So

Carvajal, or her partial memory, could focus, enhance, and permit a type of misogyny that was baked into the anti-Catholic discourses of the time.

For those enemies in England who remembered her, Carvajal's villainy was obvious. She was a walking, talking nightmare, an infiltrator of the worst sort because she was so hard to make disappear. She was, they might have vituperated, a protector of Jesuits, an insidious teacher of Catholic beliefs and practices, a supporter of Spain and its hegemony, and a teacher of treason. In all these ways they would remember her as a chaos agent, a destabilizing element of the state, and an abettor of a fifth column that could, over time, destroy England.

Luisa de Carvajal y Mendoza would have agreed.

# NOTES

## ABBREVIATIONS

*Información*   *Información de la Señora doña Luisa de Carvajal.* Archivo General de Palacio, Real Monasterio de la Encarnación, caja 104. [Testimonies from the beatification process.]

### WORKS BY LUISA DE CARVAJAL Y MENDOZA

*Epistolario*   *Epistolario y poesías.* Edited by Camilo Maria Abad. Madrid: Atlas, 1965.
*Escritos*   *Escritos autobiográficos.* Edited by Camilo Maria Abad. Barcelona: Juan Flors, 1966.
*Letters*   *The Letters of Luisa de Carvajal y Mendoza.* Edited by Glyn Redworth with Christopher Henstock. 2 vols. London: Pickering and Chatto, 2012–13.
*Life and Writings*   *The Life and Writings of Luisa de Carvajal y Mendoza.* Edited and translated by Anne J. Cruz. Toronto: Iter, 2013.
*This Tight Embrace*   *This Tight Embrace.* Edited and translated by Elizabeth Rhodes. Milwaukee, WI: Marquette University Press, 2000.

## INTRODUCTION

1. Mantel, "Royal Bodies."
2. Beard, *Women and Power.*
3. The pathbreaking book on Elizabeth is Levin, *Heart and Stomach.* On Njinga, see Heywood, *Njinga of Angola.* For previous work on queenship, see, for example, Cruz and Suzuki, *Rule of Women.*
4. Poska, "Case for Agentic Gender Norms," 355–56.
5. Mitchell, *Queen, Mother, and Stateswoman.*
6. For an English case, see Cogan, *Catholic Social Networks.*
7. For an important example of this, see Broad and Green, *History of Women's Political Thought.*
8. Poska, *Women and Authority.*
9. Luongo, *Saintly Politics.*
10. Falkeid, *Avignon Papacy Contested,* 8.
11. For example, Blumenfeld-Kosinski, *Poets, Saints, and Visions.* Of course, since Luongo's work (though not necessarily because of it), many other important books on the entwinement of religion and politics with a focus on women and gender have been

written. For example, see Warren, *Women of God and Arms*. For a classic in Spanish historiography, see Kagan, *Lecrecia's Dreams*.

12. Suzuki, *Antigone's Example*, 14.

13. I am aware that this tendency has been amply criticized, but I am using the term "sensation" here purposefully to suggest that this is an idea just beneath the surface in plenty of modern scholarship.

14. Merry Wiesner-Hanks pointed out long ago that a broader understanding of politics was a prerequisite for embedding women in political narratives. See, for example, Wiesner-Hanks, *Gender in History*, 146.

15. For one important discussion of the topic in an English context, see Lake and Pincus, "Rethinking the Public Sphere."

16. Lake and Questier, *Trials of Margaret Clitherow*, 211–12.

17. Archivo General de Palacio, Real Monasterio de la Encarnación, caja 103, no. 7: Michael Walpole, *La vida de Doña Luysa de Carvajal y Mendoça* (hereafter *Vida*).

18. Muñoz, *Vida y virtudes*, 183r.

19. Muñoz, *Vida y virtudes*, 204r.

20. Fullerton, *Life of Luisa de Carvajal*, ix.

21. Fullerton, *Life of Luisa de Carvajal*, 202.

22. Abad, *Una misionera Española*, 16.

23. Pinillos Iglesias, *Hilando oro*, 136.

24. Rees, *Writings*, 3.

25. Rees, *Writings*, 85.

26. Redworth, *She-Apostle*, 3.

27. Redworth, *She-Apostle*, 138. Chapter 11 displays this dynamic.

28. For an incisive critique along these lines, see Marshalek, "Luisa de Carvajal."

29. See *Letters*.

30. Bill-Mrziglod, *Luisa de Carvajal y Mendoza*, 239–43.

31. Rhodes, "Counter-Reformation Journey."

32. *This Tight Embrace*, 19. Here, Rhodes quotes Carvajal at some length to that effect without examining the complexities of her claim. In the source, Carvajal claims that she did not "get involved in temporal things, for I abhor a lot of war and the spilling of blood." It seems to me that her understanding of contemporary geopolitics was fundamentally about war and the spilling of blood.

33. Rhodes, review, 219–20.

34. *Life and Writings*, 1–109.

35. Cruz, "Words Made Flesh"; Cruz, "Transgendering the Mystical Voice."

36. Cruz, "Luisa de Carvajal y Mendoza."

37. Cruz, "Willing Desire," 177.

38. Iglesias, "Luisa de Carvajal y Mendoza."

39. Levy-Navarro, "Religious Warrior."

40. Pando-Canteli, "'Tentados vados'"; Romero-Díaz, "Women, Space, and Power."

41. Domínguez, "Luisa de Carvajal"; Marshalek, "Luisa de Carvajal." Marshalek's work on Carvajal was contemporaneous with mine and we arrived at our conclusions independently. I am very pleased that she asked me to read an early version of her paper, from which I learned a great deal.

42. Domínguez, *Radicals in Exile*.

43. Davis, *Passion for History*, 75.

44. Historiographical emphasis has always been on the political activism of prophetic, ecstatic women. I am currently working on the ideal of secular and politically involved pious women as expressed in the writings of Pedro de Ribadeneyra. Redworth has rightly pointed out Carvajal's eschewal of prophetic behaviors in Redworth, "A New Way of Living?"

45. For a now-classic treatment of women and Spanish mysticism, see Haliczer, *Between Exaltation and Infamy*.

CHAPTER 1

1. *Life and Writings*, 112.

2. Nader, *Mendoza Family*.

3. *Life and Writings*, 117.

4. Anne Cruz suggests that Carvajal's coolness might have something to do with her knowledge of her father's illegitimate (and thus sinful) origins. He was the illegitimate son of the bishop of Plasencia, Gutierre de Vargas y Carvajal, though he was later legitimized. Thanks to Anne for communicating this perspective.

5. *Life and Writings*, 121; Sánchez Molero, "L'educazione," 53. Note that Carvajal's queenly role-playing had, as she describes it, begun before she arrived at the Descalzas. In fact, her favorite game had once been to "sit atop a high table and have the household pages and all others I brought inside come and call me their queen, making great curtsies and humbly bowing while I showered them with apples, pears, nuts, and other treats from a basket of large cloth." *Life and Writings*, 116.

6. *Life and Writings*, 121.

7. Sánchez Molero, "L'educazione," 29.

8. Sánchez Molero, "L'educazione," 81. Martínez Hernández, "'Enlightened Queen,'" 36.

9. *Life and Writings*, 144; For Carvajal's other emphatic comments on this issue, see *Escritos*, 179.

10. *Life and Writings*, 128 (challenges to Cárdenas's authority), 144 (sanctity vs. excess).

11. *Life and Writings*, 144.

12. *Life and Writings*, 138 (women's submission to the matriarch), 125 ("and to do arithmetic"), 128 (little progress in Latin).

13. *Life and Writings*, 127 ("devotional practices"), 126–27 (Cárdenas's devotional performance).

14. *Life and Writings*, 126–27.

15. *Life and Writings*, 143.

16. *Life and Writings*, 143.

17. Introduction to M. de Guevara, *Warnings to the Kings*, 4; Bouza, *Corre manuscrito*, 257.

18. For some general comments on the marquise's service, see Marquis to Philip II, Vienna, 1574 (no date), and "Memorial y recuerdo para S.M. sobre las cosas del conde

de Monteagudo" (1575), both in *Colección de documentos inéditos*, 111:511 and 113:298, respectively.

19. Coolidge, *Guardianship, Gender, and Nobility*.
20. For a recent and exemplary account of the role that women played within Spanish bureaucratic circles, see Masters, "Influential Women."
21. Vives, *Education of a Christian Woman*.
22. Barbazza, "L'épouse chrétienne," 125–31.
23. León, *La perfecta casada*, 76v.
24. Cerda, *Vida política*, 329v–332r.
25. Salón, *Oracion panegírica*, 26. On the different visions of piety between the marquis and marquise and the purportedly dysfunctional nature of their relationship: Redworth, *She-Apostle*, 29–30.
26. Muñoz, *Vida y virtudes*, 27r–28v; testimony of the marquis of Flores, *Información*, 95v; testimony of Joan de Ceráin, *Información*, 124v and 129v.
27. Ribadeneyra, *Scisma*, 9r.
28. Ribadeneyra, *Scisma*, 118r ("prejudice her marriage"), 119r–v ("to care for his soul").
29. Ribadeneyra, *Scisma*, 23r (tertiary habit), 24r ("a thousand years older"), 120v ("fires of turbulence").
30. Ribadeneyra, *Scisma*, 50r ("judge in his own case"), 53r ("acclamation of the world").
31. Ribadeneyra, *Scisma*, 114v.
32. Ribadeneyra, *Scisma*, 190v.
33. *Life and Writings*, 149.
34. *Life and Writings*, 149.
35. Walpole, *Vida*, 10v; *Escritos*, 185.
36. Cruz, "Reading Over Men's Shoulders."
37. *Life and Writings*, 135; *Escritos*, 187.
38. Walpole, *Vida*, 10r.
39. *Escritos*, 139.
40. *Life and Writings*, 130 ("his image in many ways"; "factions and dissensions").
41. It is worth noting, however, that her comparison to David is nuanced. Especially as it related to monarchs, adulators sometimes wanted the Davidic reference to suggest a Christological comparison. David was, after all, thought to prefigure Christ. Carvajal, however, keeps David largely grounded as a historical figure, a pious monarch and not so much a quasi-divine one.
42. Ribadeneyra, *Las obras*, 286v.
43. Impressions about the marquis's time as ambassador are drawn from his correspondence transcribed in the *Colección de documentos inéditos*, vols. 111, 112, and 113. In general, for the marquis's experiences in an ambassadorial capacity, see Abad, "Un embajador español."
44. Marquis to Philip II, Prague, 18 March 1575, in *Colección de documentos inéditos*, 113:45.
45. Marquis to Philip II, Vienna, 18 April 1573, in *Colección de documentos inéditos*, 111:188.

46. Marquis to Philip II, Vienna, 17 November 1572, in *Colección de documentos inéditos*, 111:57.
47. Ávila, *Primera parte*, 60r–102r.
48. Ávila, *Primera parte*, 64r.
49. Ávila, *Primera parte*, 90r.
50. Bouza, "Docto y devoto"; González Garcia, "La colección."
51. González Garcia, "La colección," 203–4.
52. Iñurritegui Rodríguez, *La gracia y la república*.
53. Osório, *De regis institutione*; Osório, *De rebus Emmanuelis*.
54. Osório, *Epistola Hieronymi Osorii*; Anglo, *Machiavelli*, chapter 5.
55. Osório, *De regis institutione*, 207r ff.
56. *Life and Writings*, 138.
57. Carvajal to Rodrigo Calderón, London, July 1612, in *Letters*, 2:216; *Epistolario*, 351.
58. Carvajal to Rodrigo Calderón, London, 22 September 1612, in *Letters*, 2:241; *Epistolario*, 366.
59. Carvajal to Magdalena de San Jerónimo, London, 5 December 1606, in *Letters*, 1:203; *Epistolario*, 194.
60. Forteza, *Reformation in the Spanish Imagination*, esp. 54–89.
61. "Escritos anónimos sobre la vida de Luisa de Carvajal," Archivo General de Palacio, Real Monasterio de la Encarnación, caja 103, no. 9 (not foliated).
62. *Life and Writings*, 140.
63. *Life and Writings*, 140.
64. Testimony of Isabel de la Cruz, *Información*, 305v.
65. *Life and Writings*, 29.
66. Rhodes, "Counter-Reformation Journey," 893; Redworth, *She-Apostle*, 28.
67. Walpole, *Vida*, 13r. For an example of when another servant went to discipline Carvajal but wouldn't do it in light of previous mistreatment, see *Escritos*, 184.
68. Testimony of Isabel de la Cruz, *Información*, 302v.
69. Testimony of Isabel de la Cruz, *Información*, 305v.
70. *Life and Writings*, 141.

**CHAPTER 2**

1. Testimony of Margarita de Austria, *Información*, 273r.
2. Testimony of Isabel de la Cruz, *Información*, 302v.
3. *Life and Writings*, 137. Along the same lines, see *Escritos*, 210.
4. *Life and Writings*, 137.
5. *Life and Writings*, 138–39; *Escritos*, 206–7 and 210.
6. *Escritos*, 210.
7. *Escritos*, 224.
8. Domínguez, "From Saint to Sinner"; Huerga, "La vida seudomistica."
9. *Escritos*, 191.
10. Walpole, *Vida*, 49v.

11. Gregory, *Salvation at Stake*; Lake and Questier, "Agency, Appropriation and Rhetoric."
12. See the dedication in Santoro, *Flos sanctorum*.
13. *Escritos*, 245.
14. Testimony of Margarita de Austria, *Información*, 268r.
15. Kleinberg, *Prophets in Their Own Country*, 20.
16. Henstock, "Luisa de Carvajal," 23.
17. Walpole, *Vida*, 20r.
18. Walpole, *Vida*, 20r.
19. Walpole, *Vida*, 22r.
20. Testimony of Joan de Ceráin, *Información*, 118v.
21. Walpole, *Vida*, 22v.
22. Walpole, *Vida*, 28r.
23. Testimony of Joan de Ceráin, *Información*, 103v.
24. Testimony of Joan de Ceráin, *Información*, 134v–135r.
25. Walpole, *Vida*, 26v.
26. Testimony of Lorenzo da Ponte, *Información*, 31r–v.
27. Walpole, *Vida*, 27r.
28. Testimony of the duchess of Rioseco, *Información*, 64v.
29. *This Tight Embrace*, 11.
30. Carvajal to Isabel de Velasco, Madrid, 15 September 1598, in *Letters*, 1:3; *Epistolario*, 98.
31. Carvajal to Magdalena de San Jerónimo, Madrid, 29 January 1601, in *Letters*, 1:22; *Epistolario*, 109.
32. Testimony of Lorenzo da Ponte, *Información*, 89r.
33. Testimony of Lorenzo da Ponte, *Información*, 31v.
34. Testimony of Joan de Ceráin, *Información*, 116r.
35. Testimony of Lorenzo da Ponte, *Información*, 30r–v.
36. Testimony of Isabel de la Cruz, *Información*, 301r.
37. Carvajal to Alonso de Carvajal, Valladolid, 1 August 1602, in *Letters*, 1:38–39; *Epistolario*, 118–19.
38. Carvajal to Alonso de Carvajal, Valladolid, 10 March 1603, in *Letters*, 1:57–58; *Epistolario*, 129–30.
39. Carvajal to Alonso de Carvajal, Valladolid, 10 March 1603, in *Letters*, 1:59; *Epistolario*, 130.
40. A. de Guevara, *Menosprecio de corte*.
41. For example, "Y mientras miserable- / mente se están los otros abrasando / con sed insacïable / del no durable mando, / tendido yo a la sombra esté cantando." Biblioteca Virtual Miguel de Cervantes, https://www.cervantesvirtual.com/obra-visor/poesias--3/html/01e9471c-82b2-11df-acc7-002185ce6064_3.html.
42. León, *Names of Christ*, 194.
43. León, *Names of Christ*, 89.
44. Feros, *Kingship and Favoritism*.
45. See, for example, *Life and Writings*, 36.
46. *Life and Writings*, 36–48; Redworth, *She-Apostle*, 59–61; Rees, *Writings*.

47. Her poetry was printed after her death, but a manuscript survives. Its octavo format suggests devotional uses as well as easy portability. Archivo General de Palacio, Real Monasterio de la Encarnación, caja 102, no. 19.

48. Bouza, "Docto y devoto," 278–79.

49. Muñoz, *Vida y virtudes*, 207r.

50. Thus, for example, we know that Leonor de Quirós owned a book of her poetry. Carvajal to Leonor de Quirós, 31 August 1607, in *Letters*, 1:275; *Epistolario*, 229.

51. "Redondillas espirituales de Silva," in *Epistolario*, 427–28.

52. Escalante Varona, "La imagen del jardín."

53. "Romance," in *Epistolario*, 433.

54. "Romance," in *Epistolario*, 433–34.

55. "Romance a Cristo nuestro señor," in *Epistolario*, 436–37.

56. "Romance espiritual de Silva," in *Epistolario*, 446.

57. "Romance espiritual de Silva," in *Epistolario*, 443.

58. "Redondillas espirituales de Silva," in *Epistolario*, 448.

59. "Quintillas espirituales de Silva," in *Epistolario*, 451.

60. "Soneto espiritual de Silva," in *Epistolario*, 449.

61. Salón, *Oración*, sig. A5.

62. Note that while the majority of letters were from Carvajal to her cousin, there are also transcripts of letters sent to Isabel's husband.

63. Salón, *Oracion*, 103r.

64. Carvajal to Leonor de Quirós, London, 28 December 1606, in *Letters*, 1:205–6; *Epistolario*, 195.

65. Braun, *Juan de Mariana*.

## CHAPTER 3

1. Burrieza Sánchez, *Virgen de los Ingleses*; Cruz, "Vindicating the Vulnerata."

2. See, for example, Carvajal to Magdalena de San Jerónimo, Valladolid, 11 January 1602 and 4 May 1603, in *Letters*, 1:33 and 62; *Epistolario*, 166 and 132.

3. See *Recebimiento que se hizo en Valladolid*.

4. In 1600 it is still not clear that she was all in with the English project. See, for example, Carvajal to Magdalena de San Jerónimo, Madrid, 16 March 1600, in *Letters*, 1:6; *Epistolario*, 100.

5. Redworth, *She-Apostle*, 74–75.

6. This fact is mentioned throughout the *Información*.

7. Creswell to Cardinal Aldobrandini, Madrid, 24 February 1596, Archivio Apostolico Vaticano, Borghese III, 124.g.2, 89r.

8. Creswell to Cardinal Aldobrandini Madrid, 24 February 1596, Archivio Apostolico Vaticano, Borghese III, 124.g.2, 89r.

9. However, as Parker has argued, Philip's approach to England was informed by messianic impulses. See Parker, "Place of Tudor England."

10. Domínguez, "History in Action." More broadly: Domínguez, *Radicals in Exile*.

11. Carvajal to Magdalena de San Jerónimo, Madrid, 16 March 1600, in *Letters*, 1:6; *Epistolario*, 100.

12. Infanta to the marquis of Denia, Brussels, 25 October 1599, in Rodríguez Villa, *Correspondencia de la Infanta*, 266.

13. Atienza López, "Isabel Clara Eugenia." On this theme, see Romero-Díaz, "On Female Political Alliances."

14. Atienza López, "Isabel Clara Eugenia," 281–82.

15. Black, "Public Bodies," 81.

16. Carvajal to Magdalena de San Jerónimo, Madrid, 16 March 1600, in *Letters*, 1:5; *Epistolario*, 99.

17. Carvajal to Magdalena de San Jerónimo, Madrid, 16 March 1600, in *Letters*, 1:6; *Epistolario*, 100.

18. Carvajal to Magdalena de San Jerónimo, Madrid, 26 October 1600, in *Letters*, 1:16; *Epistolario*, 106.

19. Carvajal to Magdalena de San Jerónimo, Valladolid, 24 August 1602, in *Letters*, 1:41; *Epistolario*, 120.

20. Carvajal to Magdalena de San Jerónimo, Madrid, 16 March 1600, in *Letters*, 1:5; *Epistolario*, 99.

21. Carvajal to Magdalena de San Jerónimo, Madrid, 14 January 1601, in *Letters*, 1:18; *Epistolario*, 107.

22. Carvajal to Magdalena de San Jerónimo, Madrid, 14 January 1601, in *Letters*, 1:18; *Epistolario*, 107.

23. Carvajal to Magdalena de San Jerónimo, Madrid, 16 March 1600, in *Letters*, 1:7; *Epistolario*, 101.

24. Carvajal to Magdalena de San Jerónimo, Madrid, 16 March 1600, in *Letters*, 1:8; *Epistolario*, 101.

25. Carvajal to Magdalena de San Jerónimo, Valladolid, 29 May 1601, in *Letters*, 1:28; *Epistolario*, 112.

26. Carvajal to Magdalena de San Jerónimo, Valladolid, 29 May 1601, in *Letters*, 1:28; *Epistolario*, 112.

27. Carvajal to Magdalena de San Jerónimo, Valladolid, 10 September 1601, in *Letters*, 1:30–31; *Epistolario*, 114.

28. Carvajal to Magdalena de San Jerónimo, 26 October 1600, in *Letters*, 1:16; *Epistolario*, 106.

29. Carvajal to Magdalena de San Jerónimo, Madrid, 16 March 1600, in *Letters*, 1:6–7; *Epistolario*, 101.

30. Carvajal to Magdalena de San Jerónimo, 26 October 1600, in *Letters*, 1:16; *Epistolario*, 106.

31. Carvajal to Magdalena de San Jerónimo, Valladolid, 24 August 1602, in *Letters*, 1:41; *Epistolario*, 120.

32. Carvajal to Magdalena de San Jerónimo, Madrid, 1 September 1600, in *Letters*, 1:12; *Epistolario*, 103.

33. Carvajal to Magdalena de San Jerónimo, Madrid, 1 September 1600, in *Letters*, 1:12; *Epistolario*, 103.

34. Carvajal to Magdalena de San Jerónimo, Valladolid, 4 May 1603, in *Letters*, 1:65; *Epistolario*, 134.

35. Carvajal to Magdalena de San Jerónimo, Valladolid, 24 August 1602, in *Letters*, 1:41; *Epistolario*, 120.
36. Hicks, "Robert Persons, SJ"; Netzloff, "English Colleges"; Questier, "Seminary Colleges."
37. Archivo General de Simancas, Estado 166, fol. 136.
38. See, for example, Persons, *Relación de algunos martyrios*, 62r–76r.
39. Domínguez, *Radicals in Exile*, chapter 4.
40. Dractan, *Relación que embiaron las religiosas*, 11v.
41. Carvajal to Magdalena de San Jerónimo, Valladolid, 24 August 1602, in *Letters*, 1:44–46; *Epistolario*, 123.
42. Kelly, "'Suppurating Ulcer,'" 693.
43. Carvajal to Magdalena de San Jerónimo, Valladolid, 16 November 1603, in *Letters*, 1:74; *Epistolario*, 137.
44. Redworth, *She-Apostle*, 92–93.
45. English Jesuits to Philip III, circa June 1604, in Loomie, *Spain and the Jacobean Catholics*, 1:18–19.
46. Redworth, *She-Apostle*, 92–93.
47. In general, see Redworth, *She-Apostle*, 96–102.
48. Testimony of Joan de Ceráin, *Información*, 109v.
49. "Aviendo faltado la persona de la Reyna, con quien fue la guerra, cesa la causa." Philip III to Juan de Tassis, Aranjuez, 29 April 1603, Biblioteca Nacional de España, Ms. 2347, 74r.
50. Philip III to Juan de Tassis, Aranjuez, 29 April 1603, Biblioteca Nacional de España, Ms. 2347, 75r.
51. Philip III to Juan de Tassis, Aranjuez, 29 April 1603, Biblioteca Nacional de España, Ms. 2347, 73r.
52. Philip III to Juan de Tassis, Aranjuez, 29 April 1603, Biblioteca Nacional de España, Ms. 2347, 70v.
53. Persons to James I, Rome, 18 October 1603, Archivum Britannicum Societatis Iesu, Anglia III, 36; duchess of Feria to James I, Madrid, 21 October 1603, National Archives, SP 94/9/81. On Creswell, see Redworth, *She-Apostle*, 100.
54. Loomie, *English Polemics*.
55. Transcription taken from *Revista de archivos*, tome 5, 123.
56. On the political elements of Marina's prophecies, see Burrieza Sánchez, "Fundaciones y visions."
57. De la Puente, *Vida maravillosa*, introduction, not foliated.
58. Muñoz, *Vida y virtudes*, 98v; Redworth, *She-Apostle*, 177.
59. *Letters*, 1:99 (editorial note).
60. For an example of Carvajal's response to such critiques, see Carvajal to Magdalena de San Jerónimo, London, 24 July 1606, in *Letters*, 1:179; *Epistolario*, 183.
61. Carvajal to Joseph Creswell, London, 26 July 1606, in *Letters*, 1:185; *Epistolario*, 186.
62. Carvajal to Magdalena de San Jerónimo, Valladolid, 7 September 1602, in *Letters*, 1:52; *Epistolario*, 126.

63. Carvajal to Magdalena de San Jerónimo, Valladolid, 25 January 1603, in *Letters*, 1:54; *Epistolario*, 127.

64. Warren, *Embodied Word*, 97–145.

65. "Memorial sobre el medio de convertir a los ingleses al catolicismo," Real Biblioteca de Palacio, Mss. II/2165, doc. 75.

66. Bossy, *English Catholic Community*; Cogan, *Catholic Social Networks*.

67. "Avisos de Inglaterra del p.o de 8bre 1591," Archivo del Colegio de San Albano, Valladolid, Series II, Legajo 6, no. 4.

68. Basic story drawn from "Aviso de Inglaterra de 16 de Mayo 1592," Archivo del Colegio de San Albano, Series II, Legajo 6, no. 6.

69. See, for example, her testimony regarding her mother's ties to Catholic priests (National Archives, SP 12/193, fol. 72) and the testimony of her brother upon his arrival at the English College in Rome (Kenny, *Responsa Scholarum*, 19–20).

70. Pando-Canteli, "Letters, Books, and Relics," 303.

71. All extant versions survive in English, though it is not beyond reason to think that other accounts would have existed in translation. Verstegan, *Theatrum crudelitatum*, 76–77. Yepes, *Historia particular*, 602–3.

72. *A trewe reporte of the life and Marterdome of Mrs Magarete Clitherowe*, York Minster Library, T.D.1, 41v. My thanks to Mary Beth Long, who is preparing an edition of this manuscript and shared her work with me.

73. York Minster Library, T.D. 1, 19v.

74. Gondomar to Francisco de Contreras, London, 26 October 1613, Real Biblioteca de Palacio, Ms. II/2168, 27r.

75. Carvajal to the marquis of Caracena, London, 28 August 1608, in *Letters*, 2:43, 44; *Epistolario*, 270.

76. Carvajal to Joseph Creswell, London, 31 August 1607, in *Letters*, 1:270; *Epistolario*, 227.

77. *Life and Writings*, 13–14n36; *Escritos*, 128.

78. *This Tight Embrace*, 33–35.

79. Henstock, "Luisa de Carvajal," 94–99.

80. *Escritos*, 132.

81. Bilinkoff, *Related Lives*.

82. "Voto de obediencia," in *Escritos*, 242.

83. *Escritos*, 146.

84. *Escritos*, 77.

85. *Escritos*, 210.

86. *Life and Writings*, 114.

87. *This Tight Embrace*, 87.

88. *This Tight Embrace*, 73.

89. *This Tight Embrace*, 41.

90. *This Tight Embrace*, 97.

91. *This Tight Embrace*, 75.

92. *This Tight Embrace*, 189.

93. Walsham, "Luis de Granada's Mission."

## CHAPTER 4

1. Carvajal makes frequent allusions to the primitive church. See, for example, *Escritos*, 399 (from the transcript of Carvajal's "Instrucción espiritual"). For comments on this, see *Letters*, xxvi.
2. Diefendorf, *From Penitence to Charity*, 40.
3. Diefendorf, *From Penitence to Charity*, 39.
4. On their possible meeting, see Fullerton, *Life of Luisa de Carvajal*, 147.
5. Gibbons, *English Catholic Exiles*, 57.
6. Walpole, *Vida*, 56r.
7. Walpole, *Vida*, 56v.
8. See Lake and Questier's now-classic essay, "Agency, Appropriation and Rhetoric."
9. Creswell, *Historia de la vida*, 18r.
10. Creswell, *Historia de la vida*, 14r (religious disputations), 18v, 25r.
11. Creswell, *Historia de la vida*, 18v, 51v, 53r.
12. Creswell, *Historia de la vida*, 43v, 48r–49v.
13. Persons to Acquaviva, Marchena, 12 May 1594, Archivum Romanum Societatis Iesu, Rome, Hispania 136, fol. 318.
14. *A trewe reporte of the life and Marterdome of Mrs Magarete Clitherowe*, York Minster Library, T.D.1, 4v.
15. Carvajal to Magdalena de San Jerónimo, Madrid, 16 March 1600, in *Letters*, 1:6; *Epistolario*, 101.
16. Holmes, *Resistance and Compromise*.
17. Testimony of Isabel de la Cruz, *Información*, 297r.
18. Carvajal to Mariana de San José, London, December 1606, in *Letters*, 1:215; *Epistolario*, 200.
19. Lake and Questier, *All Hail to the Archpriest*.
20. Carvajal to Joseph Creswell, London, 4 October 1607, in *Letters*, 1:278; *Epistolario*, 230.
21. Carvajal to Joseph Creswell, London, 4 October 1607, in *Letters*, 1:278; *Epistolario*, 230.
22. Tutino, *Empire of Souls*, 132.
23. Marshalek, "Luisa de Carvajal," 893.
24. *Letters*, editorial note at 1:300. Questier, *Catholicism and Community*, 518.
25. Carvajal to Don Pedro de Zúñiga, London, 16 April 1611, in *Letters*, 2:134; *Epistolario*, 312.
26. Carvajal to Don Pedro de Zúñiga, London, 16 April 1611, in *Letters*, 2:134; *Epistolario*, 312.
27. Thomas Lake to Robert Cecil, 17 February 1612, National Archives, SP 14/61, 133v.
28. Gondomar to Philip III, London, 16 November 1613, in Loomie, *Spain and the Jacobean Catholics*, 2:20.
29. Carvajal to the marquise of Caracena, London, 19 October 1612, in *Letters*, 2:248; *Epistolario*, 369.
30. Carvajal to the marquise of Caracena, London, 19 October 1612, in *Letters*, 2:248; *Epistolario*, 369.

31. Carvajal to Inés de la Asunción, London, 29 June 1608, in *Letters*, 2:32; *Epistolario*, 263.
32. Carvajal to Rodrigo Calderón, London, 16 February 1612, in *Letters*, 2:203; *Epistolario*, 345.
33. Carvajal to Inés de la Asunción, London, 29 June 1608, in *Letters*, 2:33; *Epistolario*, 263.
34. This is not to say, of course, that the state controlled the drama at the gallows but only that state authorities set the stage.
35. Carvajal to Inés de la Asunción, London, 29 June 1608, in *Letters*, 2:33; *Epistolario*, 263.
36. Carvajal to Inés de la Asunción, London, 29 June 1608, in *Letters*, 2:33; *Epistolario*, 263.
37. Carvajal to Inés de la Asunción, London, 29 June 1608, in *Letters*, 2:34; *Epistolario*, 264.
38. Carvajal to Joseph Creswell, London, 29 June 1608, in *Letters*, 2:4; *Epistolario*, 247.
39. Carvajal to Inés de la Asunción, London, 29 June 1608, in *Letters*, 2:34; *Epistolario*, 264.
40. Carvajal to Inés de la Asunción, London, 29 June 1608, in *Letters*, 2:35; *Epistolario*, 265.
41. Carvajal to Inés de la Asunción, London, 29 June 1608, in *Letters*, 2:39; *Epistolario*, 267. Carvajal to Lorenzo da Ponte, London, 29 June 1608, in *Letters*, 2:20; *Epistolario*, 260.
42. Carvajal to Lorenzo da Ponte, London, 29 June 1608, in *Letters*, 2:25; *Epistolario*, 256.
43. Marshalek, "Luisa de Carvajal," 897.
44. Carvajal to Inés de la Asunción, London, 29 June 1608, in *Letters*, 2:36; *Epistolario*, 265.
45. Carvajal to Inés de la Asunción, London, 29 June 1608, in *Letters*, 2:37; *Epistolario*, 266.
46. Carvajal to Joseph Creswell, London, 4 July 1610, in *Letters*, 2:115; *Epistolario*, 303.
47. Carvajal to Lorenzo da Ponte, London, 29 June 1608, in *Letters*, 2:23; *Epistolario*, 258.
48. Carvajal to Inés de la Asunción, London, 29 June 1608, in *Letters*, 2:33; *Epistolario*, 264.
49. "Escritos para sus compañeras," in Abad, *Una misionera Española*, 399.
50. "Escritos para sus compañeras," in Abad, *Una misionera Española*, 399.
51. "Escritos para sus compañeras," in Abad, *Una misionera Española*, 399.
52. "Escritos para sus compañeras," in Abad, *Una misionera Española*, 401.
53. "Escritos para sus compañeras," in Abad, *Una misionera Española*, 403.
54. "Escritos para sus compañeras," in Abad, *Una misionera Española*, 406.
55. Carvajal to Inés de la Asunción, London, 22 November 1609, in *Letters*, 2:94; *Escritos*, 294.

56. Extracts from a letter written 14 September 1610, Archivo General de Palacio, Real Monasterio de la Encarnación, caja 102, no. 24.

57. George Abbot to William Trumbull, London, 29 October 1613, British Library, Ms. Add. 72242-3 (Trumbull Papers, vol. 1), 19v.

58. Carvajal to Rodrigo Calderón, London, 16 February 1612, in *Letters*, 2:202; *Epistolario*, 344.

59. Gondomar to the marqués de la Inojosa, London, 29 November 1613, Real Biblioteca de Palacio, II/2168, 37r.

60. Carvajal to Rodrigo Calderón, London, 5 September 1613, in *Letters*, 2:320; *Epistolario*, 400.

61. Marshalek, "Luisa de Carvajal," 902–3.

62. Testimony of Richard Brouch [sic], *Información*, 390v.

63. Marshalek, "Luisa de Carvajal," 904.

64. Gondomar to Philip III, London, 16 November 1613, in Loomie, *Spain and the Jacobean Catholics*, 2:21.

CHAPTER 5

1. For example, Carvajal to Inés de la Asunción, London, 29 April 1607, in *Letters*, 1:244; *Epistolario*, 215.

2. Carvajal to Lorenzo da Ponte, London, 29 June 1608, in *Letters*, 2:23–24; *Epistolario*, 258.

3. Carvajal to Don Pedro de Zúñiga, London, 16 April 1611, in *Letters*, 2:134; *Epistolario*, 312.

4. Carvajal to the marquise of Caracena, London, 16 April 1611, in *Letters*, 2:151; *Epistolario*, 321–22.

5. Carvajal to Joseph Creswell, London, 16 April 1611, in *Letters*, 2:144; *Epistolario*, 318.

6. Carvajal to the marquise of Caracena, London, 10 May 1611, in *Letters*, 2:159; *Epistolario*, 325.

7. Vicente Melo and Working, "'Means of Persuasion.'"

8. Carvajal to the marquise of Caracena, London, 10 May 1611, in *Letters*, 2:159; *Epistolario*, 325.

9. Carvajal to Rodrigo Calderón, London, 21 June 1612, in *Letters*, 2:206; *Epistolario*, 316.

10. Carvajal to Magdalena de San Jerónimo, London, 26 May 1606, in *Letters*, 1:156–57; *Epistolario*, 173.

11. Carvajal to Magdalena de San Jerónimo, London, 26 May 1606, in *Letters*, 1:156–57; *Epistolario*, 173.

12. Carvajal to Magdalena de San Jerónimo, London, 26 May 1606, in *Letters*, 1:156–57; *Epistolario*, 173.

13. Questier, *Catholics and Treason*, 354–55.

14. Carvajal to Joseph Creswell, London, 16 February 1612; *Letters*, 2:195. This text does not appear in Abad's defective transcription.

15. Carvajal to Joseph Creswell, London, 16 February 1612, in *Letters*, 2:195. This text does not appear in Abad's defective transcription.

16. Carvajal to Joseph Creswell, London, 16 February 1612, in *Letters*, 2:195–96. This text does not appear in Abad's defective transcription.

17. For one version of the story, see Edward Kenion to Thomas More, 2 March 1612. Questier, *Newsletters from the Archpresbyterate*, 136–37, and 137n587 on variant versions.

18. Carvajal to Joseph Creswell, London, 16 April 1611, in *Letters*, 2:144; *Epistolario*, 318.

19. Carvajal to Joseph Creswell, London, 5 November 1608, in *Letters*, 2:54; *Epistolario*, 276.

20. Carvajal to Joseph Creswell, London, 6 March 1609, in *Letters*, 2:60; *Epistolario*, 279.

21. Carvajal to Mariana de San José, London, 5 July 1609, in *Letters*, 2:79; *Epistolario*, 288.

22. Carvajal to Mariana de San José, London, 5 July 1609, in *Letters*, 2:79; *Epistolario*, 288.

23. Carvajal to Joseph Creswell, London, 6 March 1609, in *Letters*, 2:60; *Epistolario*, 279.

24. Carvajal to Joseph Creswell, London, 4 July 1610, in *Letters*, 2:115; *Epistolario*, 303.

25. Carvajal to Joseph Creswell, London, 4 July 1610, in *Letters*, 2:117; *Epistolario*, 305.

26. Carvajal to Joseph Creswell, London, 4 July 1610, in *Letters*, 2:113; *Epistolario*, 302.

27. Sanz Camañes, "Las instrucciones diplomáticas," 18.

28. Don Alonso to Philip III, London, 22 March 1611, in Loomie, *Spain and the Jacobean Catholics*, 1:171.

29. Prefatory note in *Letters*, 2:133.

30. Carvajal to Don Pedro de Zúñiga, London, 16 April 1611, in *Letters*, 2:134; *Epistolario*, 312.

31. Carvajal to Don Pedro de Zúñiga, London, 16 April 1611, in *Letters*, 2:135; *Epistolario*, 312.

32. Carvajal to Don Pedro de Zúñiga, London, 16 April 1611, in *Letters*, 2:136; *Epistolario*, 313.

33. Carvajal to Don Pedro de Zúñiga, London, 16 April 1611, in *Letters*, 2:137; *Epistolario*, 314.

34. Carvajal to Don Pedro de Zúñiga, London, 16 April 1611, in *Letters*, 2:137; *Epistolario*, 314.

35. Carvajal to Don Pedro de Zúñiga, London, 16 April 1611, in *Letters*, 2:135; *Epistolario*, 313.

36. Carvajal to Alonso de Carvajal, London, 5 July 1609, in *Letters*, 2:83–85; *Epistolario*, 290–91.

37. Redworth, *She-Apostle*, 208.

38. Colón Calderón, "Linajes de mujeres."

39. See, for example, Carvajal to Rodrigo Calderón, London, 31 December 1612, in *Letters*, 2:294; *Epistolario*, 389.
40. Carvajal to Joseph Creswell, London, 29 June 1608, in *Letters*, 2:7; *Epistolario*, 249.
41. Carvajal to Rodrigo Calderón, London, 4 July 1609, in *Letters*, 2:76; *Epistolario*, 287.
42. Levy-Navarro, "Religious Warrior."
43. Carvajal to Rodrigo Calderón, London, 15 August 1611, in *Letters*, 2:166; *Epistolario*, 328.
44. Carvajal to Rodrigo Calderón, London, 30 August 1612, in *Letters*, 2:228; *Epistolario*, 356.
45. Carvajal to Rodrigo Calderón, London, 30 August 1612, in *Letters*, 2:228; *Epistolario*, 356.
46. Carvajal to Rodrigo Calderón, London, July 1612, in *Letters*, 2:218; *Epistolario*, 352.
47. Carvajal to Rodrigo Calderón, London, July 1612, in *Letters*, 2:217; *Epistolario*, 351.
48. Carvajal to Rodrigo Calderón, London, 5 August 1612, in *Letters*, 2:226; *Epistolario*, 356.
49. Carvajal to Rodrigo Calderón, London, 22 September 1612, in *Letters*, 2:242; *Epistolario*, 366.
50. Carvajal to Rodrigo Calderón, London, 16 February 1612, in *Letters*, 2:200; *Epistolario*, 343.
51. Carvajal to Rodrigo Calderón, London, 22 September 1612, in *Letters*, 2:242; *Epistolario*, 366.
52. Carvajal to Rodrigo Calderón, London, 22 September 1612, in *Letters*, 2:242; *Epistolario*, 366.
53. Carvajal to Rodrigo Calderón, London, 23 May 1613, in *Letters*, 2:309; *Epistolario*, 396.
54. Carvajal to Rodrigo Calderón, 23 May 1613, in *Letters*, 2:308; *Epistolario*, 396.
55. Carvajal to Rodrigo Calderón, London, 21 June 1612, in *Letters*, 2:205; *Epistolario*, 345.
56. Carvajal to Rodrigo Calderón, London, 16 February 1612, in *Letters*, 2:200; *Epistolario*, 343.
57. Carvajal to Rodrigo Calderón, London, 19 October 1612, in *Letters*, 2:252; *Epistolario*, 360.
58. Carvajal to Rodrigo Calderón, London, 19 October 1612, in *Letters*, 2:252; *Epistolario*, 360.
59. Carvajal to Rodrigo Calderón, London, 5 October 1613, in *Letters*, 2:339; *Escritos*, 412–13.
60. Gondomar to Francisco de Contreras, London, 26 November 1613, Real Biblioteca de Palacio, II/2168, 27v.
61. Gondomar to Juan Hurtado de Mendoza, 13 February 1614, Real Biblioteca de Palacio, II/2168, 92r.

62. Gondomar to the count of Oliva, 12 February 1614, Real Biblioteca de Palacio, II/2168, 95r.
63. Gondomar to Philip III, London, 9 May 1614, in Loomie, *Spain and the Jacobean Catholics*, 2:31.
64. Walpole, *Vida*, 125r.

CONCLUSION

1. "Interrogatorio de preguntas," *Información*, 10v–11r. Walpole, *Vida*, 124v–127r.
2. Giraldo Orano, *Vita Aloysiae Carvajaliae virginis Hispane martyrii candidatae in Anglia fidem professae*, University of Valladolid Library, Valladolid, Ms. 293. For one take on the manuscript, see Mañas Núñez, "La *Vita Aloysiae Carvajaliae*."
3. Orano, *Vita Aloysiae Carvajaliae*, not foliated.
4. Isabel de Bórbon to the duke of Pastrana, 25 January 1626, Archivo General de Palacio, Real Monasterio de la Encarnación, caja 102, no. 31.
5. On Ávila, see Rowe, *Saint and Nation*.
6. Muñoz, *Vida y virtudes*, sig. 2.
7. Muñoz, *Vida y virtudes*, not foliated.
8. Pineda, *En las honras de Doña Luisa de Carvajal*, 18r.
9. Pineda, *En las honras de Doña Luisa de Carvajal*, 8v.
10. Pineda, *En las honras de Doña Luisa de Carvajal*, 18r.
11. "Memorial sobre el medio de convertir a los ingleses al catolicismo," Real Biblioteca de Palacio, Mss. II/2165, doc. 75.
12. Middleton, *Game at Chess*.

# BIBLIOGRAPHY

Abad, Camilo Maria. "Un embajador español en la corte de Maximiliano II, Don Francisco Hurtado de Mendoza." *Miscelánea Comillas: Revista semestral de estudios históricos* 43 (1965): 21–94.

———. *Una misionera Española en la Inglaterra del siglo XVII: Doña Luisa de Carvajal y Mendoza (1566–1614)*. Comillas: Universidad Pontificia, 1966.

Anglo, Sydney. *Machiavelli: The First Century; Studies in Enthusiasm, Hostility, and Irrelevance*. Oxford: Oxford University Press, 2005.

Atienza López, Ángela. "Isabel Clara Eugenia, la corte de Bruselas, y el mundo religioso femenino." In *Mujeres en la corte de los Austrias: Una red social, cultural, religiosa y política*, edited by María Leticia Sánchez Hernández, 275–314. Madrid: Polifemo, 2019.

Ávila, Juan de. *Primera parte del epistolario espiritual, para todos estados*. Alcalá: Juan de Lequerica, 1579.

Barbazza, Marie-Catherine. "L'épouse chrétienne et les moralistes espagnols des XVIᵉ et XVIIᵉ siècle." *Mélanges de la Casa de Velázquez* 24 (1988): 99–137.

Beard, Mary. *Women and Power: A Manifesto*. New York: Liveright, 2017.

Bilinkoff, Jodi. *Related Lives: Confessors and Their Female Penitents, 1450–1750*. Ithaca, NY: Cornell University Press, 2005.

Bill-Mrziglod, Michaela. *Luisa de Carvajal y Mendoza (1566–1614) und ihre "Gessellschaft Mariens": Spiritualität, Theologie, und Konfessionspolitik in einer semireligiosen Frauengemeinschat des 17. Jahrhunderts*. Hamburg: Dr. Kovač, 2014.

Black, Georgina Dopico. "Public Bodies, Private Parts: The Virgins of the Magdalens of Magdalena de San Gerónimo." *Journal of Spanish Cultural Studies* 2, no. 1 (2001): 81–96.

Blumenfeld-Kosinski, Renate. *Poets, Saints, and Visions of the Great Schism*. University Park: Penn State University Press, 2006.

Bossy, John. *The English Catholic Community, 1570–1850*. Oxford: Oxford University Press, 1973.

Bouza, Fernando. *Corre manuscrito: Una historia cultural del Siglo de Oro*. Madrid: Marcial Pons, 2001.

———. "Docto y devoto: La biblioteca del Marqués de Almazán y Conde de Monteagudo (Madrid, 1591)." In *Hispania-Austria II: Die Epoche Philipps II. (1556–1598)*, edited by Friedrich Edelmayer, 247–310. Vienna: Verlag für Geschichte und Politik; Munich: Oldenbourg, 1999.

Braun, Harold. *Juan de Mariana and Early Modern Spanish Political Thought*. Aldershot: Ashgate, 2007.

Broad, Jacqueline, and Karen Green. *A History of Women's Political Thought in Europe, 1400–1700*. Cambridge: Cambridge University Press, 2009.
Burrieza Sánchez, Javier. "Fundaciones y visions de Marina de Esobar." In *Donne, potere, religione: Studi per Sara Cabibbo*, edited by Marina Caffiero, Maria Pia Donato, and Giovanna Fiume, 97–110. Milan: FrancoAngeli, 2017.
———. *Virgen de los Ingleses, entre Cádiz y Valladolid: Una devoción desde las guerras de religion*. Valladolid: Real Colegio de Ingleses, 2008.
Carvajal y Mendoza, Luisa de. *Epistolario y poesías*. Edited by Camilo Maria Abad. Madrid: Atlas, 1965.
———. *Escritos autobiográficos*. Edited by Camilo Maria Abad. Barcelona: Juan Flors, 1966.
———. *The Letters of Luisa de Carvajal y Mendoza*. Edited by Glyn Redworth with Christopher Henstock. 2 vols. London: Pickering and Chatto, 2012–13.
———. *The Life and Writings of Luisa de Carvajal y Mendoza*. Edited and translated by Anne J. Cruz. Toronto: Iter, 2013.
———. *This Tight Embrace*. Edited and translated by Elizabeth Rhodes. Milwaukee, WI: Marquette University Press, 2000.
Cerda, Juan de la. *Vida política de todos los estados de mugeres*. Alcalá de Henares: Juan Gracián, 1599.
Cogan, Susan. *Catholic Social Networks in Early Modern England: Kinship, Gender, and Coexistence*. Amsterdam: Amsterdam University Press, 2021.
*Colección de documentos inéditos para la historia de España*. Vols. 111–13. Madrid: José Perales y Martínez, 1895.
Colón Calderón, Isabel. "Linajes de mujeres y linajes nobiliarios: Rodrigo Calderón, Bernardo de Sandoval y Rojas, el duque e Lerma y su entorno femenino en los textos de Luisa de Carvajal." In *El duque de Lerma: Poder y literatura en el Siglo de Oro*, edited by Juan Matas Caballero, José María Micó, and Jesús Ponce Cárdenas, 317–40. Madrid: CEEH, 2011.
Coolidge, Grace E. *Guardianship, Gender, and Nobility in Early Modern Spain*. Farnham: Ashgate, 2011.
Creswell, Joseph. *Historia de la vida y martyrion que padecio en Inglaterra, este año de 1595 el P Henrique Valpolo*. Madrid: Pedro de Madrigal, 1596.
Cruz, Anne J. "Luisa de Carvajal y Mendoza y su conexión jesuita." In *Actas de XI Congreso de la Asociación Internacional de Hispanistas*, edited by Juan Villegas, 97–104. Irvine, CA: Asociación Internacional de Hispanistas, 1992.
———. "Reading Over Men's Shoulders: Noblewomen's Libraries and Reading Practices." In *Women's Literacy in Early Modern Spain and the New World*, edited by Anne J. Cruz and Rosilie Hernandez, 41–56. London: Routledge, 2011.
———. "Las redes sociales creadas por Luisa de Carvajal y Mendoza a través de su correspondencia." In *Mujeres en la corte de los Austrias: Una red social, cultural, religiosa y política*, edited by María Leticia Sánchez Hernández, 615–36. Madrid: Polifemo, 2019.
———. "Transgendering the Mystical Voice: Angela Foligno, San Juan, Santa Teresa, Luisa de Carvajal." In *Echoes and Inscriptions: Comparative Approaches to Early Modern Spanish Literatures*, edited by Barbara A. Simerka and Christopher B. Weimer, 127–41. Lewisburg, PA: Bucknell University Press, 2000.

———. "Vindicating the Vulnerata: Cádiz and the Circulation of Religious Imagery as Weapons of War." In *Symbolic and Material Circulation Between Spain and England, 1554–1604*, edited by Anne J. Cruz, 39–60. Aldershot: Ashgate, 2008.

———. "Willing Desire: Luisa de Carvajal y Mendoza and Feminine Subjectivity." In *Power and Gender in Renaissance Spain: Eight Women of the Mendoza Family, 1450–1650*, edited by Helen Nader, 177–93. Champaign: University of Illinois Press, 2004.

———. "Words Made Flesh: Luisa de Carvajal's Eucharistic Poetry." In *Studies on Women's Poetry of the Golden Age*, edited by Julian Olivares, 255–69. Woodbridge: Boydell & Brewer, 2009.

Cruz, Anne J., and Mihoko Suzuki, eds. *The Rule of Women in Early Modern Europe*. Champaign: University of Illinois Press, 2009.

Davis, Natalie Zemon. *A Passion for History: Conversations with Denis Crouzet*. Kirksville, MO: Truman State University Press, 2010.

Diefendorf, Barbara. *From Penitence to Charity: Pious Women and the Catholic Reformation in Paris*. Oxford: Oxford University Press, 2004.

Domínguez, Freddy. "From Saint to Sinner: Sixteenth-Century Perceptions of 'La Monja de Lisboa.'" In *A New Companion to Hispanic Mysticism*, edited by Hilaire Kallendorf, 297–320. Leiden: Brill, 2010.

———. "History in Action: The Case of Pedro de Ribadeneyra's *Historia ecclesiastica del cisma de Inglaterra*." *Bulletin of Spanish Studies* 93, no. 1 (2016): 13–38.

———. "Luisa de Carvajal, Her 'Life,' and the Place of Women in Counter-Reformation Politics." In *Political and Religious Practice in the Early Modern British World*, edited by William J. Bulman and Freddy C. Domínguez, 203–19. Manchester: Manchester University Press, 2022.

———. *Radicals in Exile: English Catholic Books During the Reign of Philip II*. University Park: Penn State University Press, 2020.

Dractan, Thomas. *Relacion que embiaron las religiosas del monasterio de Sion de Inglaterra*. Madrid: Viuda de Pedro de Madrigal, 1594.

Escalante Varona, Alberto. "La imagen del jardín espiritual como medio de evangelización en la obra politica de Luisa de Carvajal y Mendoza." *Cauriensia* 10 (2015): 91–111.

Falkeid, Unn. *The Avignon Papacy Contested: An Intellectual History from Dante to Catherine of Siena*. Cambridge, MA: Harvard University Press, 2017.

Feros, Antonio. *Kingship and Favoritism in the Spain of Philip III, 1598–1621*. Cambridge: Cambridge University Press, 2000.

Forteza, Deborah R. *The Reformation in the Spanish Imagination: Rewriting Nero, Jezebel, and the Dragon*. Toronto: University of Toronto Press, 2022.

Fullerton, Georgiana. *The Life of Luisa de Carvajal*. London: Burnes and Oates, 1873.

Gibbons, Katy. *English Catholic Exiles in Late Sixteenth-Century Paris*. Woodbridge: Boydell & Brewer, 2011.

González Garcia, Juan Luis. "La colección, librería y relicario de D. Francisco Hurtado de Mendoza, primer marqués de Almazán (1532–1591)." *Celtiberia* 48, no. 92 (1998): 193–228.

Gregory, Brad. *Salvation at Stake: Christian Martyrdom in Early Modern Europe*. Cambridge, MA: Harvard University Press, 2001.

Guevara, Antonio de. *Menosprecio de corte y alabança de aldea*. Barcelona: Hieronymo Margarit, 1613.

Guevara, María de. *Warnings to the Kings and Advice on Restoring Spain*. Edited and translated by Nieves Romero-Díaz. Chicago: University of Chicago Press, 2007.

Haliczer, Stephen. *Between Exaltation and Infamy: Female Mystics in the Golden Age of Spain*. Oxford: Oxford University Press, 2002.

Henstock, Christopher. "Luisa de Carvajal: Text, Context, and (Self-) Identity." PhD diss., Manchester University, 2012.

Heywood, Linda M. *Njinga of Angola: Africa's Warrior Queen*. Cambridge, MA: Harvard University Press, 2017.

Hicks, Leo. "Robert Persons, SJ, and the Seminaries in Spain." *The Month* 157, no. 801 (1931): 193–204.

Holmes, Peter. *Resistance and Compromise: The Political Thought of the Elizabethan Catholics*. Cambridge: Cambridge University Press, 1982.

Huerga, Alvaro. "La vida seudomistica y el proceso inquisitorial de Sor Maria de la Visitacion." *Hispania Sacra* 23 (1959): 35–125.

Iglesias, Miguel. "Luisa de Carvajal y Mendoza: Catolicismo y estrategia política en la Inglaterra jacobina." In *Luisa de Carvajal en sus contextos*, edited by María Luisa García-Verdugo, 47–74. Madrid: Pliegos, 2008.

Iñurritegui Rodríguez, José María. *La gracia y la República: El lenguaje político de la teología católica y el "Príncipe Cristiano" de Pedro de Ribadeneyra*. Madrid: UNED, 1998.

Kagan, Richard. *Lucrecia's Dreams: Politics and Prophecy in Sixteenth-Century Spain*. Berkeley: University of California Press, 1995.

Kelly, James E. "'A Suppurating Ulcer': Religious Orders and Transnational Conflict in Valladolid at the Start of the Seventeenth Century." *Seventeenth Century* 37, no. 5 (2022): 693–716.

Kenny, Anthony, ed. *The Responsa Scholarum of the English College, Rome, Part 1: 1598–1621*. London: Catholic Record Society, 1962.

Kleinberg, Aviad M. *Prophets in Their Own Country: Living Saints and the Making of Sainthood in the Later Middle Ages*. Chicago: University of Chicago Press, 1992.

Lake, Peter, and Steve Pincus. "Rethinking the Public Sphere in Early Modern England." *Journal of British Studies* 44, no. 2 (2006): 270–92.

Lake, Peter, and Michael Questier. "Agency, Appropriation and Rhetoric Under the Gallows: Puritans, Romanists and the State in Early Modern England." *Past & Present* 153 (November 1996): 64–107.

———. *All Hail to the Archpriest: Confessional Conflict, Toleration, and the Politics of Publicity in Post-Reformation England*. Oxford: Oxford University Press, 2019.

———. *The Trials of Margaret Clitherow: Persecution, Martyrdom, and the Politics of Sanctity in Elizabethan England*. London: Bloomsbury, 2019.

León, Luis de. *The Names of Christ*. Edited by Manuel Duran and William Kluback. New York: Paulist Press, 1984.

———. *La perfecta casada*. Salamanca: Guillelmo Faquel, 1587.

Levin, Carol. *Heart and Stomach of a King: Elizabeth I and the Politics of Sex and Power*. Philadelphia: University of Pennsylvania Press, 2013.

Levy-Navarro, Elena. "The Religious Warrior: Luisa de Carvajal y Mendoza's Correspondence with Rodrigo Calderón." In *Women's Letters Across Europe, 1400–1700: Form and Persuasion*, edited by Ann Crabb and Jane Couchman, 263–73. New York: Routledge, 2005.
Loomie, Albert, ed. *English Polemics at the Spanish Court: Creswell's Letter to the Ambassador from England*. New York: Fordham University Press, 1993.
———. *Spain and the Jacobean Catholics: 1603–1612*. 2 vols. London: Catholic Record Society, 1973.
———. *Spanish Elizabethans*. New York: Fordham University Press, 1963.
Luongo, F. Thomas. *The Saintly Politics of Catherine of Siena*. Ithaca, NY: Cornell University Press, 2006.
Mañas Núñez, Manuel. "La *Vita Aloysiae Carvajaliae* de Gerardo Van Der Berghe." In *La mujer en la Europa Renacentista y en el nuevo mundo*, edited by Rosa María Martinez de Codes and César Chaparro Gómez, 299–325. Yuste: Fundación Academia Europea e Iberoamericana de Yuste, 2020.
Mantel, Hilary. "Royal Bodies." *London Review of Books*, 21 February 2013. https://www.lrb.co.uk/the-paper/v35/n04/hilary-mantel/royal-bodies.
Marshalek, Kathryn. "Luisa de Carvajal in Anglo-Spanish Contexts, 1605–14." *Renaissance Quarterly* 75, no. 3 (2022): 882–916.
Martínez Hernández, Santiago. "'Enlightened Queen, Clear Cynthia, Beauteous Moon': The Political and Courtly Apprenticeship of the Infanta Isabel Clara Eugenia." In *Isabel Clara Eugenia: Female Sovereignty in the Courts of Madrid and Brussels*, edited by Cordula van Wyhe, 21–53. Madrid: CEEH; London: Paul Holberton, 2011.
Masters, Adrian. "Influential Women, New World Riches, and Masculine Anxieties in the Development of the Spanish Council of the Indies, 1524–1598." *Renaissance Quarterly* 74, no. 1 (2021): 94–136.
Melo, João Vicente, and Lauren Working. "'Means of Persuasion': The Material Culture and Oppositional Politics of Two Counter-Reformation Female Agents, Jane Dormer and Luisa de Carvajal." *Sixteenth Century Journal* 53, no. 1 (2022): 135–68.
Middleton, Thomas. *A Game at Chess*. Edited by T. H. Howard-Hill. Manchester: Manchester University Press, 2003.
Mitchell, Sylvia. *Queen, Mother, and Stateswoman: Mariana of Austria and the Government of Spain*. University Park: Penn State University Press, 2019.
Muñoz, Luis. *Vida y virtudes de la venerable virgen Doña Luisa de Carvajal*. Madrid: Imprenta Real, 1632.
Nader, Helen. *The Mendoza Family in the Spanish Renaissance, 1350–1559*. New Brunswick, NJ: Rutgers University Press, 1979.
Netzloff, Mark. "The English Colleges and the English Nation: Allen, Persons, Verstegan, and Diasporic Nationalism." In *Catholic Culture in Early Modern England*, edited by Ronald Corthell, Frances E. Dolan, Christopher Highley, and Arthur Marotti, 236–60. South Bend, IN: University of Notre Dame Press, 2007.
Osório, Jerónimo. *De rebus Emmanuelis regis Lusitantiae invictissime virtute et auspicio gestis libri duodecim*. Lisbon: Antonium Gondisaluum, 1571.
———. *De regis institutione et disciplina, Lib. VIII*. Lisbon: Ioannis Hispani, 1571.

———. *Epistola Hieronymi Osorii ad serenissimam Elisabetam Angliae regina*. Venice: Iordani Ziletti, 1563.
Pando-Canteli, María J. "Letters, Books, and Relics: Material and Spiritual Networks in the Life of Luisa de Carvajal y Mendoza (1564–1614). In *Devout Laywomen in the Early Modern World*, edited by Alison Weber, 294–312. New York: Routledge, 2016.
———. "'Tentado vados': The Martyrdom Politics of Luisa de Carvajal y Mendoza." *Journal of Early Modern Culture* 10, no. 1 (2010): 17–25.
Parker, Geoffrey. "The Place of Tudor England in the Messianic Vision of Philip II of Spain." *Transactions of the Royal Historical Society* 12 (December 2002): 167–221.
Persons, Robert. *Relacion de algunos martyrios, que de nuevo han hecho los hereges de Inglaterra*. Madrid: Pedro de Madrigal, 1590.
Pineda, Juan de. *En las honras de Doña Luisa de Carvajal, defunta en Londres por Enero de 1614*. N.p., 1614.
Pinillos Iglesias, María Nieves. *Hilando oro: Vida de Luisa de Carvajal*. Madrid: Laberinto, 2001.
Poska, Allyson. "The Case for Agentic Gender Norms for Women in Early Modern Europe." *Gender and History* 30, no. 2 (2018): 354–65.
———. *Women and Authority in Early Modern Spain: The Peasants of Galicia*. Oxford: Oxford University Press, 2006.
Puente, Luis de la. *Vida maravillosa de la venerable virgen doña Marina de Escobar*. Madrid: Francisco Nieto, 1665.
Questier, Michael. *Catholicism and Community in Early Modern England*. Cambridge: Cambridge University Press, 2006.
———. *Catholics and Treason: Martyrology, Memory, and Politics in the Post-Reformation*. Oxford: Oxford University Press, 2022.
———. *Newsletters from the Archpresbyterate of George Birkhead*. Cambridge: Cambridge University Press, 1998.
———. "Seminary Colleges, Converts, and Religious Change in Post-Reformation England, 1568–1688." In *College Communities Abroad: Education, Migration and Catholicism in Early Modern Europe*, edited by Liam Chambers, 142–73. Manchester: Manchester University Press, 2017.
*Recebimiento que se hizo en Valladolid a una imagen de nuestra Señora*. Madrid: Imprenta de la Tina, 1600.
Redworth, Glyn. "A New Way of Living? Luisa de Carvajal and the Limits of Mysticism." In *A New Companion to Hispanic Mysticism*, edited by Hilaire Kallendorf, 273–95. Leiden: Brill, 2010.
———. *The She-Apostle: The Extraordinary Life and Death of Luisa de Carvajal*. Oxford: Oxford University Press, 2008.
Rees, Margaret. *The Writings of Doña Luisa de Carvajal y Mendoza, Catholic Missionary to James I's London*. Lewiston, NY: Edwin Mellen, 2002.
Rhodes, Elizabeth. "Luisa de Carvajal's Counter-Reformation Journey to Selfhood (1566–1614)." *Renaissance Quarterly* 51, no. 3 (1998): 887–911.
———. Review of *The She-Apostle: The Extraordinary Life and Death of Luisa de Carvajal*, by Glyn Redworth. *Gender and History* 22, no. 1 (2010): 218–20.

Ribadeneyra, Pedro de. *Historia ecclesiastica del scisma de Inglaterra*. Madrid: Pedro de Madrigal, 1588.

———. *Las obras del P. Pedro de Ribadeneyra*. Madrid: Viuda de Pedro Madrigal, 1595.

Rodríguez Villa, Antonio, ed. *Correspondencia de la Infanta Archiduquesa D.a Isabel Clara Eugenia de Austria con el duque de Lerma*. Madrid: Boletín de la Real Academia, 1906.

Romero-Díaz, Nieves. "On Female Political Alliances: Sor María de Ágreda's Communities of Letters." *Hispanic Review* 86, no. 1 (2018): 91–111.

———. "Women, Space, and Power in Early Modern Spain." *Early Modern Women* 11, no. 2 (2017): 42–58.

Rowe, Erin. *Saint and Nation: Santiago, Teresa of Ávila, and Plural Identities in Early Modern Spain*. University Park: Penn State University Press, 2011.

Salón, Miguel. *Oracion panegírica*. Valencia: Pedro Patricio Mey, 1616.

Sánchez Molero, José Luis Gonzalo. "L'educazione devozionale delle Infante." In *L'infanta: Caterina d'Austria duchessa di Savoia (1567–1597)*, edited by Blythe Alice Raviola and Franca Varallo, 25–96. Rome: Carocci, 2013.

Santoro, Juan Basilio. *Flos sanctorum y vida de los santos*. Madrid, 1576.

Sanz Camañes, Porfirio. "Las instrucciones diplomáticas de los embajadores españoles en Inglaterra durante el siglo XVII." *Revista de historia moderna* 33 (2015): 11–31.

Suzuki, Mihoko. *Antigone's Example: Early Modern Women's Political Writing in Times of Civil War from Christine de Pizan to Helen Maria Williams*. Cham: Palgrave, 2022.

Tutino, Stefania. *Empire of Souls: Robert Bellarmine and the Christian Commonwealth*. Oxford: Oxford University Press, 2010.

Verstegan, Richard. *Theatrum crudelitatum haereticorum nostri temporis*. Antwerp: Adrian Hubert, 1587.

Vives, Juan Luis. *The Education of a Christian Woman: A Sixteenth-Century Manual*. Edited and translated by Charles Fantazzi. Chicago: University of Chicago Press, 2000.

Walsham, Alexandra. "Luis de Granada's Mission to Protestant England: Translating the Devotional Literature of the Spanish Counter-Reformation." In *Publishing Subversive Texts in Elizabethan England and the Polish-Lithuanian Commonwealth*, edited by Teresa Bela, Clarinda Calma, and Jolanta Rzegocka, 129–54. Leiden: Brill, 2016.

Warren, Nancy Bradley. *The Embodied Word: Female Spiritualities, Contested Orthodoxies, and English Religious Cultures, 1350–1700*. South Bend, IN: University of Notre Dame Press, 2010.

———. *Women of God and Arms: Female Spirituality and Political Conflict, 1380–1600*. Philadelphia: University of Pennsylvania Press, 2011.

Wiesner-Hanks, Merry. *Gender in History*. Oxford: Blackwell, 2005.

Yepes, Diego de. *Historia particular de la persecucion de Inglaterra*. Madrid: Luis Sanchez, 1599.

# INDEX

Abad, Camilo, 7, 8, 79
Abbot, George, 106–9, 130
Acarie, Barbe, 87, 88
Acarie, Pierre, 87–88
Acquaviva, Claudio, 91
Albert (archduke), 59, 66
Archpriest Controversy, 92–93
Augustinians, 20, 48, 69
Ávila, Juan de, 28–30, 32, 67
Ayllón, Isabel de, 17, 19

Beard, Mary, 2
Benedictines, 69, 96, 117
Bilinkoff, Jodi, 80
Bill-Mrziglod, Michaela, 9–10
Birgitta of Sweden, 4
Birkhead, George, 117
Blackwell, George, 93–95, 115–17
Blumenfeld-Kosinski, Renate, 4
Boleyn, Anne, 2
Boulogne conference (1600), 59
Bouza, Fernando, 29

Calderón, Rodrigo, 11, 114, 123–25, 127–28, 130, 133
Calvinism, 27, 84
Campion, Edmund, 57
Cárdenas, Ana María de (aunt of Luisa)
    charity and, 18, 19
    death of, 41
    in household hierarchy, 18, 31–32
    personality of, 17, 18
    piety of, 18–19, 21, 142n25
    politics and, 19–20, 141–42n18
    spiritual influence of, 20–21
Carmelites, 60, 87
Carvajal, Alonso de (brother of Luisa), 46–48, 70, 122–23, 133
Carvajal, Francisco de (father of Luisa), 14, 46, 141n4

Carvajal y Mendoza, Luisa de
    autobiographical writings, 17, 24, 31, 75, 79–84
    beatification proceedings, 6, 45, 134
    birth and early life, 14–17, 141n5
    bodies of martyrs collected by, 97–98, 113–14
    charity and, 42, 43, 47, 54, 70, 80, 96
    critiques against, 74–75, 147n60
    death and return of body to Spain, 6, 130–33
    decision to go to England, 57, 71, 73–75, 85–86, 145n4
    diplomacy and, 11, 21, 36, 64–65, 73, 85, 102–3, 108, 118–27, 132
    education of, 15–18, 25
    on Elizabeth I, 63–65, 91, 99
    exemplarity of, 79, 81, 82, 92, 130, 134, 135
    fame of, 39–45, 134
    family background, 14–15, 141n4
    on good governance, 66, 123
    imprisonment of, 6, 98, 101–3, 108, 111, 128–29
    inheritance of, 10, 46–47, 62, 70–71
    Jesuits and, 11, 41, 69, 74, 105, 114, 137
    kinship networks of, 6, 15, 24, 123
    lay community of women established by, 6, 104–7
    letters written by, 7–11, 32, 47, 54, 61–69, 91, 110–24, 130–31, 145n62
    literature review, 6–11, 133–34
    Louvain novitiate established by, 46, 70–71, 130
    martyrdom aspirations of, 39, 40, 57, 70–71, 83–84, 89, 105, 111
    meeting with Blackwell, 93–95
    missionary work of, 6, 7, 74–76, 79, 135
    mistreatment of, 34, 143n67
    penitential practices of, 34–35, 82

Philip III and, 44–46, 55, 129, 132, 133
piety of, 9, 13, 36, 41, 44–46, 49, 70–71, 123, 135
poetry written by, 8, 10, 49–53, 145n47, 145n50
politics of, 8–13, 30–33, 60–67, 99, 113, 140n32
on primitive church, 87, 105, 149n1
privacy desired by, 82–83
relationship with Magdalena de San Jerónimo, 60–69
spiritual counsel provided by, 42, 45, 54, 60, 112
spiritual growth of, 19, 21, 24–25, 31, 34, 37, 41
spiritual roadblocks for, 18, 81
vow of martyrdom taken by, 10
voyage to England, 87–89
wealth and power shunned by, 5, 48
Catalina Micaela (daughter of Philip II), 16
Catherine of Aragon, 21–24, 99
Catherine of Siena, 3–4, 39
Catholics and Catholicism
  Archpriest Controversy and, 92–93
  Augustinians and, 20, 48, 69
  Benedictines and, 69, 96, 117
  Counter-Reformation, 10, 60, 84
  defense against Protestant attacks, 22, 28, 59, 88
  diplomatic promotion of, 111
  exiled English Catholics in Spain, 6, 57–58, 66, 68
  Franciscans and, 20, 23
  Fullerton on silence of, 7
  Gunpowder Plot organized by, 89, 114, 115
  imprisonment in England, 76–77, 93–96
  intra-Catholic conflicts, 92–93, 105
  lay communal living and, 6, 104–7
  Marian devotion in, 56–57
  papal authority and, 93, 94, 98–99, 101, 112, 115, 127
  penitential practices in, 34–35, 82
  persecution in England, 7, 39, 57–58, 64, 78, 121
  politics and, 9, 27, 91
  primitive church, 87, 105, 149n1
  relics in, 6, 97, 113–14, 130

  state conflicts with, 5, 91, 92
  Wisbech Stirs and, 94
  *See also* heresy; Jesuits; martyrs and martyrdom; missionary work; piety
Ceráin, Joan de, 41–42
Cerda, Juan de la, 20
Chacón, María (aunt of Luisa), 15
Champney, Mary, 75
charity
  Ávila on, 28
  Barbe and, 88
  Carvajal y Mendoza and, 42, 43, 47, 54, 70, 80, 96
  for monastic institutions, 60
  networking skills and, 19
  piety and, 18, 19, 114
  Zúñiga and, 122
Charles II (king of Spain), 3
Charles V (Holy Roman Emperor), 22–23, 27
Clitherow, Margaret, 5, 77–78, 91
Copley, William, 77, 148n69
Cortés, María, 68–70
Counter-Reformation, 10, 60, 84
court/country dichotomy, 48–51
Creswell, Joseph, 57–58, 66–67, 72–73, 89–92, 113, 116–19
Cruz, Anne J., 10–11, 25, 34, 79, 141n4
Cruz, Isabel de la, 35, 92
Cruz, San Juan de la, 49

David (king of Israel), 26, 29, 142n41
Davis, Natalie Zemon, 12
Descalzas Reales, 15–16, 18, 25, 82, 141n5
Diana (princess of Wales), 1
Dickenson, Roger, 76–77
diplomacy
  ambassadors and, 118–25, 127, 129
  backroom forms of, 73
  Boulogne conference and, 59
  Catholicism promoted through, 111
  compromise and, 28, 64
  counter-diplomacy, 73
  détente and, 118, 126
  diplomatic immunity, 5, 101
  epistolary exchanges and, 11
  *A Game at Chess* and, 135–36
  international, 21, 23, 132

diplomacy (*continued*)
  peace treaty and, 71, 73, 85
  power and, 25, 126
  in release of Carvajal y Mendoza, 102–3, 108, 129
divorce, 22–23
domesticity, sphere of, 21
Dormer, Jane, 72
Dylan, Bob, 12–13

elites, 3, 11, 24, 55, 68
Elizabeth I (queen of England)
  Boulogne conference and, 59
  Carvajal y Mendoza on, 63–65, 91, 99
  debates regarding legitimacy of, 91, 99
  gender role navigated by, 3
  James I as successor to, 71–72
  Osório's book offering counsel to, 30
  persecution of Catholics under, 57, 58, 64
  relationship with Philip II, 126
Elizabeth II (queen of England), 1
Encarnación, Inés de la, 74
England
  Archpriest Controversy in, 92–93
  decision of Carvajal y Mendoza to go to, 57, 71, 73–75, 85–86, 145n4
  diplomacy with, 59, 64–65
  divorce issue in, 22–23
  Gunpowder Plot in, 89, 114, 115
  imprisonment of Catholics in, 76–77, 93–96
  lay communal living in, 6, 104–7
  missionary work in, 13, 57, 68, 74–76, 90
  monarchical bodies of women in, 1–2
  peace treaty with Spain, 71, 73, 85
  persecution of Catholics in, 7, 39, 57–58, 64, 78, 121
  Philip II's actions against, 58, 145n9
  political landscape in, 67–75
  voyage of Carvajal y Mendoza to, 87–89
  Wisbech Stirs in, 94
English College, 46, 56–58, 68–69, 76, 77, 119, 134
Escalante Varona, Alberto, 50
Escobar, Marina de, 74, 147n56

Falkeid, Unn, 4
females. *See* women
Fernando (son of Philip II), 16

Flanders, 59–66, 69–70, 75, 122–26, 133
Forest, John, 23
France
  Carvajal y Mendoza's journey through, 87–88
  heretical activity within, 27, 68
  Jesuit murder of king of, 120
  monarchical bodies of women in, 2
Franciscans, 20, 23
Fullerton, Georgiana, 7

Gage, Margaret, 77, 148n69
Gallo, Juan Bautista, 68
*A Game at Chess* (Middleton), 135–36
Garnet, Henry, 114–15
gender
  norms related to, 31, 76
  power and, 2–3, 11, 31–32
  public–private sphere distinctions based on, 21
  questioning of Carvajal y Mendoza, 102
  roles based on, 3, 10
  *See also* men; women
geopolitics, 10, 59, 65–67, 103, 111, 122, 125–28, 140n32
Gervase, George, 100, 101
Gondomar, count of, 78, 107–9, 128–30, 132
Góngora, Luis de, 73
good governance, 20, 28–30, 66, 123
Granada, Luis de, 16, 38–40
Gregory, Brad, 39–40
Guevara, Antonio de, 48
Gunpowder Plot, 89, 114, 115

Henry IV (king of France), 88
Henry VIII (king of England), 1, 2, 22, 23, 99
Henstock, Christopher, 40, 79
heresy
  Blackwell's actions and, 93
  combating, 27, 39, 56–58, 65, 71, 75, 91, 105, 110
  Gondomar's public stance against, 129
  papal actions against heretics, 115
  rituals associated with, 127
  threats associated with, 66, 73, 84
  unexpected persons in battle against, 79
Holmes, Peter, 92
Holy League, 87–88

holy women
 characteristics of, 3, 74
 confessorial persona of, 23
 invitations to royal courts, 45
 political scholarship and, 4
 public sphere and, 5
 spiritual autobiographies of, 80
Hurtado de Mendoza, Francisco (uncle of Luisa)
 as ambassador to the empire, 19–20, 26–28, 142n43
 art collection of, 29
 death of, 30, 38, 41
 estates held by, 17, 19
 in household hierarchy, 31–32
 library of, 25, 29–30
 on marriage, 24–25
 on penitential practices, 34–35, 82
 piety of, 20–21, 24–27, 142n25
 poetry written by, 49
 politico-religious efforts against heresy, 71
 politics and, 26, 27, 57
 Ribadeneyra on, 26–27
 shortcomings of, 37–38, 81
 social order as understood by, 33
 in spiritual growth of Carvajal y Mendoza, 19, 25, 31, 37

Iglesias, Miguel, 11
Iñurritegui Rodríguez, José María, 30
Isabel Clara Eugenia (daughter of Philip II), 16, 59–62, 65–66, 100

James I (king of England)
 on Carvajal y Mendoza, 96, 130–31
 count of Gondomar and, 107, 129, 132
 Creswell's attempted rapprochement with, 73
 death of son, 126
 ecclesiastical establishment under, 99
 in *A Game at Chess*, 136
 legitimization of rule, 99–100
 marriage agreements considered by, 127–28
 Oath of Allegiance required by, 93–94
 Philip III's ambassadors to court of, 118, 120
 as successor to Elizabeth I, 71–72
 tepidity toward regime of, 125

Jesuits
 anti-Jesuit sentiments, 96, 102, 106–7
 Archpriest Controversy and, 93
 Benedictine conflict with, 69, 117
 Carvajal y Mendoza and, 11, 41, 69, 74, 105, 114, 137
 on church-state separation, 55
 education provided by, 41, 46
 exiled in Spain, 57, 66
 French king murdered by, 120
 Hurtado de Mendoza and, 26
 Juana of Austria and, 15
 missionary work and, 41, 57, 70
 persecution in England, 57–58
 Wisbech Stirs and, 94
Joseph of Arimathea, 113
Juana of Austria, 15
Juana of Jacincourt, 62

Kelly, James, 69
kinship networks, 3, 6, 15, 24, 76, 123
Kleinberg, Aviad, 40

Lake, Peter, 5, 93
Laynez, Diego, 26
León, Luis de, 20, 48–49
Levy-Navarro, Elena, 11
Louvain novitiate, 46, 70–71, 130
Luongo, F. Thomas, 3–4, 139–40n11

Machiavelli, Niccolò, 30
Mantel, Hilary, 1–2
Manuel I (king of Portugal), 30
Margaret (queen of Spain), 45
Mariana of Austria, 3
Marian devotion, 56–57
Marie Antoinette (queen of France), 2
marriage, 20, 22, 24–25, 41, 46, 121, 127–28
Marshalek, Kathryn, 11, 94, 102, 107, 108, 140n41
martyrs and martyrdom
 aspirations for, 13, 39–40, 57, 70–71, 77, 83–84, 89, 94, 104–5, 111
 bodies collected by Carvajal y Mendoza, 97–98, 113–14
 canonization of, 6, 7
 defense of true faith by, 21, 23
 desacralization of bodies by authorities, 97, 98

martyrs and martyrdom (*continued*)
   Elizabeth I and, 63, 64
   Gervase case and, 100, 101
   literature on, 57–58, 75–78, 89, 92
   missionary work and, 67, 68, 90
   physical evidence of, 56
   politics of, 22, 113
   primitive church and, 87, 105
   prison visits by Carvajal y Mendoza, 95–97, 112
   relics of, 6, 97, 113–14, 130
   scripts for, 89–91, 99, 103, 150n34
   significance of, 113–17, 135
   vow of martyrdom, 10
Mary I (queen of England), 3, 22, 23
Mary Stuart (queen of Scotland), 22, 99–100, 126
Medici, Catherine de, 3
men
   Holy League for, 87–88
   marriage and, 20, 22, 24–25, 41, 46, 121, 127–28
   patriarchy and, 2, 85
   politics as domain of, 9, 21
   *See also* gender
Mendoza y Chacón, María de (mother of Luisa), 14, 82
Middleton, Kate (princess of Wales), 1
Middleton, Thomas, 135
Milner, Ralph, 76–77
misogyny, 2, 137
missionary work
   education for, 67–68
   Jesuits and, 41, 57, 70
   martyrdom and, 67, 68, 90
   by women, 6, 7, 13, 74–76, 79, 135
Mitchell, Silvia, 3
Molina, Melchor de, 45–46
Moses (biblical figure), 29, 61
Muñoz, Luis, 6, 7, 134
Mush, John, 78
mysticism, 8, 141n45

Nader, Helen, 11
Neville, Mary, 79
Njinga of Angola, 3

Oath of Allegiance, 93–94, 105, 108, 116–17
Orano, Giraldo, 133–34, 154n2

Osório, Jerónimo, 30
Ovid, 2

Padilla, Martin de, 56
Pando-Canteli, María, 11
papal authority, 93, 94, 98–99, 101, 112, 115, 127
Parker, Geoffrey, 145n9
patriarchy, 2, 85
patronage, 3, 59–60, 62, 68, 70
Paul (saint), 20
Persons, Robert, 69, 70, 72, 91, 94
Philip II (king of Spain)
   anti-English actions by, 58, 145n9
   Calderón and, 123
   children of, 16, 59
   claims to Portuguese crown, 30
   Copley as pensioner of, 77
   critiques against, 44, 58, 125–26
   geopolitical landscape under, 59
   Hurtado de Mendoza as ambassador for, 19, 27, 28
   Juana of Austria as sister to, 15
   missionary work supported by, 68
   relationship with Elizabeth I, 126
   Spanish Armada and, 44, 58
Philip III (king of Spain)
   ambassadors to court of James I, 118, 120
   anti-English actions by, 58–59
   Calderón and, 123
   Carvajal y Mendoza and, 44–46, 55, 129, 132, 133
   factional disputes during reign of, 49
   geopolitical landscape under, 59, 125, 126
   marriage agreements considered by, 127, 128
   missionary work supported by, 68
   piety of, 132, 134
   policies following death of Elizabeth I, 72
Philip IV (king of Spain), 134, 136
piety
   of ambassadors, 122
   beatification proceedings and, 134
   of Cárdenas, 18–19, 21, 142n25
   of Carvajal y Mendoza, 9, 13, 36, 41, 44–46, 49, 70–71, 123, 135
   of Catherine of Aragon, 22, 23
   challenges posed by, 83, 84
   charity and, 18, 19, 114

Clitherow as exemplar of, 5
of David (king of Israel), 26, 142n41
domestic expectations at odds with, 81
of Hurtado de Mendoza, 20–21, 24–27, 142n25
of Magdalena de San Jerónimo, 62
marriage and, 20, 24–25
performances of, 19, 21, 36, 44, 88
of Philip III, 132, 134
politics and, 4, 30, 33, 41n44, 63, 103, 131
power and, 15–16
public, 21, 23, 36, 40–42, 104
transformative nature of, 105
of Velasco y Mendoza, 54
visions of, 142n25
Vulnerata sculpture and, 56
Pineda, Juan de, 134–35
Pinillos Iglesias, María Nieves, 8
politics
  ambassadorial, 118, 122
  corruption and, 48, 49, 117
  decision-making and, 67, 128
  definition of, 4–5
  dichotomy between devotion and, 53
  ecclesiastical, 72
  education and, 15–17
  in England, 67–75
  in the flesh, 33–35
  friendship and, 60–67
  *A Game at Chess* and, 135
  geopolitics, 10, 59, 65–67, 103, 111, 122, 125–28, 140n32
  of martyrdom, 22, 113
  as men's domain, 9, 21
  networks related to, 57
  piety and, 4, 30, 33, 63, 103, 131, 141n44
  power and, 6, 12, 20, 24, 27–28, 30, 49
  religion and, 8–16, 24, 27–33, 71, 91, 110, 113, 122, 134, 139–40n11
  of spiritual direction, 95–97
  women and, 2–4, 16, 19–20, 60, 99, 139–40n11, 140n14
  *See also* diplomacy
Poska, Allyson, 3
poverty, 42, 92, 101, 105, 118
power
  for anti-English action, 58
  Carvajal y Mendoza's shunning of, 5, 48
  circles of, 50, 124

diplomacy and, 25, 126
distribution of, 31, 32
dynamics of, 4, 80, 85
gender and, 2–3, 11, 31–32
lust for, 127
piety and, 15–16
political, 6, 12, 20, 24, 27–28, 30, 49
prophetic, 67
of relics, 114
private sphere, 18, 21
prostitution, 60–61
Protestants and Protestantism
  challenges posed by, 27
  conversion opportunities for Catholics, 7
  deciphering thoughts of, 33
  defense of Catholicism against attacks by, 22, 28, 59, 88
  suffering by Carvajal y Mendoza at hands of, 6
  *See also specific denominations*
public sphere, 2, 5, 12–13, 18, 21, 55, 61
Puente, Luis de la, 74

Questier, Michael, 5, 93, 94
Quirós, Leonor de, 54, 145n50

Redworth, Glyn, 8–11, 121, 141n44
Rees, Margaret A., 8
relics, 6, 97, 113–14, 130
religion
  family differences in, 78, 81
  modernization as distinct from, 4
  politics and, 8–16, 24, 27–33, 71, 91, 110, 113, 122, 134, 139–40n11
  *See also* Catholics and Catholicism; Protestants and Protestantism
Rhodes, Elizabeth, 10, 79, 140n32
Ribadeneyra, Pedro de, 21–24, 26–27, 141n44
Ribera, Juan de, 134
Roberts, John, 95–97, 106, 112, 113, 117, 121
Romero-Díaz, Nieves, 11
Rudolf II (Holy Roman Emperor), 19–20

Salón, Miguel, 53–54
Sander, Elizabeth, 75
San Jerónimo, Magdalena de, 60–69, 77, 133
San José, Mariana de, 119

Santoro, Juan Basilio, 40
Sebastian (king of Portugal), 30
Shakespeare, William, 2
social order, 33, 51, 93
Society of Jesus. *See* Jesuits
Somers, Thomas, 95–97, 106, 117, 121
Spain
    Carvajal y Mendoza's body returned to, 132–33
    Descalzas Reales in, 15–16, 18, 25, 82, 141n5
    English Catholic exiles in, 6, 57–58, 66, 68
    English College in, 46, 56–58, 68–69, 76, 77, 119, 134
    geopolitical strategy of, 125
    landed nobility in, 14
    peace treaty with England, 71, 73, 85
    social ills in, 60–61
    urban areas within, 41–46
    women in bureaucratic circles in, 19–20, 142n20
Spanish Armada, 44, 58
Spencer, Diana (princess of Wales), 1
Stapleton, Anne, 75
Stuart, Mary (queen of Scotland), 22, 99–100, 126
Suárez, Francisco, 108
Suzuki, Mihoko, 4

Teresa of Ávila, 49, 134
Trumbull, William, 106
Tudor, Mary (queen of England), 3, 22, 23

Vargas y Carvajal, Gutierre de, 141n4
Velasco, Alonso de, 119–22, 125, 129
Velasco y Mendoza, Isabel de, 52–54
Versteghen, Richard, 78
Visitaçao, Maria da, 39
Vives, Juan Luis, 20
Vulnerata sculpture, 56–57

Walpole, Henry, 57–58, 89–90
Walpole, Margaret, 75
Walpole, Michael, 6, 41
Ward, Mary, 136
Wiesner-Hanks, Merry, 140n14
Wisbech Stirs, 94
women
    Carmelites, 60, 87
    diplomacy and, 11, 21, 23, 25, 36, 59, 64–65
    exiled English Catholics in Spain, 68
    in household hierarchy, 18
    lay communal living by, 6, 104–7
    limitations imposed on, 9, 76
    marriage and, 20, 22, 24–25, 41, 46, 121, 127–28
    misogyny and, 2, 137
    missionary work by, 6, 7, 13, 74–76, 79, 135
    monarchical bodies of, 1–2
    motherhood and, 1, 17
    mysticism and, 8, 141n45
    politics and, 2–4, 16, 19–20, 60, 99, 139–40n11, 140n14
    power and, 2–3, 11
    in prostitution, 60–61
    as sources of spiritual uplift, 20–21
    in Spanish bureaucratic circles, 19–20, 142n20
    in sphere of domesticity, 21
    *See also* gender; holy women

Yepes, Diego de, 78, 148n71

Zúñiga, Juan de, 16
Zúñiga, Pedro, 89, 102–3, 116, 118–22, 124–25, 127–29

www.ingramcontent.com/pod-product-compliance
Lightning Source LLC
Chambersburg PA
CBHW022014290426
44109CB00015B/1168